WHAT HAPPENED TO
ELLEN?

WHAT HAPPENED TO ELLEN?

AN AMERICAN MISCARRIAGE OF JUSTICE

NANCY GRACE

with BENÉE KNAUER

A REGALO PRESS BOOK

What Happened to Ellen?:
An American Miscarriage of Justice
© 2025 by Nancy Grace with Benée Knauer

ISBN: 979-8-88845-532-6
ISBN (eBook): 979-8-88845-533-3

Cover design by Cody Corcoran
Interior design and composition by Greg Johnson, Textbook Perfect

Publishing Team
Founder and Publisher: Gretchen Young
Editorial Assistant: Caitlyn Limbaugh
Managing Editor: Madeline Sturgeon
Production Manager: Alana Mills
Production Editor: Rachel Paul
Associate Production Manager: Kate Harris

A portion of the author's proceeds will go to the National Center for Missing and Exploited Children, a private, nonprofit organization that provides services nationwide for families and professionals in the prevention of abducted, endangered, and exploited children.

This book, as well as any other Regalo Press publications, may be purchased in bulk quantities at a special discounted rate. Contact orders@regalopress.com for more information.

This is a work of nonfiction. All people, locations, events, and situations are portrayed to the best of the author's memory.

Regalo Press
New York • Nashville
regalopress.com

Published in the United States of America
1 2 3 4 5 6 7 8 9 10

In remembrance of Ellen Rae Greenberg,
June 23, 1983–January 26, 2011

*The best way to get away with homicide
is to have it ruled a suicide.*

—THOMAS BRENNAN JR., FBI behavioral science trained,
veteran Pennsylvania State Police,
and retired Dauphin County detective

*First, rule out homicide. Second, rule out homicide.
Third, rule out homicide.*

—GRAHAM HETRICK, Dauphin County Coroner

AUTHOR'S NOTE

On April 17, 2024, a Pennsylvania court ruled former Philadelphia prosecutor, Guy D'Andrea, an assistant district attorney who worked on Ellen's case, could be deposed by Ellen Greenberg's family. The Greenbergs have been entrenched, for thirteen years, in a heartbreaking battle against the City of Philadelphia over the official manner of then twenty-seven-year-old Ellen's death. It was ruled a suicide in 2011, but Ellen's parents, Josh and Sandee, along with a long and steadily growing list of experts, are absolutely certain Ellen was murdered.

The facts leave no room for doubt. I agree with a host of professionals who tirelessly studied the case and whose expertise and ethics I respect. This conclusion is without question and brings me here, to this battle.

The Greenbergs have used every legal weapon at their disposal on behalf of their beautiful daughter, but the war they now wage is not against Ellen's killer. The war is against representatives for a major metropolis, seemingly willing to move Heaven and Earth to make this all go away.

When I first learned about this case and read, with shock and sadness, that this beautiful young woman, wedding date set, had been stabbed twenty times and that manner of death was ruled a suicide,

I was stunned. I could not believe what I was reading…surely I had missed some critical fact, surely I would discover that fact and feel a sense of relief wash over me, assured that justice had been sought. That never happened. Instead, the more I learned, the more distraught I became.

In all my many years on the job, having been mired in more wrenching cases than I can count, I have never witnessed such an obvious miscarriage of justice. The "investigation" into Ellen's death is replete with layer upon layer of evidentiary fails.

What I have discovered makes it impossible for me to let this case go. Why? Because the longer the saga continues and the more I learn, the more disturbing the "official" investigations and judicial maneuvering of Ellen's case have become.

Understand. Ellen was an incredibly vivacious young woman, deeply loved, deeply admired and respected, a beloved teacher to tender young children, a cherished daughter, granddaughter, and friend, with her whole life ahead of her. Ellen Greenberg was barbarically snuffed out, violently stabbed over and over again. Most probative, at least one of Ellen's wounds is shown to have been inflicted postmortem. Repeat. At least one of Ellen's stab wounds is shown to have been inflicted postmortem, AFTER DEATH. A basic truth is being shouted into the ether: Without oversight, scrutiny, and a willingness to say we got it wrong and must fix it, this could happen to anyone.

Ellen's family fights on. They are battle fatigued, weary, drained in mind, body, and soul. They cannot fully mourn their daughter's passing because the fight still rages. They are broke and nearly broken, their resources gone. And yet, they stand. I now stand with them in their pursuit of justice. Will you join me?

PROLOGUE

A striking revelation was recorded on April 16, 2024, at a motions hearing in the Philadelphia Court of Common Pleas. A key witness in the lawsuit filed by Ellen's parents against the City of Philadelphia was prepared to testify that Ellen died by homicide, not suicide, and that a ten-inch knife was found still plunged deep into her chest.

This news was reported before Judge Linda Carpenter by Joseph Podraza, the Greenbergs' lawyer. The key witness, Guy D'Andrea, a former Philadelphia assistant district attorney, as reported by *Penn-Live Patriot-News*, had "carefully reviewed and organized" the official death investigation file on Ellen Greenberg after it "had been all-but discarded in a closet of the District Attorney's office once her January 2011 stabbing had been ruled a suicide."

The Greenberg family formally asked to question D'Andrea, who had been in the DA's office at the time Ellen's case was investigated. For thirteen years, the Greenbergs, along with a legion of supporters, have waged this endlessly uphill battle, while reps for the city seem interested only in burying facts, evidence, and their own mishandling of the case.

Podraza argued before Judge Carpenter that former ADA D'Andrea had very specialized firsthand knowledge of the evidence and witnesses. Podraza referred to findings of then Medical Examiner Dr. Samuel Gulino, who bluntly stated Ellen had been murdered, telling D'Andrea "this is a homicide."

Dr. Gulino, asserts Podraza, explained that Ellen's body was absolutely moved after she succumbed to twenty unspeakably brutal stab wounds. Gulino told prosecutor D'Andrea that Ellen had been in a "supine position for a period of time." Translation? Gulino infers Ellen was lying flat on her back, not sitting up from mid-chest, her corpse slumped against the kitchen cabinet as reported to authorities. Was Ellen's body moved postmortem and if so, why?

"That's the first I've heard of it," Sandee Greenberg told *PennLive* afterward. How could that be, given years investigating Ellen's death, the family's lawyers, forensics experts, my team, and those following the case obsessively (podcasters, bloggers, reporters, true crime watchers, and social media devotees, just to name a few) digging into every available file, document, and bit of evidence? Where was this pivotal fact hidden? And why?

"I feel pleased, and so should every parent in America, that Judge Carpenter is allowing this to proceed," Sandee told *PennLive* after learning the judge would allow prosecutor D'Angelo's deposition to go forward. "The city's fighting awfully hard (against us)," she stressed.

What other new light is yet to be shed on this profoundly misdirected investigation? I wonder what new evidence will be revealed and how it's been kept from prying eyes all these many years.

CHAPTER ONE

On a stormy winter night, January 26, 2011, just days after sending out save-the-dates for her upcoming wedding, a beautiful twenty-seven-year-old elementary school teacher, Ellen Greenberg, was found dead in the apartment she shared with her twenty-eight-year-old fiancé, Sam Goldberg. According to court records, Goldberg voluntarily spoke with police and told them he was downstairs at the building's gym at the time Ellen was killed. When he came back upstairs to their Manayunk, Philadelphia, apartment, he found their front door deadbolted, with the swing bar locked from inside.

Unable to gain entry with his keys, Sam said he banged on the door repeatedly, to no avail. After trying in vain to reach Ellen by phone for an hour, he explained he was ultimately able to force open the door by breaking the inside lock.

Fiancé Goldberg reports he discovered Ellen seated on the kitchen floor, her body slumped, propped up against the kitchen cabinets with her legs splayed out in front of her, the kitchen awash with blood. According to the medical examiner's report, Goldberg called 911 and was "instructed to start CPR until he noticed a knife in her chest, then was instructed to stop."

3

When police arrived, they honed in on only a few key elements, almost as if they were looking to rule something out. Finding no defensive wounds, evidence of a struggle, or forced entry, they deemed amongst themselves, rank and file, the manner of death was suicide. Case closed. Easy.

Though they were using words like "suicide," foot patrol cops, first on the scene, called for backup of a higher echelon. They contacted the Northwest detectives, who then called in homicide detectives. Two detectives and their supervisor arrived to the luxury condos in Manayunk, a town which hadn't had a single homicide that year. The gathering of law enforcement went on over a period of three hours.

It was only when the Philadelphia Medical Examiner's Office got involved, however, that the investigation began in earnest. During the autopsy, it was ascertained that Ellen had been stabbed twenty times. Yes, twenty times. There were knife wounds to her head, the back of her head, the back of her neck, and to her chest. The medical examiner also found bruises in "various stages of resolution" on her arms, abdomen, and leg, according to the autopsy report. When police arrived on scene, a ten-inch kitchen knife was still deeply anchored ten centimeters into Ellen's chest. And here's a most remarkable finding: At least one, if not more, of the stab wounds had not bled, which means they'd occurred postmortem, after Ellen's heart had stopped beating, after she was dead.

Then there is the issue of the blunt and brutal force of many of the stabs. Could Ellen have continued to stab herself over and over with such power and velocity, there on the floor of her own kitchen? And there is the issue of stabs and cuts to the back of the neck and head, seemingly impossible to have been self-inflicted.

CRITICAL FACT: Naturally then, Philadelphia Medical Examiner Dr. Marlon Osbourne's initial finding was homicide, Ellen Greenberg had been murdered. The obvious was stated by a certified pathologist hired by the government. I am in awe of the work of forensic experts and so grateful they do it. The best of them—and I've had the great honor of working with so many of these brilliant people—break down then put back together the death scene as if they were there to witness what originally transpired. But the assessment of Ellen's death was by no means rocket science. At the time, Dr. Osbourne stated the clear and definitive truth. Homicide.

You'd think.

On March 7, 2011, the Philadelphia Medical Examiner's Office had a seismic shift in position; they officially reclassified Ellen Greenberg's death as a suicide.

There was immediate backlash. Many people in the know were flabbergasted, scratching their heads and wondering how this could possibly be explained. Well, how do you explain the inexplicable? The Greenberg family was distraught and bewildered. Ellen's father, Josh, is convinced that the medical examiner was pressured to reclassify the death to align with the official police assessment.

The response of the Greenbergs and Ellen's close-knit legion of loved ones? After they dealt with the immediate shock—leaving them feeling utterly betrayed by the justice system, their already raw pain now exponentially multiplied—they vowed to fight back. They set out on a mission and their outrage would not be squelched. Driven by haunting grief, crushing heartache, and the powerful certainty Ellen did not take her own life, they acted.

Convinced the alleged suicide was the complete antithesis of who Ellen was and how she lived her life, they knew the MOD, manner of death, made no sense. There was also the overarching impossibility that she committed all these atrocities to her own body, much less in light of the pain she was suffering in the last minutes of her life. Ellen's parents began the fight of their lives, starting by putting together their own team of experts.

The loss of Ellen and the ghastly way she left this world, alone, terrified and terrorized was already a worst-case scenario. What should have been an obvious homicide determination followed by an intense manhunt for a cold-blooded killer was anything but. There was no search for the monster responsible for a vicious stabbing spree, no deep-rooted investigation, no detailed forensics or intensive interrogations. Instead there was the sense of, "Everybody go home, nothing to see here. Just your run-of-the-mill female suicide. Let's move on."

Ellen's parents and loved ones had no idea what lay ahead, that they were entering the most grueling and seemingly endless battle of their lives. It's overwhelming to comprehend they are still engaged in the same fight, all these years and all this evidence later. What they continue to learn along this journey will disturb your sense of justice and your belief in a system designed to protect us all.

CHAPTER TWO

Ellen Rae Greenberg was born on June 23, 1983, in New York City. A beautiful, healthy baby, she was instantly the love of her parents' lives and warmly welcomed into their close-knit extended family. Always cheerful and energetic, Ellen was the very first grandchild on both sides and the center of a growing brood of cousins. Her girl cousins, especially, gravitated toward and looked up to the raven-haired beauty with the deep brown eyes and gorgeous, megawatt smile.

The Greenbergs were happily living in Tenafly, New Jersey, but when Ellen started middle school, they headed to Harrisburg, Pennsylvania, Sandee's home state. Josh sold his periodontal practice and bought into a new one, and they settled in, a happy trio. Young Ellen took to Harrisburg like a duck to water and quickly embraced her new home and school.

Sandee's mom was thrilled to have her granddaughter close. After Sandee went back to work, Ellen's grandmother picked her up from school to go on adventures together. Josh's parents adored their granddaughter; their sun rose and set on Ellen. They were besotted with little Ellen, becoming like children themselves around her. They simply loved being part of the joy that surrounded her.

From early on, Josh and Sandee instilled into their girl the importance and empowerment of hard work, determination, and the confidence to go after her dreams. "Ellen always had the incentive to work and play hard," says her mom.

A gifted and enthusiastic athlete, Ellen loved being part of a team and practiced intensely, always trying harder than the time before. She excelled at softball, tennis, and swimming. She was her father's football sidekick and partner, the two faithfully attending Jets and Giants games all season. At the same time, she was very much a "girlie girl," loving the fashion trends.

Friends were a huge part of Ellen's life. In middle school, she met and instantly befriended Alyson, one year older than Ellen. The two besties were always together, sharing secrets, dreams, and crushes; laughing, growing, and engaging in one experience after the next. They went to Hebrew school together, and the two even signed up for a Penn State summer program while still in high school.

Debbie, whose husband is Sandee's cousin, married into the family in 1989, when Ellen was a little girl. Debbie and her family celebrated Ellen's bat mitzvah and loved having her over to visit. Debbie was deeply moved when at the party, her father-in-law described Ellen as "one of the ten happiest people in life," along with her natural warmth and sweetness, how she had the knack of bringing people together, how deeply Ellen was loved.

Debbie and Ellen would become extremely close over the years, sharing a special, sister-like bond that would last until the final day of Ellen's life.

It became easily evident as she grew that Ellen had a soft spot for children. She loved their energy and playfulness and did a lot of babysitting to earn pocket money. A summer job at a law firm didn't appeal to her; she knew instantly that a corporate gig was not for her.

With silky brunette hair, a light dusting of freckles, and a dazzling smile, Ellen was so pretty, so charming and magnetic, she could make anyone feel welcome and important. Growing up, she always had schoolgirl boyfriends, and true to character, she remained friendly with her beaus even after they'd gone their separate ways. A decade later, three of those young sweethearts traveled from across the country to her funeral, to mourn and remember her bright light.

After graduating from high school, Ellen headed to Penn State to join her friend Alyson. Ellen took instantly to the social life at college but also understood it was critical that she throw herself into her studies. She became driven to achieve high grades and extend her education.

In 2005, Ellen graduated from Penn State with a major in communications and set out for Washington, DC, to study speech pathology. Alyson, who settled in Philadelphia after college, visited often until Ellen joined her back in Philly. While there, Ellen refined her career path and decided to pursue her teaching degree at Temple University. She worked tirelessly and with intense focus, ultimately earning not one but two master's degrees. By day, she worked as an aide at Colonial Middle School, and at night she took classes.

Ellen promptly moved into Alyson's Philadelphia apartment building and the two besties were again inseparable. They did everything together. It was a golden time, their bright futures in front of them, the world theirs for the taking.

In short order, the two rented an apartment together and became roommates. "She was always positive, everybody's biggest cheerleader…supportive, and in touch," Alyson says of Ellen. But as much as Ellen was involved in the daily life details of those she loved, always there to help at the drop of a hat, she somehow kept her own life details, including potential romances, close to the vest. Alyson says

Ellen would definitely talk about boyfriends and dating, divulging surface details, but deeper, personal particulars seemed off-limits.

It was when Ellen moved to Philadelphia that she became more a part of cousin Debbie's life, visiting Debbie's home often and regularly, even staying with Debbie's children when Debbie and her husband went out of town. To Debbie's children, she morphed into an adored big sister. They loved having her over and being in her happy, positive circle. There was always a ton of laughter.

Teaching degrees in hand, Ellen began teaching first grade at the Juniata Park Academy in Philadelphia. She loved her students and threw herself wholeheartedly into teaching. Organized and conscientious, she put great thought into daily class lesson plans. And she fit in with Juniata staff and colleagues. It was perfect.

Then, one early evening in 2007, an excited Ellen phoned Debbie with news: Ellen had been set up for a blind date with a guy who sounded great. Ellen was thrilled when it just so happened that Debbie knew this guy's very prominent family fairly well and thought highly of them. Debbie was so happy for Ellen that, in the midst of their call, she encouraged Ellen to go for it! And she did.

CHAPTER THREE

Sandee Greenberg recalls her daughter's excitement as palpable and her energy high. Ellen was buzzing, really looking forward to meeting this new guy who came so highly regarded. His name was Sam Goldberg and he worked for NBC Golf. Ellen thought it sounded fantastic. And she could travel with him when he went away for NBC!

"We'd tried to raise our daughter to make the right choices in life. We weren't micromanaging. We trusted her, had faith in her decision-making," Sandee says. She and husband Josh had always been supportive of Ellen's passions and all she pursued to follow her dreams. That support and cheerleading wasn't limited to education and career, but, of course, included love! They wanted happiness for Ellen. Was this Sam Goldberg "Mr. Right"?

Ellen was into Sam from the get-go, and they started spending a ton of time together. He hailed from a wealthy and connected family; they were "Main Line," Philadelphia, in wealth, education, economic class, and sensibility. She was impressed and seemed hungry for his approval. Always beautiful and slim, she suddenly began watching her own appearance including every calorie, as if she felt inferior somehow. The Goldbergs seemed in another league altogether.

Ellen began sleeping at Sam's more and more…that is…at his parents' home. Her friends found it odd that Sam, given his family's wealth, didn't have his own place. When Ellen was home, things started to feel increasingly "off" to Alyson. One day after arriving back from school, after she hadn't been to their apartment for a while, Ellen became tense when she found her pile of mail waiting for her in her bedroom. "She said that the next time I should leave it in the kitchen, that she didn't want the 'dirty mail' on her bed." Micromanaging a detail like where to place the mail? Much less being upset about it? That, or anything like it, had never happened before.

* * *

Debbie recounts how a mutual friend introduced Sam and Ellen. They exchanged numbers and quickly fell into a regular pattern of long phone calls since Sam was often on the road for work. Eventually, Sam asked Ellen to join him and sent her a plane ticket to Arizona where he was working. Ellen didn't like to fly, but she was smitten with Sam and decided to go.

Debbie says Goldberg was "warm, funny, charming…knew how to talk to people." Sam didn't seem concerned with his appearance. "It's funny," Debbie says, "after they got involved, Ellen began to drop weight, and she was already thin, while Sam, who had been thin, started to gain." Debbie never saw the two argue publicly, and all was portrayed as blissful.

As time went on, Debbie saw less and less of the two, as Ellen spent nearly all her time, when Sam was not on the road, with his friends and his family and rarely her own. She notes that Sam stated that he loved to cook and his father bought him an expensive and highly rated set of chef knives. "One of those was used to kill Ellen," Debbie says, her voice cracking.

* * *

Ellen continued to present their coupledom as perfect and Sam as a devoted boyfriend. Ellen's struggle with Sam's family, however, grew. Usually close-lipped about life with Sam Goldberg, she was ultimately unable to hold in all of her feelings about his family and their treatment of her. She vented enough to make an impression on her mother and close friends.

The Goldbergs lived an exclusive, upscale lifestyle and had the best of everything. They resided on Philadelphia's Main Line and had a real estate fortune inherited from his mother's family. Mindy Hankin Goldberg came from money, and lots of it. Ellen sensed they didn't think she measured up, that her own accomplished and successful family was not, and never would be, of their same ilk. She found his mother, in particular, to be very difficult to get close to or gain approval from. This, coming from a young woman who'd never before failed to impress or touch the lives around her.

Sandee remembers Ellen felt she was always the "last person on the chain" with Mindy. "We thought we brought prestige to the table. We were educated, Josh is a doctor," Sandee says. Sandee's convinced that the Goldbergs considered themselves superior and that Ellen was not treated kindly by them. Was this real?

Josh says he also sensed that the Goldbergs looked down on them, like they were "hicks" from Harrisburg, not shiny, elite Main Line types. He didn't like the stories he heard about how his daughter was being treated by them.

Ellen attended numerous weddings and celebrations with Sam's family as his plus-one. She told a close friend that his mother and sisters were fake-looking and obsessed with fashion, makeup, and hair…that they seemed to fancy themselves as the Main Line Kardashians. And yet, Ellen then seemingly followed suit to please

Sam and his family… getting her hair done just like Sam's sisters and imitating the sisters' fashion and clothing choices. She deeply yearned to fit in and be accepted, even though the group was a tight, closed clique, and seemingly not interested in inviting her in.

She then became extremely concerned about the day her parents would have to meet Sam's. She worried that the Goldbergs would look down their noses at Sandee and Josh, that her own mom and dad wouldn't gel with his.

Though according to Ellen, Sam's mother, Mindy, was cold and distant to her, and kept her out of the loop, Ellen tried valiantly to fit in, to win her support and convince her that she, Ellen Greenberg, was, indeed, good enough. Ellen continued to lose weight, though already extremely thin. Those close to her noticed her taste in fashion had turned toward more expensive, more sought-after labels and styles typically sported by the privileged and elite. She stressed about wearing the right thing, saying the right thing, doing the right thing. The trend continued… as Sam Goldberg gained more and more weight, Ellen did the opposite and became painfully thin.

Delighted their daughter had found love, Josh and Sandee took a trip together with the young couple to the beautiful Caribbean island of St. Kitts. Ellen's parents picked up on nothing troubling or off. Yes, there was some anxiety bubbling up about Sam's parents, but if Ellen's worst problem was getting Sam's mother to warm up to the woman he loved, Josh and Sandee figured their girl could handle blending families. She'd be fine, they thought. She always was, right?

CHAPTER FOUR

As Ellen got deeper and deeper in with Sam, she put greater and greater distance between herself and her longtime friend, Alyson. She largely stopped socializing with Alyson and her fiancé and instead, turned almost exclusively to Sam's friends, other young Main Line couples. It was clear that Ellen was trying to become part of a rich, elitist crowd. "She went from Nordstrom's to Bloomingdale's and then to Saks Fifth Avenue," Alyson says. Ellen would attempt to hide luxury purchases she couldn't afford on a teacher's pay and didn't want to talk about them. She seemed desperate to make the right impression.

According to her close friends, Ellen had always "worn the pants" with her boyfriends, had always been the boss. No one pushed her around and never did she feel the need to explain herself. "The relationship with Sam was the first time I ever saw her ask a guy's permission for anything," says Alyson. "We were shopping for brides-maid dresses for my wedding and had been to many stores. I wanted to go to one more, and Ellen got nervous, said she had to ask Sam." Ellen asking permission to go to a bridesmaids' shop? This was a first. "That was bizarre behavior for her."

Ellen had always seemed relaxed and carefree to be around, including when with former beaus. In 2010, Ellen brought Sam to a party at an old friend's house and was observed to have seemed extremely tense, as if worried. "The whole time," the friend recounts, "she never took her eyes off him. She waited on him, constantly, couldn't sit still. It was noticeable to everyone. So not like her."

By this point, Ellen seemed to embrace a wholesale "don't tell" policy about her relationship with Sam. There was not a single negative word uttered now, not even in the silly, jovial way women complain about romantic partners and vice versa. Ellen conveyed everything was wonderful, actually. Ellen insisted Sam was generous and charming, attentive and affectionate, she'd say, and she was so incredibly happy.

Then, Ellen moved out of the apartment she shared with Alyson, got her own, and ultimately moved in with Sam. In June 2010, the month of Ellen's birthday, they got engaged. Ellen sensed it was coming; she and Sam had talked about a future together. She even knew he planned to use his grandmother's diamond ring to propose to her.

Ellen had gone along with Sam on a business trip to California. Debbie happened to be out on the West Coast at the same time and spent a day with Ellen, who excitedly confided that she felt Sam could pop the question at any moment. She'd just finished the school year and seemed so happy about what was ahead. Two and a half years after they'd started dating, Sam proposed in a beautiful setting, out on the ocean rocks at the shore.

Ellen was giddy when she texted the big news the next day, and Debbie was so happy for her, delighted to give the marriage her blessing. Josh and Sandee's only concern was that their daughter should be happy and well cared-for. It was instinctive on their part; Ellen was spending nearly all her time with Sam's family, keeping her parents distinctly separate from the Goldbergs. Sandee and Josh decided to stay well out of the way and not present any impediment to the happiness of their only child.

* * *

After weeks of excitement, the wedding planning got underway in earnest. The marriage was going to take place in August 2011. Josh and Sandee were very surprised to learn that Sam's parents, coming from great wealth, would not be financially contributing to the wedding. They would host a brunch and rehearsal, but otherwise, everything would be covered by the bride's parents.

Then, the first shock came. Ellen's longtime best friend learned that she would not be in the bridal party...at all. This blow stung deeply. The two had been so close since childhood, their friendship spanning nearly two decades. They had been roommates, college buddies and more for twenty years...as close as sisters. And, of course, Ellen had been one of Alyson's bridesmaids. The bridal party would be all family...Sam's family, that is. Ellen offered no excuses for having none of her own friends in her wedding party. It was not to be discussed.

Then, the second shock. It became painfully clear that no one on Ellen's side would be told any of the wedding plans. If friends even tried to approach the subject with Ellen, she'd be standoffish in response, making it obvious they shouldn't even ask. All of it felt odd, completely off-kilter, so unlike the Ellen her friends and loved ones had always known and cherished.

CHAPTER FIVE

But Sandee and Josh tried their best to stay involved in the wedding planning, trying to accommodate their daughter and make her happy, to ensure her wedding day would be everything she'd dreamed. The venue was chosen and secured. Ellen had successfully completed another year of teaching at Juniata Park Academy, another dream come true. She loved children and wanted to help them; being a teacher allowed her to achieve that, to really make a difference.

As she did with others in her life, anytime the subject of Sam and their relationship came up, Ellen painted a rosy picture for her parents. Ellen had always been affectionate with everyone she loved, and the same was true regarding Sam. Sandee steadfastly encouraged Ellen to share anything that was troubling her, making it crystal clear Ellen could always come to her and tell her anything. Occasionally, in a peripheral way, Ellen let details slip out.

Ellen deeply appreciated the kindness Sam's father extended toward her. She loved going to their house, especially when she first started dating Sam. Sam's dad was warm and welcoming to her, but her future mother-in-law and sisters-in-law were just the opposite.

While she never would reveal blatant disrespect aimed at her by the women closest to Sam, Ellen did feel very slighted, glossed over. "I got the feeling that with Sam's mother and sisters, my daughter did not matter," Sandee says. Ellen was oftentimes excluded, which was hurtful and confusing. She felt pushed to the side during the wedding planning of another family member. For one celebration, a makeup artist and hairstylist was brought in to pamper every one of Sam's sisters. Ellen was there on the scene with the sisters, had assumed she would be part of the group, one of the sisters. But instead, she was excluded again, left embarrassed for having assumed they wanted to include her. That must have stung.

Again, she got the message. They hadn't even considered her; she didn't even cross their minds. She knew then that what she had felt instinctively all along was right: They didn't approve of her, and she didn't belong.

Hearing their daughter was even a bit unhappy with her treatment by members of Sam's family was painful and infuriating for Sandee and Josh. Their priority was their daughter's joy, so with much self-control, Sandee and Josh remained tight-lipped, even to Ellen, about their feelings for the Goldbergs.

Josh was more outspoken, if not to his daughter, to Sandee and trusted friends. He didn't like the Goldbergs, found their obvious feelings of superiority distasteful, and their judgment of his daughter ugly and unacceptable. "Unkind things were said that I didn't understand. It was like she wasn't good enough for their son, for their family. She seemed to be trying too hard with people who could be snotty toward her."

The wedding was teeing up to be very fancy…and an expensive affair. "We had given deposits everywhere," Sandee remembers. "It was going to be big. Ellen was happy and excited. And she was marrying a nice Jewish boy. Sam seemed nice enough, reasonable. We didn't know much more than that."

They had to go with it. Sandee and Josh were committed to Ellen, and that meant helping her get the life she wanted. Period. They loved and adored her and would never interfere or put their own feelings before hers. They had the difficult task of keeping their opinions to themselves and making her happiness the most important thing. It was all that mattered.

CHAPTER SIX

In the fall of 2010, things took a worrisome and ultimately drastic turn. Ellen, always so polished, poised, outgoing, and in complete control of herself, was obviously unraveling. She was suffering... something was terribly wrong. But what?

After months of planning, everything was set in stone. Ellen, soon to be married, was back to school for another year of teaching her precious first graders. By all accounts, it should have been a joyous time filled with anticipation and wonder at all the possibilities before them. She should have been watching the clock, excited for the days to pass, until the biggest day of them all.

Ellen's father was the first to sense something was wrong. He couldn't put his finger on it, but he knew his daughter and she was not herself. She was skittish, on edge, newly nervous, all things she'd never before been. Josh didn't want to worry his wife, so he didn't share his concerns or let on he was worried about Ellen. "I didn't know what I was dealing with," Josh says now, looking back.

Then, it hit. Ellen called her parents to say that she wanted to come home, right in the middle of the school term. She wanted to move out of the apartment she shared with Sam Goldberg and come back to Harrisburg. What? It couldn't be. Leave paradise with the man of your dreams to move back in with Mom and Dad? They wanted to chalk it up to pre-wedding jitters but they immediately asked if she was okay. Were there problems with Sam? Had plans changed? In other words...was the wedding off?

As always, Ellen projected everything with Sam was great. But she wanted to move out and come home? Even leave her job to move out? Sandee, surprised and concerned, tried to get to the bottom of it. She pressed and prodded in order to help her daughter, but as was her way, Ellen avoided questions she didn't want to answer.

It would come to light after her death that Ellen had also asked Debbie if she could move into her guest room. Debbie had been confused. She'd asked, "Oh, is Sam going to move in too?" Ellen wouldn't answer, and the odd subject was dropped.

Deeply concerned, Josh and Sandee put their heads together, searching for the meaning of all this. As far as they knew, their daughter had never taken drugs or had any bout of depression even in the slightest degree. In fact, Ellen had never even been indecisive. If anything, she always had a clear sense of what she wanted. She'd never displayed erratic behavior, not even once. She had never, in all her years, fallen prey to those kinds of life stressors. Moreover, she'd always remained composed, kept her personal issues close, despite the efforts of her loved ones to get her to open up. But now, things were altogether different.

Puzzled, Josh told his daughter that it didn't make sense for her to pick up and leave a job she loved so much, a job at which she was so gifted and so appreciated by students and parents alike. The school loved her...it was her calling. And after all, the school term was almost finished. Josh advised her to stick it out a few more months and come home at the end of the school year, which he and her mother would love.

When pressed again about possible troubles with Sam, Ellen denied any. She instead claimed her problems were related to school, that she was worried about her students' grades.

Her students' grades? They were in the first grade, not applying to Harvard Law School. It didn't make sense. Josh and Sandee urged Ellen to be specific regarding what was upsetting her about the children's grades. But Ellen wouldn't explain why she wanted to come home... she shut down.

Sensing Ellen's unhappiness, Josh and Sandee insisted Ellen see someone to get counseling. They reached out to a very respected psychiatrist who came highly recommended, Dr. Ellen Berman. Berman prescribed meds for Ellen for anxiety (Xanax, Klonopin) and for sleep (Ambien) and asked Ellen to journal about her feelings day to day. In her own, copious notes, Dr. Berman was crystal clear: Ellen showed absolutely no signs of suicidal thoughts or suicidal ideation. None. Zero.

At first, Ellen texted her mom with good news. She told Sandee the meds were helping. It didn't take long, though, for Ellen to push back against the prescribed pills, texting Sandee that she didn't like the way they made her feel. Ellen didn't like the sense of not being in control, of feeling different somehow. Ellen had never dabbled in drinking or drugs, so she wasn't, by nature, comfortable with being medically altered in any way. And importantly, Ellen was worried that the pills would make her gain weight.

After her death, when her computer searches were explored, it was discovered Ellen had been looking online for anxiety meds that didn't cause weight gain. According to the FBI, we've been told, there was no evidence whatsoever of any searches for how to end your life, painlessly or otherwise. There was nothing related to even depression, much less suicide. Bearing that out, nothing, absolutely nothing other than Ellen's prescribed meds was found in her system during the autopsy.

* * *

Leading up to the wedding, Ellen's anxiety did not improve. Sandee and Josh continued attempting to ask, but they got nowhere.

"About two months before she died, I noticed she was not herself," Debbie says. "She said it was all about school, but that made no sense." Debbie knew well that Ellen had moved through her time teaching school with ease. She glided, making it look effortless; she loved it! But now she was suddenly gravely concerned about the children's grades...but "This was first grade."

When Debbie pressed Ellen, urging her to open up, to let her in, Ellen would go silent. She'd completely turn off. "It never occurred to me that this was about her relationship. She made it all about her," Debbie says. Seemingly, according to Ellen herself, it was all Ellen's own problem, her making. Ellen blamed herself.

Though Debbie's relationship with Ellen never changed, everything surrounding it did. She said Ellen was no longer bubbly, her zest for life drained. Looking back, Debbie poignantly recalls it all and says, "I wished I could do something to help."

As the wedding date inched closer, Alyson also became concerned about Ellen's anxiety. When Ellen mentioned moving home, Alyson counseled her friend that she didn't need to go back to her parents. All of Ellen's friends pressed her for answers. "There was this huge shift from a happy, positive person," Alyson says, sounding sad and reflective. Why was there anxiety that had never existed before? Why the secrecy? Why the obsessive dieting?

It was then that Ellen let loose a few more details to her friends. For instance, just months before the big wedding, there was still no bridal shower in the works. Ellen definitely noticed Sam's mother had not helped the move-in at their new apartment. In fact, she'd shown no interest at all. These little confessions were few and far between. But they were there and slowly bubbled up.

A friend shares that Ellen spoke glowingly of her mother, Sandee, and was a daddy's girl all the way. But when it came to Sam's family, "she seemed to want to keep her parents and Sam's apart. She was impressed by the status that Sam's family enjoyed and worried that they wouldn't approve of her parents, their personalities, and how they navigated in a world far apart from the one the Goldbergs moved in."

Ellen's friends also found it odd that with all the Goldberg wealth, Sam didn't have his own place. They found it even stranger that given that wealth and the fact that Sam had a great job, he remained at home, still living with his mom and dad. Even when the relationship intensified and Ellen began spending nights with him under his parents' roof, it seemed they obviously would enjoy privacy in their own apartment. Ellen's friends found it odd she would sleep at the Goldbergs' house in the same bed with him, while his parents were there.

Could Ellen ever possibly fit in?

CHAPTER SEVEN

In the days leading up to Ellen's wedding save-the-dates mailout and her stabbing death, she seemed to have lost herself, overwrought. Even a friend's father-in-law, who worked with Ellen at school, reported that her behavior was not at all normal.

"There was clearly something awful going on," Alyson says now. Ellen's parents believe their daughter was protecting Sam, that she loved him and didn't want to lose him, in spite of whatever was transpiring. "She was stuck. I see that now," a friend reflects.

In her last days on Earth, Ellen was emotionally unkempt and physically disheveled, which was the most surprising thing of all. She'd always been so meticulous about her appearance, wouldn't even entertain the very notion of walking out of the house without full hair and makeup, clothing just right and looking perfect head to toe. This was a complete departure; Ellen had ceased being herself. She couldn't deal with whatever was happening, as if unable to reach for help.

In between tearful sobs she told Alyson that she was taking medication for her anxiety and that she was trying a new one, hoping it would be easier to take. She hated the side effects, complained about them bitterly, and said, "You don't want to know." Alyson pushed for clarification, and Ellen finally revealed, among other things, she "dreaded gaining weight." She seemed so worried about remaining thin for the wedding.

The day before Ellen's body was found, riddled with stab wounds and notably covered in bruises all over, in varied stages of healing, Alyson received an alarming call from her nearly lifelong friend. "It was President's Day, and I was standing in front of CVS. My phone rang, and Ellen was hysterical from the moment I answered." She was crying about the job, and how terrible things had become. Ellen stuck with the story…it was all about the job. This level of misery was all about teaching first grade? "She said she just wanted to go home."

The next morning, Alyson woke to the worst. Ellen's mom, Sandee, called with devastating news: Ellen was dead. At first, Alyson didn't second-guess when Sandee told her Ellen had taken her own life, but once Alyson learned the cause of death, multiple stab wounds with a kitchen knife, she instantly knew it was all wrong. "Once I knew the severity…there was no way. No. Not a suicide." Within hours the word spread and all agreed…this was no suicide.

* * *

Josh and Sandee were shattered, inconsolable. Their grief was, and is, unspeakable, beyond anything imaginable. Nothing could be worse than losing a child. No one should ever know that kind of crushing pain and loss.

The Greenbergs knew their daughter was suffering anxiety over her beloved teaching position, or so they thought, or some other unnamed and more secretive dilemma. But nothing…nothing… signaled that Ellen wanted to stop living. How could she be that distraught? She had just sent out her save-the-dates for her wedding. She had huge plans, fantastic dreams, and a bright, shiny future.

Ellen Greenberg loved life.

"Did I believe what the police were saying? Only because I had been raised to trust the police," Josh laments. At that terrible time, both he and Sandee had no reason not to trust the police, unquestionably. "We took them at their word. Even if we were truly shocked and couldn't imagine on a logical or emotional level that she would have ended her own life. Not Ellen."

And, of course, they didn't have yet a clue as to how their girl had left this world, what she'd endured, obviously so alone and terrorized, helpless. They were tortured by the thought of Ellen so distraught and so alone…or was she?

CHAPTER EIGHT

"I knew of Ellen quite some time before we met. My aunt and Ellen's mom, Sandee, had been college roommates and were still very close. My aunt really wanted the friendship between us for a long time," says Pam.

They officially met in 2005, after college. Pam was a year older than Ellen and living in Washington, DC. "We connected and really hit it off." Ellen, who had just moved to the capital city, went with her mom and her grandmother (Sandee's mom) to Pam's apartment and was impressed; soon thereafter, Ellen took a place in the same building.

It really all started with an invitation from Ellen for a weekend at the beach. "After that, we were inseparable in our DC lives," Pam says. The fast friends spent a chunk of the summer at the shore, at least two or three days at the beach. They got along so well and always had so much fun together. Pam found Ellen effusive, always smiling that wide, toothy grin that lit up her face, always up for a good time. Her spiritedness was contagious.

"Ellen wanted everyone to be happy around her. She wanted me to be happy. She was generous and thoughtful. She made a great effort to go out and find what I loved, like chocolate-covered strawberries, and buy them for me. She liked to bring different people together, to help establish new networks and friendships," Pam says.

During that summer of 2005, Ellen had been dating a guy named John, with whom she was on-and-off. It never got ugly, according to Pam, but remained carefree and casual. Ellen dated regularly and remained in touch and on good terms with guys after they stopped seeing each other romantically. From John, she moved on to Jason, whom Pam is still friendly with today.

Jason introduced Ellen to his friends and vice versa. It was all very inclusive. "We all spent time together at the beach as a group," Pam remembers. "I was often the third wheel, having gone through a break-up of my own, but was never treated that way. I was always included, never, ever left out for the couples to go it alone."

Pam says that Ellen treated Jason very well. She would tease him about how he dressed—sloppily and not with any up-to-date fashion sense at all—and threaten to give him a makeover, but it was all in fun. He didn't mind the teasing and seemed to actually get a kick out of it. "He didn't care and didn't change his style for her. He laughed along, and it was kind of like their thing, good-naturedly."

Pam says that Jason really liked Ellen, that she was so kind to him and made him feel good. She was very loving and affectionate to him in front of others and always seemed mindful of how he felt. They dated until Ellen moved back to Philadelphia, in the fall of 2006, to go to graduate school. They parted on the best of terms, with no resentment, bad blood, or hurt feelings between them.

Pam hated seeing Ellen leave. The two dear friends would miss each other, but it was clear that their friendship would remain solid. "We had to be more intentional about staying in touch," Pam says. "My brother went to Penn, and Ellen hung out with him. I made trips to Philly every month and spoke to her every day. We kept up lots of contact and remained very close."

Settled in Philadelphia, Ellen was working and going to school, her social life as active as ever. She dated different guys. "Every time I went to visit, she introduced me and included me, as she always had," Pam remembers warmly. "When she met Sam, though, it was different."

It was in 2008, at a celebration of Ellen's twenty-fifth birthday, that Pam met Sam for the first time. Pam had heard about him, about how into him her friend was, about their traveling and romantic adventures, how he doted on her. What she'd noticed from the start, however, was how carefully Ellen seemed to guard the more personal details of this relationship and how much she seemed to be catering to her new boyfriend. With other guys, Ellen called her own shots, was her own boss.

The excited planning for Ellen's June birthday had started back in April. "We all went to the Jersey Shore," Pam says. "Sam's family had a house there, and we arranged for a celebration dinner." It started as a girls' weekend, including their mutual friend, Alyson, and others. They were all out at a restaurant, partying and having a blast. Suddenly, things got weird and took a strange turn. "I remember that Sam told us that he was taking Ellen back to his house. He suggested that she was too drunk."

Ellen's friends were stunned and taken aback. Nothing had seemed to be wrong or in any way worrisome. Sam had insisted Ellen leave with him on the night that her closest friends had gathered for her, on the night that they were going to sleep, dorm-style, in the cramped, one-bedroom house together—a special night for the girls. "We thought she'd be up early and back joining us for breakfast. We didn't hear from her until after noon the next day," Pam says.

* * *

That night at the Jersey Shore aside, Pam's take on Sam was positive. "He was super charming. I was dating someone that summer, and we went to Philly for a dinner date with them. Sam seemed like a great fit. Family was very important to Ellen, as it is for me. We loved each other's cousins and relatives and parents," Pam says. She calls Ellen a "great role model for her cousins, who loved and adored her."

"Sam had a golf tournament in Baltimore. We met him there and went for dinner. My aunt came along to meet him. He was incredibly friendly, and took an interest in my date… Ellen was telling me that she was spending an extraordinary amount of time with Sam's family. She was always there," Pam says.

On the occasions, few that they were, Pam was together with Ellen and Sam, the couple was always affectionate…but "I didn't see that sillier, more free side of her. Ellen could be so silly and joyful."

What Ellen wasn't doing was spending as much time as she always had with her people and at her apartment. Her friends found that "a little weird." She had her own place and was still spending nights under his parents' roof when they could have had privacy. Their time with Ellen's parents was far more regimented and planned in advance; there wasn't a lot of that. The same goes for their time with Ellen's friends.

"Ellen was trying to make it work and fit in. She still prioritized me, but it was around Sam's schedule," Pam remembers. "She was different with Sam than with other guys she'd dated. At the time, I guess I just thought she was in love with him and wanted to make it work. He was offering things others hadn't. He came from wealth, and not having to worry about money was nice. I mean, she came from a financially comfortable family, but this was on another level."

Ellen never, ever complained about Sam, but Pam says "by the time they got engaged, she felt judged by his sisters…she said that even when they were at the beach, around Sam's family, she felt pressured to put herself together, pristinely, even first thing in the morning.

Like she wouldn't meet them for breakfast without doing her hair and makeup and choosing the perfect outfit."

Ellen was thrilled when she told Pam that she and Sam had gotten engaged. Everyone was happy for them; no member of Ellen's close circle was surprised. They'd been dating for a few years and had been dropping little comments about marriage for a while by then. Pam got engaged three weeks later. "We had been doing everything in lock-step. It was thrilling!"

When Ellen started mentioning her stress and anxiety to Pam, she, unlike as she had with her other friends and parents, blamed it all on the wedding planning. She'd said she was worried about the arrangements not being good enough for his family, about getting her parents and Sam's together, that it wouldn't be an easy fit. "I knew she was seeing a psychiatrist," Pam says. "The one thing that's always been weird to me was that she had an appointment the day she died."

They went back to the beach to celebrate Ellen's engagement. Pam was helping her to gather emails for her invitations and save-the-dates. Ellen picked a date to get married when Pam's fiancé had another wedding, and the same in reverse, so they were going to stay with each other's families and attend the celebrations solo.

The close friends shared a Google calendar. "I knew what she was doing and where she was going all the time," says Pam. "I wrote Ellen a letter for her birthday and she wrote one back to me. She was really excited about my wedding... she didn't seem to have the same excitement about her own wedding."

Ellen confided to Pam that she'd gone on Klonopin. Pam had started ADD medications to help her focus. "We talked about our meds, if they were really helping, the side effects. I noticed that she was getting unhealthily thin. She'd always been thin. This was different."

Pam says, "I'd never before been worried about her. She was strong, knew what she wanted, could speak her mind, had a loving and supportive family, had a great life. Hey, Sam, I thought, was just an added bonus. In my eyes, she was okay, if a bit changed. I still saw her alone, but only when Sam was traveling. When he was home, she was with him every possible second. Everyone we both knew only saw Ellen alone, when she was not with Sam. She invited me there when he was away and never brought him when she visited me. At the time, I didn't see that as a problem. I actually appreciated that I got more of her."

* * *

On the morning of January 27, 2011, Alyson called Pam at work at 9:30 AM. Pam, a CPA, was struck; it was unusual to get a random and, especially, early call from her. "I walked out of my office as Alyson told me that Ellen had been murdered. A UPS guy who was making a delivery was standing there, watching me. I was in disbelief. I thought that this made no sense.

"I hung up, called my aunt, who was speaking with Sandee on the other line. Of course, I knew that I was going straight to Harrisburg from DC. That was my only clear thought. My heart left my body, one hundred percent. I was crying. The UPS guy asked how he could help me. I was in shock, wanted to know what had happened, how this could actually be real."

"I texted my fiancé and friend; they dropped everything and met me at the office. I called my brother to tell him. Everyone was in shock.

"We drove to Harrisburg. I stayed at Alyson's house. My aunt went also. I called one of the DC guys Ellen had dated. He came to the funeral. My parents flew up from Kentucky. We watched a lot of news, but none of it made sense. Who would have killed her? For what? Why? I was shocked when I learned about the bruises all over her body. Total shock."

Pam rescheduled her wedding. She was traumatized and heart-broken, missing Ellen profoundly.

"I heard from Sam after Ellen's death," Pam says. "He reached out within the month. The most interesting thing he said to me: 'Sometimes people just snap.' I was distressed by that. I felt chilled."

Memories flooded back. Pam thought about happier times, when Ellen was hoping to get engaged to Sam. She and he would tease each other about a future together, and she and Pam would send him photos of beautiful rings. Pam says that he was good-natured about the photos, that it seemed quite obvious that he wanted to marry her friend. She thought about the surprise birthday dinner Sam had thrown for Ellen in 2009 in Philadelphia, before he proposed. It had all felt "super-normal" then. Everyone had seemed happy, especially Ellen.

On September 13, 2011, eight months after they lost Ellen, Sam reached out to Pam on Facebook, for a private chat. "We went back and forth a few times, very unspecifically and not discussing anything of import. I created a website for people to share stories about Ellen." It was bittersweet.

CHAPTER NINE

Many believe that on the night of January 26, 2011, Ellen Greenberg's apartment became a crime scene. Many agree that there is no question that Ellen Greenberg was murdered.

As in all cases, let's review the evidence.

First and foremost, there is no statute of limitations on murder. It is never too late to start again, to reopen the case and fully assess the facts. Under the law, it is never too late to give Ellen Greenberg and her family a shot, albeit a long shot at this juncture, at justice. It is never too late under our system of jurisprudence to examine ALL the facts and to allow a Pennsylvania jury to do the same.

* * *

It all started with a call to 911. At roughly 6:30 PM, Sam Goldberg, sounding panicked, was seeking help. He explained to the dispatcher that he came up to the couple's apartment that frigid evening, January 26, 2011, after leaving the building's gym downstairs. His fiancée, Ellen Greenberg, had arrived home early that day, having left Juniata Park Academy when the school closed due to a large-scale storm blanketing the region with snow.

But upon reaching their sixth-floor apartment, Goldberg states he could not open the front door with his key, that the deadbolt was engaged from the inside. Goldberg explained he repeatedly banged on the door, ultimately spending a full hour pounding away ever harder, screaming out Ellen's name while texting and calling her.

Weeks later, Goldberg stated he went to the front desk, explained what was happening, and was accompanied back to his apartment's front door by a building staffer. Goldberg says that with Philip Hanton, who worked security for the complex, as his witness, Goldberg managed to break into the apartment, forcing the door open, pulling the extra lock away from the frame. Then, with the witness still present, Goldberg found his fiancée, soaked with blood, partially sitting up, slumped against the kitchen cabinets, legs splayed out on the floor in front of her. Goldberg called 911.

Here are excerpts of that 911 call:

Sam Goldberg: *"I went downstairs to go work out. I came up and the door was latched. My fiancée's inside. She wasn't answering so after about a half hour, I decided to break it down. I see her now. She is on the floor—bloody. She's not responding."*

The 911 operator asks what happened.

Sam Goldberg: *"She may have slipped. There is blood on the table, and her face is a little purple."*

The 911 operator instructs Sam to look at Ellen's chest, to see if she is breathing.

Sam Goldberg: *"I don't think she is. I really don't think she is. She's on her back. I don't see her moving."*

The 911 operator tells Sam to attempt CPR. Moving closer to Ellen's body, Sam makes sounds that suggest he is shocked and/or distressed by what he sees.

Sam Goldberg: *"Oh my God. Ellie, please!"*

The 911 operator instructs Sam to bare Ellen's chest, to perform CPR.

Sam Goldberg: *"Her shirt won't come off. It's a zipper."*

He is quiet for a few seconds.

Sam Goldberg: *"Oh my God, she stabbed herself."*

"Where?" the 911 operator asks.

Sam Goldberg: *"The knife's sticking out. There's a knife sticking out of her heart."*

"She stabbed herself?" the 911 operator asks.

Sam Goldberg: *"I guess so. Or she fell on it."*

In the very first moments after the discovery of Ellen's body, accident or suicide comes up.

The call goes on:

911 operator: *"Okay, with a knife in her chest, it's going to be kind of hard for you to do CPR. Don't touch it. Don't touch anything."*

Sam is then asked to check for "signs of life."

Sam Goldberg: *"Her hands are still warm. I don't know what that means. But there's blood everywhere.… I'm not touching anything. I can't believe this, though. We're the only ones here."*

The operator inquires about any signs of a break-in.

Sam Goldberg: *"No, no, no, no. No sign of a break in. There will be when you get here because I had to break the latch to get in. I went downstairs to work out. When I came back, the door was latched. It was like locked from the inside. And I'm yelling.… "*

While Ellen stood at the kitchen counter preparing a fruit salad, she devised a suicide plan and executed it? In that short time? Having just sent out save-the-dates for her wedding, in the midst of preparing a meal, she suddenly killed herself? This scenario is entirely contrary to our working knowledge of the manner and assessments of homicide and suicide.

The police arrived and began to investigate. Over several hours, higher-level officers were called in and arrived to the scene, including homicide detectives. Sam Goldberg spoke to police downstairs in the lobby; his parents and uncle, James Schwartzman, an attorney and judge, and other Goldberg friends were also on the scene. Amazingly, they had gotten there in the midst of a blizzard... and quickly.

When Sam Goldberg arrived at the station to voluntarily speak to police, he told his story of what happened, but made no mention of Philip Hanton being present when he broke the lock and entered the apartment.

Let me be clear, Goldberg was not, nor has ever been charged in connection to Ellen's death. He has never been named as a suspect or as a person of interest. Neither he nor his family have ever been accused of any wrongdoing in connection with Ellen's death.

That night, it was accepted that no forced entry, no defensive wounds, and no evidence of a struggle could only mean one thing: Ellen Greenberg had committed suicide. But shouldn't an autopsy rape kit be performed before suicide is pronounced by cops at the scene? Were there microscopic cells of someone's skin or blood under her nails where she fought back? What was the temperature of Ellen's body? How long had she been slumped dead against the kitchen cabinets? What exactly did the rivulet of blood trickling and dried horizontally across her face, from nose to ear, mean? Certainly it meant something. Had she been lying prone on the floor for a period of time that let the blood dry horizontally across her face while she was found with her face vertical to her body? Was she moved after death? Shouldn't the sheer number of stab wounds and their locations, including to the back of the head and neck as well as at least one stab wound inflicted postmortem, after death, be taken into account?

These are just a very few of the questions that should have been answered before a manner of death was entertained. Should have, would have, could have. None of it mattered. It had to be suicide. Right?

CHAPTER TEN

Declaration of Philip Hanton Pursuant to 42 P.A.C.S.6206

I, Philip Hanton, declare of my own personal knowledge:

1. My name is Philip Hanton and I reside at _____, Philadelphia, PA.
2. In January 2011, I was employed as a front desk clerk providing security at the Venice Lofts Apartments located at 4601 Flatrock Road, Philadelphia, PA 19127.
3. I worked the afternoon and evening shift at the Venice Lofts on January 26, 2011, and was on duty when Ellen Greenberg was found dead in the sixth floor Apartment #603.
4. I was the only desk clerk/security person working on the premises during the afternoon and evening of January 26, 2011.
5. Before I learned Ms. Greenberg was dead, Samuel Goldberg, her fiancé, had come to the concierge desk where I was stationed on the first floor of the apartment building.
6. Mr. Goldberg asked if I could help him get into Apartment #603 and I told him I could not.
7. I did not accompany or escort Mr. Goldberg up the elevator, stairs, or otherwise, at any time on January 26, 2011.
8. Had he been accompanied or escorted, it would have been by me.

9. I have reviewed the videotapes taken from the facility for January 26, 2011, which record activity in the first-floor elevator lobby and other common areas of the facility from about 3:00 p.m. until 7:00 p.m. on January 26, 2011.

10. The video confirms that neither I nor anyone else accompanied Mr. Goldberg to his apartment at any time during the full length of the videotape.

11. If I had accompanied or escorted Mr. Goldberg to his apartment, I would have done it using the elevator, and it would be captured on the video.

12. I did not see Mr. Goldberg enter Apartment #603 at any time on January 26, 2011.

13. I did not witness anything Mr. Goldberg did or did not do on the sixth floor of the facility at any time on January 26, 2011.

14. Because I was not with him, I could not observe anything Mr. Goldberg did or did not do on the sixth floor of the facility.

15. I do not know how Mr. Goldberg entered Apartment #603 at any time on January 26, 2011, because I was not with him.

16. I did not see Ms. Greenberg's body in Apartment #603 at any time on January 26, 2011.

17. If anyone says I was with or able to observe Mr. Goldberg on the sixth floor when or just prior to when he claimed to enter Apartment #603 on January 26, 2011, they would be wrong, because I was not with him or otherwise in a position to observe him.

I hereby certify that the facts set forth above are true and correct to the best of my personal knowledge, subject to the penalties of 42 Pa.C.S. & 6206 for unsworn declarations.

Executed this 28th day of June, 2021.

*** Signature of Philip Hanton.

CHAPTER ELEVEN

A t 7:31 PM, according to the Philadelphia medical examiner's official report written by Investigator Stephen Olszewski, "Detective Sierra 9103 of Homicide called to report the death of the above decedent in her apartment with a knife in her chest."

Olszewski arrived at the scene at 8:27 PM, where he was met by Fifth District Police, including sergeants. Also present were Ellen Greenberg's fiancé, Sam Goldberg, and members of his family and some of Goldberg's friends. Olszewski noted that "PFD Medic-5 responded and pronounced death at 1840."

Working the death scene, Olszewski noted that the apartment was "well kept, clean," the front door's inside lock was broken, the screws were still on it but loose, and that it was "obviously forced in when in a locked position." The screws were still attached even though the door had been broken in? He observed that the screws were loose. Had they simply become loosened during the break-in? This is just one of many issues that were not investigated.

Throughout the apartment, he wrote, "there is no evidence of a struggle. Furniture and items appear in place, nothing is obviously missing or disturbed. There are numerous valuables present, money, keys, 3 laptop computers; one in the kitchen on the island (appears to be Goldberg's), one in the master bedroom suite on the floor (appears to be the decedents, [*sic*] as evidenced by wedding material and one on an additional bedroom desk (appears to be the decedents [*sic*] work computer, as evidenced by numerous teaching materials)." He noted that the only way to exit the apartment with the front door locked was through a sliding door to the patio, and that there was no snow present there, no tracks or footprints. Summing up his investigation of the vicinity, he wrote, "There is no note found or anything indicative of suicide on the computer or in the rest of the apartment."

In the bedroom, the investigator found Ellen's prescribed medications: alprazolam, clonazepam, and zolpidem. He found the journal Dr. Berman had asked Ellen to keep. Ellen's cell phone was in the master bedroom. Her last outgoing calls and texts were made that afternoon, the details of which have been redacted. Her last incoming emails and texts were from Sam, nine in total.

They are as follows:

"Hello"

"open the door"

"what r u doin"

"im getting pissed"

"hello"

"you better have an excuse"

"what the fuck"

"ahhhhh"

"u have no idea"

Investigator Olszewski focused next on Ellen's body. He noted that her legs were splayed out on the hardwood floor, just inside the entrance to the apartment. "The decedent is found supine with her head and some of her upper body/shoulders resting against the lower half of the white kitchen cabinets next to the range. Her body, starting with the head is facing north and the legs west. She is clad in a zipper up dark colored shirt overtop a t-shirt, grey sweatpants, underwear and light brown UGG boots. A pair of eyeglasses are on the floor to the right of the decedent. A white towel is grasped in her left hand. A hair tie or scrunchie is on her right wrist. There are no personal effects on the body."

A kitchen towel still in her hand? Indicating that she was in the midst of still making the fruit salad when she died?

Olszewski noted that Ellen had "a knife embedded in her chest, through her clothing. There are multiple stab wounds examined at the scene; at the chest where the knife is located, a few superficial grouped nearby, one to the left upper chest near the clavicle, 2 more at the mid chest between and just below the breasts. There are defects to the shirts consistent with the underlying wounds. There are no defense injuries to the hands, wrists, or forearms. The right hand is closed in a loose fist." He added that the body was cool to the touch in the extremities and warm to the touch at the torso, front and back.

I question why her body would already be cool to the touch, especially in light of the fact that the heat was on in the apartment and she was in the kitchen as well? If she were stabbed dead in such a brief space of time, shouldn't her entire body still have been warm to the touch? Do bodies cool that quickly when in a heated apartment, the kitchen in fact, and when wearing two layers on the upper torso and sweatpants below? Why was her body already cool to the touch?

Olszewski noted blood was present on Ellen's head, on her neck, in her hair, and on her right hand. There was blood along the front of her pants and on both boots. The blood was mostly confined to her body, but there was some on the floor and cabinets; there were also a few drops on the granite kitchen counter.

Blood drops on the kitchen counter? Does this indicate, since they are drops, that Ellen was standing at the kitchen counter prepping food when she was stabbed and that blood dripped down onto the counter? Why would she stop, mid-fruit-salad-prep, dish towel in her left hand, and kill herself? According to one source, there were blood droplets in the bathroom as well.

Adjacent to the body, Olszewski noted two kitchen knives in the sink, both free of blood and tissue. The knife block on the counter was turned on its side, all its utensils also free of evidence. The steak knife in Ellen's chest was consistent with the knife block and the knives in the sink, "a single edged serrated blade approximately 12.5 cm in length."

According to the police officers Investigator Olszewski questioned at the scene, no neighbors reported hearing any noise or arguments. Sam Goldberg went voluntarily to "NWDD for further interviews." Sam's father, Richard Goldberg, meanwhile, notified Sandee and Josh Greenberg that their daughter had died. Sandee answered the call and heard, "Something terrible has happened."

The next morning, Stephen Olszewski called Sandee and Josh to complete the investigation and identification processes:

"Mom states she last talked to the decedent the same day at 0700 when they were both on their way to work. They had a pleasant conversation. She gave no indication that something was imminently wrong. The decedent has been battling issues with anxiety since the end of last year. Mom states she was 'struggling with something,' for which she urged her to seek help. She was seeing a Psychiatrist, Ellen Berman, in Merion Station. The decedent was described as anxious, insecure, not sure of herself and not liking how she felt, characteristics that were not the norm her entire life. The decedent expressed to her parents that she was a bit overwhelmed with her classroom work."

At the time, the Greenbergs stated that they had no reservations about their daughter's relationship with her fiancé. They were emphatic that there had been no previous suicide attempts by Ellen or any mention whatsoever of taking her own life. Ever.

Later that day, January 27, Olszewski interviewed Dr. Berman, who was very upset. She explained that she'd only seen Ellen three times and that they were actually scheduled for the next appointment the very same day. Dr. Berman reiterated that Ellen, who presented with anxiety, complained of pressure at school with a few problematic students and district school regulations changes.

Dr. Berman mentioned that when she asked Ellen about her relationship, her patient would smile, insist everything was great and that he was "wonderful." Ellen denied any issues with abuse when asked. They had been experimenting with medications in an attempt to find the right fit for Ellen, who didn't like certain side effects.

Ellen body was "ordered for transportation to the MEO via Police Wagon for further postmortem examination."

It is here that the mystery deepens.

CHAPTER TWELVE

Beside themselves with grief, Sandee and Josh Greenberg had funeral plans to make. They were heartsick, under the impression that their daughter must have been so utterly desperate and they had missed it. They tried their best to reconcile that something in her life was so awful she couldn't face living anymore but couldn't bring herself to reach out to parents who loved her so dearly. They were so incredibly close, in near constant contact…yet never a word? What was so awful she couldn't share?

None of it aligned with the girl they'd raised and loved. Ellen, the bubbly young woman with an endless appetite for life, who had so much to live for, who brought them such pride and joy, who made their lives and little family complete and who could hardly wait to walk down the aisle to Sam Goldberg.

Sandee and Josh would bury their daughter, their heart. They would sit shiva and mourn their only child. They would try to find strength to go on. And they would try to make sense of it all.

Without their daughter, who were they?

It had always been the three of them. Everything they'd done since the day of Ellen's birth was for their sweet girl, who, with all that vibrancy and boundless energy, embraced every adventure and possibility.

But as confused as they were, counting all the details that didn't add up, Sandee and Josh did not publicly question anyone…yet. They trusted the professionals. And why not?

"We believed in the justice system. No longer," Sandee says now.

CHAPTER THIRTEEN

It was not until the morning after Investigator Stephen Olszewski worked the scene that Dr. Marlon Osbourne, while conducting Ellen Greenberg's autopsy for the Philadelphia Medical Examiner's Office, discovered all twenty of her stab wounds. Shockingly, there were ten to the back of her neck. Repeat, there were ten stabs to the back of Ellen's neck, in an upward trajectory.

Eight more stabs to her chest were documented at autopsy. The stabs to the chest ranged from ".2 centimeters to the final 4-inch wound of the knife still embedded in her chest." Repeat. A four-inch knife wound deep into her chest. There was also a "2-inch wound to her stomach." This was followed by a "2.5-inch-long gash across her scalp." A two-and-a-half-inch gash across her scalp? How did she do that?

There were also eleven bruises in various stages of severity found across Ellen's body, including her "arm, abdomen, and leg," according to the *Philadelphia Inquirer*.

Osbourne's report cited "multiple stab wounds by an unknown person." And with that, Dr. Osbourne of the Philadelphia Medical Examiner's Office officially ruled Ellen's death a HOMICIDE.

Autopsy showed Ellen had suffered eleven stab wounds to the back of her head and neck, which are not visible in the photos. Oddly, only a very limited number of photos were taken by police and the assistant ME at the scene.

This, however, shined a very bright light on a major problem. Yes, another problem. Before Osbourne's ruling changed the entire complexion of the case, investigating members of the police left Ellen and Sam's apartment late on January 26 without sealing it as a crime scene. Wait for it…

The apartment was cleaned and sanitized the very next day. Disaster. Yes, disaster on a monumental scale. A homicide scene as declared by the Philly medical examiner was professionally cleaned and sanitized before detectives and, more critically, forensics teams secured a search warrant to return. The apartment was officially a crime scene as of January 28.

The cleaning took place after Melissa Ware, the building's senior property manager, called police on January 27, asking for instructions about cleaning the bloody apartment. Police referred Ware to a company specializing in crime scene sanitation. James Schwartzman, Sam's uncle, had contacted Ward, to gain entry to the apartment and retrieve a funeral suit for his nephew, and other personal effects, he said. Ward ran this by the police and was given the okay to let civilians onto the scene. No problem; according to police, Ellen's apartment was not a crime scene. Remember? The police on the scene had decided it was a suicide.

Sam Goldberg's uncle, James Schwartzman, along with his son, entered the apartment. In addition to a suit for Goldberg, they also took work and personal laptops, phones, and credit cards belonging to Sam and Ellen to, they said, safeguard them.

The police requested and received items removed by Schwartzman. The electronic equipment was later analyzed by the FBI. But once evidence escapes police possession and is outside police purview, the so-called chain of custody is broken.

Think of a necklace with a beautiful diamond and pearl cluster pendant hanging on a delicate, gold chain. If a single link is broken, the chain is worthless. The diamond and pearl cluster slips off and is gone forever. Much the same with evidence. Once the chain is broken, the evidence will almost certainly be inadmissible at trial. The evidence is no good. Its authenticity is gone. Even if the evidence in question is beyond reproach, pristine, still no one can vouch that it has not been tampered with. It's as if the evidence is gone forever.

CHAPTER FOURTEEN

Melissa Ware, the senior property manager at the Venice Lofts Apartments, worked both the afternoon and evening shifts on January 26, 2011. Melissa was on duty when Ellen was found dead in her sixth-floor apartment, #603.

The following day, on January 27, Ware received a call "from a male family member of Samuel Goldberg requesting to enter the apartment to gather some personal effects for the funeral, including photographs," Ware stated in a legal declaration filed on July 1, 2021. "I then contacted the Philadelphia Police Department and asked permission to let the family member into the apartment."

At that time, Ware was told that there were no restrictions regarding entering the apartment. When she sought information about the condition of the apartment, she was told that any cleaning was not the responsibility of police and that she should contact a third party. Police even went a step further and referred Melissa to "Crime Scene Cleanup."

Ware made arrangements with Crime Scene Cleanup, then advised the Goldberg family member who requested entry that he was permitted to go into Ellen's apartment. She also relayed details about cleanup costs and scheduling and got the Goldberg family members' approval to move forward.

It was only thereafter Melissa learned, through news reports believe it or not, that Ellen Greenberg's death was declared a homicide. When police returned to the scene on January 28, 2011, she informed them that the cleanup had been done and that she had recorded a video of the apartment prior to the cleaning service and before anyone else entering the apartment. The police requested the video; Melissa complied and gave them a copy.

"Before Crime Scene Cleanup arrived, I arranged and was present for the videotaping of the inside of Apartment #603 to preserve a record of the condition and contents of the apartment before anyone else could have access to the premises, primarily to protect the company in the event of theft or damage," Ware explained.

She was present when Crime Scene Cleanup arrived and let them into Apartment #603. "Upon completion, I notified the family member, whom I believe to have been Samuel Goldberg's uncle, that the apartment was clean, and he was able to retrieve the desired personal effects." Ware was present when the man she understood to be Sam's uncle removed several items at his own discretion. We are not in any way suggesting wrongdoing by the family regarding the items taken. The point is, the apartment was the scene of a death and still very much part of an ongoing investigation. Removal of items such as computers, laptops and other devices should not have been allowed by law enforcement.

CHAPTER FIFTEEN

Then there is Ellen's funeral. It's difficult to know where to start. I could see it was very painful, even now, for Sandee and Josh to recall it and speak of it.

The day of Ellen's funeral was one of the most tragic in the lives of Ellen's parents and loved ones. It was also a moment in time, however, according to multiple witnesses, that seemed to shine a bright spotlight on reactions that day.

* * *

The mourners were gathering to grieve with Sandee and Josh Greenberg. Sam Goldberg arrived separately with his own family. Most of Ellen's circle genuinely liked Sam Goldberg; some even loved him. Surrounded on either side by his sisters, who seemed to be physically holding him up as his body was apparently threatening collapse. "Sam was bawling his eyes out. He was hysterical," says a close friend of Ellen's.

At the outset of the funeral, everyone was functioning under the police decision that Ellen had committed suicide. Dad Josh Greenberg was about to eulogize his daughter at their Harrisburg synagogue when he received startling news: His girl Ellen's death had just officially been ruled a homicide by the Philly medical examiner. Significantly, this news, this watershed moment in everyone's lives, came courtesy of a Greenberg family friend, not police, not prosecutors.

I had to double-check that fact, and it is absolutely correct. Neither police nor prosecutors, detectives nor investigators, advised Ellen's family that their daughter was the victim of a brutal homicide. A family friend bore the news. "Once again, we were out of the loop, not deemed important enough to share information with," says Josh.

Bold as ever, instead of eulogizing his daughter as he'd originally intended, Josh Greenberg, in front of a packed gathering, announced the news to all those gathered to mourn Ellen. Gasps were audible, shock throbbing in the air. Can you imagine? Attending the funeral of a vibrant young woman who had tragically taken her own life, or so you thought, and then learning from her dad, at the pulpit, that she'd been murdered and there was a killer walking free?

Needless to say, Josh Greenberg's announcement reverberated through the synagogue and left many in extreme discomfort, as it should have.

I place myself in that position. Of course, I knew at my fiancé's funeral that he had been murdered. But I try to imagine that, at my beloved dad's funeral, our pastor had announced from the pulpit that my dad, my soulmate, had been murdered. What shock Ellen's loved ones must have felt.

Homicide? Lovely Ellen? Killed? Why? By whom?

Ellen's cousin says that after the gasps, "You could hear a pin drop." The beautifully appointed chamber went dead silent.

* * *

After the funeral, mourners gathered at Sandee and Josh's home. The homicide ruling hung like a heavy cloud over an already painful day. As grim as news of the homicide ruling was, it actually brightened the otherwise very darkest of days for the Greenbergs. They were burying their only child.

"I was happy," Josh said shortly after. "That's what I thought it was. Murder. We never believed suicide. We didn't think her problems were so great. She didn't have depression. She had anxiety. And now we could clear her name and seek justice."

Greenberg told *PennLive* that he didn't get word of the abrupt change in the case from investigating police. In fact, he relayed that he'd heard very little from them throughout the case.

"'Do you think your daughter committed suicide?' Nobody ever asked me that," Greenberg said. "No contact, even that day. We had little contact with any of the detectives."

During Ellen's eulogy that day and the bombshell announcement, Josh had told those gathered, 'Everybody close your eyes. The spirit of Ellen is with you now, and she will always be there,'" assuring them all there would be justice for Ellen, that it was just a matter of time before her killer was caught. But as he stood there in that pulpit, neither Josh nor Sandee had any idea of the heartaches ahead.

CHAPTER SIXTEEN

After the shiva, Sandee and Josh went to the apartment where their daughter's life had been snuffed out. They went to retrieve Ellen's personal belongings. It was wrenching, but making it worse, their pain was compounded by an odd series of events.

Sandee and Josh were so upset. "We were distressed but also very angry. We felt violated. [They] never had our permission to take Ellen's possessions. Her phone, pocketbook, wallet, engagement ring, computers…" Sandee remembers, her tone shaky.

Josh says, "We had to go through a whole chain of command to get those back. They said she had psychological problems and killed herself. They did not help from the beginning to find the killer."

Ellen's cousin relayed that Goldberg clung to the original suicide ruling, even after the finding was changed to homicide.

CHAPTER SEVENTEEN

After the flurry of the homicide manner of death determination, the police investigation into Ellen's murder appeared to stall, grinding to a near standstill. Police updates to Josh and Sandee barely existed, and the media reported little progress in the case.

Philly police and prosecutors were saddled with a high-profile homicide of a pretty, wholesome first-grade schoolteacher from a loving, all-American family, who had one foot down the aisle to marry into a wealthy and prominent Main Line clan, yet there were no answers.

Then, a cruel twist of the knife. On March 11, 2011, the official manner of death ruling was inexplicably changed, renaming the manner of death as suicide. The rug was yanked out from under the homicide investigation and out from under Sandee and Josh as well.

Dr. Osbourne, who performed the autopsy and ruled it a homicide, in a stunning about-face, amended Ellen's death certificate to officially change manner of death to suicide. Once again, without a single word or any explanation to Sandee and Josh.

The Greenbergs openly insist that the evidence they've amassed shows that Ellen's death ruling was changed only after a secret meeting among the police, at least one prosecutor, and two medical examiner officials. This evidence is highly disturbing, and even includes the ME officials' sworn depositions describing the meeting.

The Greenbergs have discovered, after years of investigating and using their life savings to do it, that a female assistant district attorney, a prosecutor representing the DA's office at that meeting, has been granted "high immunity." Translation? In exchange for telling what she knows about the secret meeting and any other goings-on connected to the case, she will never be prosecuted.

Whatever happened in that meeting resulting in Ellen's manner of death being changed from homicide to suicide is so incendiary, a prosecutor was given immunity from prosecution to find out the truth? What does she know? And why and how has this been kept secret from so many for so long?

The suicide ruling completely shut down the homicide investigation, of course. Ellen's twenty stab wounds and all the bruises were discounted as self-inflicted. They were to be buried with her battered body, done away with and dismissed.

The Greenbergs quickly concluded the medical examiner had reclassified the ruling to match with police department investigators. According to the *Philadelphia Inquirer*, the medical examiner was told authorities were "leaning" toward suicide and looking at "mental issues" Ellen may have been suffering.

It was a crushing blow, yes. But going away quietly was the last thing Josh and Sandee had on their minds. They were ready to fight for the justice, already so elusive. They knew it would be an uphill battle, but little did they know it would be so treacherous. Quitting wasn't an option. Getting justice for their daughter, their only child, was the only thing left they could do for her.

* * *

When Josh and Sandee went to file theirs and Ellen's taxes that April, their accountant notified them that a check made out to their daughter had been cashed after her death. What?

Goldberg moved out of the apartment he'd shared with Ellen. The Greenbergs had still not been able to get their daughter's personal effects back. They went to Philadelphia City Hall to file paperwork and sign documents seeking permission to gain access to their daughter's apartment—to get her belongings and pick up her car and drive it back home. "We had to have her things boxed and shipped back to Harrisburg," Sandee says.

Waiting in the lobby, Sandee visited the ladies' room. She spotted what appeared to be specks of blood. The blood triggered a panic... had blood in Ellen's apartment been photographed, was luminol used? What steps had police taken? These thoughts collided in her mind... no one had ever filled them in on so many aspects of the investigation, such as it was.

Josh weighs in: "The police did nothing. They never used luminol on the night Ellen was murdered." Forensic investigators use luminol to detect trace amounts of blood at crime scenes, as it reacts with the iron in hemoglobin. When luminol is sprayed, trace amounts of an activating oxidant make it emit a blue glow. Importantly, luminol can often detect whether there has been a cleanup of a crime scene as well.

Josh continues: "The way they handled the scene and the whole case so far is malpractice."

Sandee says, "I just knew that something was very wrong here. That my daughter would never have done this." Sandee and Josh's increasing certainty Ellen was murdered was fueled by far more than gut feelings or how well they knew their daughter. It was all the secrecy, how they were left out of everything, how they couldn't get a straight answer on anything, how they were treated by police and all the investigating agencies, how they were the last to know anything about Ellen's death.

Sam Goldberg's calls to Sandee and Josh continued for a year until he called to say that he was getting married.

CHAPTER EIGHTEEN

Josh and Sandee Greenberg still knew nothing about the details of Ellen's death. "We ordered the autopsy report, read it, with a metric ruler in hand, trying to understand the depths of the wounds," Josh says. It would take years of consultations and examinations to put everything together, to fully comprehend the science, not to mention the unthinkable nature of it all. "You're grieving, you're in shock, gathering evidence, hiring experts, fighting to keep our heads on straight."

Sandee reflects: "I cannot even begin to illustrate how difficult… What our daughter had to endure is beyond words. It was vicious. Shocking!"

And making it all the worse, if that is possible, was that no justice was being sought. "The police wouldn't treat any other victim's family member like this," Sandee says. "How could they? How was this happening? There was almost no communication with us, with the victim's family. And the media coverage seemed to reflect only how Philly PD was working to shift their position and the public narrative, to change the slant from homicide to suicide. As if this were not a big story."

But the Greenbergs remained determined. They wouldn't and couldn't just stay quiet, resigned to simply paging through scrapbooks and left with nothing but memories of Ellen.

* * *

Unable to get answers from Philadelphia authorities, Josh and Sandee purchased photos of their daughter's death scene. Their goal? To amass a team of attorneys, forensic experts, pathologists, crime scene investigators, and blood spatter specialists to investigate and challenge the suicide ruling.

They did it. Sandee and Josh, surrounded by friends and loved ones, gathered their team of experts. Attorney Walter Cohen, the Pennsylvania Attorney General from 1989 to 1994, came on board first. The next legal mind to join the team was attorney Larry Krasner, and then, attorney Joseph Podraza Jr. joined forces. Podraza remains as their chief counsel.

They secured the brilliant pathologist Cyril Wecht and then, renowned forensic scientist Henry Lee. After conducting their own intensive investigations, both Wecht and Lee disputed the medical examiner's suicide ruling.

Cyril Wecht said he was "suspicious" initially. Why? Because statistically, an incredibly small percentage of women at this age use violent means to take their own lives. Pills or carbon monoxide poisoning is by far more common a choice. Josh states, "I wasn't surprised" at Wecht's suspicions, as they confirmed his own.

The Greenbergs also contacted Graham Hetrick, the Dauphin County coroner, a medical legal death investigator and member of the American Academy of Forensic Sciences. Hetrick is also an expert on violent crimes and forensic methodology. He is also highly trained in blood pattern analysis, crime scene management, forensic sculpting, and shallow grave recovery.

Hetrick knew the Greenbergs from the Harrisburg area and was deeply saddened by Ellen's death, remembering her as a wonderful young woman. He sensed something was very wrong from the moment he heard about the case.

Hetrick readily agreed to help and brought in longtime colleague, Tom Brennan Jr., a veteran Pennsylvania State policeman and former Dauphin County detective who'd trained with the FBI's Behavioral Sciences Unit, now working as a private investigator. "The best way to get away with homicide is to have it ruled a suicide," says Brennan. He goes on to say that the chances for victims' families to legally challenge a manner of death ruling in Pennsylvania are slim to none.

In fact, if Josh and Sandee prevail, it will be the first time a medical examiner's ruling in such a case is successfully challenged in Pennsylvania, according to Podraza. "A ruling in the family's favor could advance Ellen's death investigation, clearing the way for the evidence the Greenbergs collected to be presented in court. It also could help set a new legal standard, establishing specific grounds for appealing manner of death rulings in Pennsylvania," Podraza says.

Podraza went on: "We believe when the coroner acts arbitrarily and capriciously, the court can step in and correct the error and the arbitrary and capricious conduct by the coroner."

Hetrick and Brennan agree: "The fastest way to prepare a good investigation is through a scientific process of good collection of evidence and data. We must look at hypotheses, must challenge each one; if it doesn't stand up, it can't be a working theory," Hetrick says. "We must establish the standard for what is real evidence and who are real witnesses, and, in turn, what and who are not."

Hetrick and Brennan studied all the evidence, police and medical examiner's reports, and the scene of the death. Together, they studied the on-scene photographs and notes. "We mapped them out by engineering all the wounds of the body," Hetrick explains.

Brennan and Hetrick met with the Greenbergs at their Lower Paxton home. They listened to their heartbreaking and infuriating story and reviewed files, reports, and photos the family obtained through many modes. In short order, they spotted a number of "troubling inconsistencies." For instance, the condition of Ellen's door latch, the trajectory of blood on Ellen's face, which dried horizontally despite the fact that she was discovered sitting up and, distressingly, more.

They then shared with the Greenbergs that evidence had been withheld, kept from them. They discovered there was bruising on Ellen's wrists, along with all the other bruises on Ellen's body that were deemed to have occurred at various times.

COULD THESE BRUISES HAVE BEEN DEFENSIVE WOUNDS, PARTICULARLY THE ONES ON HER WRISTS AND ARMS?

"They [the police at the scene] said she lacked defense wounds," Brennan said. "In looking at the autopsy photographs, I take a look at the victim's wrists. Both wrists show trauma."

All these findings and more would later be documented in forensic exhibits for the Greenbergs' court cases. Not conjecture, this is evidence gained from the crime scene photos themselves.

Brennan and Hetrick faced Ellen's parents and rendered their verdict: "From what I've looked at and everything you've given me, this is, in fact, a homicide."

Since then, Brennan says he has unearthed even more evidence that Ellen was killed and that the evidence is overwhelming. This is what the Greenbergs and their team are fighting to present in court. They have just one question: Why are Philly officials battling so hard to stop them? Josh Greenberg asks, "Why are the officials so afraid to get into court with us?"

CHAPTER NINETEEN

One of the first things to capture Graham Hetrick and Tom Brennan Jr.'s attention were police and medical examiner's photos of the apartment door and its internal latch lock, a swing latch, like those found in hotel rooms. When the lock is engaged, the unlocked door can be opened a crack, but the metal latch stops entry from the hallway."

The two experts noted the 911 operator and the police on the scene were told that after roughly an hour of struggling to reach his fiancée, in a panic, Goldberg wrestled the door open by breaking the latch. In both Hetrick and Brennan's professional opinions, the police and medical examiner photos reflect a different situation.

"The state police sent me to lock-picking school. I used to do all of the surreptitious entries," Brennan said. "The only way you can open that lock is if one or the other piece is completely dismounted from where it's mounted, okay? That bar isn't going to open up for you any other way." The photos show the latch was only partially dislodged. Both sides of it were still fastened to the door and the jamb with a number of screws. "Three of those screws are still mounted. There's one that's out," Brennan said. He concludes the damage to the latch was not extensive enough for the apartment door to have been forced open.

Cyril Wecht and Henry Lee, crime scene experts also working for the Greenbergs, reach similar results. Could the police and their detectives have reached a different result? Is there a plausible explanation? Yes, various possibilities are absolutely plausible, but the issue is, it was never investigated.

This passage is from a Henry C. Lee Institute of Forensic Science at the University of New Haven report: "Some damage appears to be in the area of this lock in the close-up photograph. There does not appear to be damage to the doorjamb or evidence of a break-in at the latch lock from the other side of the door." The report is signed by Henry C. Lee and Elaine M. Pagliaro.

PennLive reports that "a second report by Det. Scott Eelman of Lititz, a veteran detective employed by the East Lampeter Township Police Department and a court-qualified expert on crime scene analysis and blood spatter, states: 'There is damage noted to the door side of the security latch which is still attached to the door. The screws are still present in the screw hole. The doorjamb side of the security latch does not appear to show any damage.'"

This does not name guilt on anyone's part and we know nothing of the sort. The complex was full of residents, employees, and more. We have no idea who may have had access to those hallways or who may have come in contact with Ellen. Simply put, these experts say evidence does not support the door and lock being forced open as police describe. What it does prove could be one of many scenarios. Moreover, neither Brennan nor the Greenbergs point fingers. Both civil cases brought by the family are against Philadelphia officials, not an alleged perpetrator. They refer simply to an "unknown assailant." Again, it must be made clear that these issues are simply part of a cadre of facts that must be resolved.

Brennan and Hetrick next focused on photos of Ellen's body taken by the medical examiner's team at the scene, prompting another important observation. Though Ellen was said to be found slumped in an upright sitting position, a horizontal line of dried blood was visible on her face.

"The police and medical examiner photos taken at the scene show coagulated blood that runs straight across to her ear," Brennan noted. The blood, he explained, should have run down her face, based on the position of her body when she was found.

Similar findings were made by Cyril Wecht and Henry Lee, working independently of Brennan and Hetrick. These findings were issued in the written reports and filed as exhibits in the Greenbergs' lawsuits.

Detective Scott Eelman's assessment of the state of Ellen Greenberg's body at the scene of her death is as follows: "Ms. Greenberg was found in the corner of the kitchen area of the apartment between the sink and the stove. Her back was leaning against the corner cabinet, she was slumped downward with her feet and arms extended. Her head was found to be tilted slightly forward and to the right, with her chin resting against her right shoulder.... The bloodstains on her face are inconsistent with the position in which she was found. Specifically, the bloodstain flow pattern diagonally across her forehead from the right to the left and terminating in the left eyebrow would move against the law of gravity.... It is my opinion that the blood stain evidence in this case is inconsistent with the position in which Ms. Greenberg was found."

In his report, Henry Lee stated: "The view of the decedent in Photo #2 shows a female on the kitchen floor with her head and shoulders against the corner cabinets near the stove and sink.... The blood is flowing in different directions on her face. This could mean she moved after receiving the initial bleeding injuries to her head."

Brennan had other ideas. "Or it could mean that someone moved her body."

Henry Lee went on to write without doubt: "The number and type of wounds and bloodstain patterns observed are consistent with a homicide scene."

Hetrick was struck by the fact there were no patterns of the knife moving from one wound to another—no blood castoff. "In my opinion," he says, "an average detective going into that case with those multiple stab wounds, with the absence of blood trails, would have immediately called in a blood pattern analyst. Ellen would have to have been moving around. Someone would have to have cleaned the scene. You see this scene, you'd think, maybe this thing was cleaned up."

Hetrick still can't figure out why luminol wasn't used at the scene. "This in itself is astounding," he says.

"From the very beginning, I was convinced. To this day I am convinced…she was murdered," Hetrick says.

CHAPTER TWENTY

Hetrick reached out to a respected colleague, Charlie Hall, a veteran crime scene investigator and now the Cumberland County coroner. "Charlie agreed with us after we looked at it from the aspect of scene investigation," Hetrick says. He then brought Dr. Wayne K. Ross, a legendary forensic neuropathologist, onto the team.

Dr. Ross, who frequently conducts autopsies for county coroners across central Pennsylvania, wrote: "It is my opinion that the investigating authorities should pursue this case as a homicide. It is further my opinion to a reasonable degree of medical certainty that the manner of death is a homicide.... The scene findings were indicative of a homicide."

Additionally, Cyril Wecht concluded in his written report that: "It is my professional opinion that the manner of death of Ellen Greenberg is strongly suspicious of homicide." In reaching this conclusion, Wecht cited the following:

1. The absence of a suicide note.
2. What he referred to as "unlikely suicidal stab wounds" to the back of Ellen's upper neck and lower head.

3. The unlikelihood of suicidal stab wounds made through clothing.

4. The rarity of multiple wounds in a suicidal stabbing.

* * *

Graham Hetrick remains profoundly bothered by this case and the shocking way it was, and continues to be, handled. The deeper he looks, the more questionable it all becomes and the more certain he is that the investigation was totally botched. He still doesn't know why.

Hetrick loves data. When he approaches any case, he thinks about the day in question and what might have been different about it. On the day Ellen Greenberg died, schools were closed early because of a snowstorm. Ellen saw to it that her students got home safely and then returned to her apartment—hours earlier than she normally would have. Did the police investigate who, if anyone, knew Ellen would be home early? Was anyone observing her leave her car and enter the building? Was she followed? Did she have a delivery? Was she visited by a neighbor? Were there crank calls to the apartment? Was anyone lurking in the parking lot that day? Had there been any disagreement with anyone in the building? Who had access to the hallways, mechanical or maintenance rooms? Did police inquire as to discrepancies regarding various versions of events?

"The apartment was too much in order. Everything was pristine, as if no one were living there or using anything. Ellen's position, as per the photos taken at the scene, was not consistent with moving around if she were, in point of fact, actually cutting herself," Hetrick explains. "You have that many cuts, the absence of blood patterns, a postmortem cut… Well, the simplest explanation is usually the truth."

Some things are elementary, including rules and protocols for crime scene investigation. A layperson, as it pertains to autopsies and death scene investigations, is aware of a few basic facts. Common sense dictates that a potential crime scene cannot be compromised in any way. In other words, no touching!

Which brings us to the scene at the apartment on that terrible day, January 26, 2011, and in the days and weeks following. Once Goldberg called 911 and police were dispatched, many, many cardinal rules were ignored or broken altogether.

Why and *how* were civilians given permission to (a) enter the scene and (b) remove items? Not to mention personal effects belonging to the deceased, personal effects that could have contained evidence. This is not allowed!

Then there is the very serious question of why Ellen's bruises were not explored and investigated. The bruises were said to have been in various stages of healing, but this makes Hetrick furious. "There should have been an intense analysis of this," he says.

Hetrick, a stickler for protocol, is all about the timeline, especially as it relates to the time of death. "You start by concentrating on what is on or about the body," he explains. You determine body temperature. "While you can never get exactitude, that is unless you have a witness who saw everything unfold, you can get ranges."

Then, there is lividity…or livor mortis, postmortem lividity, hypostasis, or suggillation, which is recognized by many as the second stage of death. It amounts to a settling of blood in the lower portion of the body after death, resulting in a purplish-red coloring of the skin. The skin appears to be deep red or blue where the blood settles once the heart stops pumping it throughout the body. "If the heart stops pumping, then blood will flow simply from gravity," Hetrick states. "When the heart is not pumping, lividity will become quite pronounced, which is a good indicator. After death, that lividity will be important. It will give you a timeline." Lividity often becomes perceptible within three to four hours of death.

Rigor mortis simply means the body's postmortem rigidity. The human body becomes stiff for a period of time after death. This is considered to be the fourth stage of death and one of the most recognizable signs of death, characterized by stiffening of the limbs. This is caused by chemical changes in the muscles postmortem. Rigor can occur as soon as four hours after death, but it can take as long as six hours for a body to reach full rigor. Hetrick, who teaches lividity and rigor mortis to the Pennsylvania State Police, says a death investigator can absolutely achieve a timeline based on the degree of, or lack of, rigor.

Which brings us to the stunning question whether Ellen's body was moved after her death and before the police were called. Moving a body tampers with evidence and changes what the investigator will find. It's called "staging" the scene.

Blanching, or a white discoloration to the skin when pressure is applied, can happen when circulation is cut off. Blanching can occur after death within a certain time frame if pressure is applied to the skin, forcing blood from the capillaries. The bluish skin turns white until the pressure is released.

If a person were lying down on their back, there would be blanching on their back and buttocks, because blood can't get there. The position of the body in a death scene is crucial. If the body is moved a few hours after the heart has stopped, shadows on the skin can be visible. These are the fundamentals of a crime scene.

And yet, there is no reason to believe that any of these rudimentary steps were followed.

Hetrick argues there are many questions left unanswered. For instance, what was the ambient temperature in the room when they did the investigation? Was the body already in full rigor? Was the lividity fixed?

"The first thing you do in any death investigation," Hetrick explains, "is we send our investigators to the scene and they follow protocol.

What drives our work? What is our axiom? What do we teach forensic interns? First, rule out homicide. Second, rule out homicide. Third, rule out homicide.

"Once we leave the scene, the evidence is no longer evidence. It's not valid, it's not legitimate or pure. You cannot go back a day or two later to analyze a death scene."

These are the basics. The scene of a death is to be treated with delicacy and the utmost of care. Until such time as any kind of foul play is ruled out, or until the cause of death is ascertained, it is strictly off-limits. That yellow police tape we see on TV and which many of us have seen in person has a purpose. It tells us to "keep out," to stay away, don't touch, don't leave footprints, don't disturb delicate evidence such as DNA, fingerprints, hair follicles, fibers, or debris invisible to the naked human eye. It is critical in the search for the truth.

Hetrick went on to say, "We do see 'hesitation wounds' in suicide. There were no significant hesitation wounds here." He added, "It's pretty unusual for someone to stab themselves repeatedly. Twenty times?"

CHAPTER TWENTY-ONE

Based on all the above and more, the Greenbergs filed a civil suit. In it, they accuse police, prosecutors, and medical examiner's officials involved in the meeting of "individual and willful misconduct and participating in a conspiracy to cover-up the murder of Ellen R. Greenberg." The suit seeks unspecified monetary damages. This becomes the second suit filed by attorney Joseph Podraza Jr. on behalf of Josh and Sandee Greenberg.

Did investigators who worked the scene of death for the City of Philadelphia take notice of details described in the various forensic and crime scene reports privately commissioned by the Greenbergs? We don't know. The police incident report dated January 26, 2011, stated simply: "Homicide and ME processed scene and ruled a suicide."

Larry Krasner, a lawyer on the Greenbergs' team, became the Philadelphia district attorney in 2018. They asked him to reopen their daughter's case, but citing a conflict of interest, Krasner recused himself and referred the case to the Pennsylvania Attorney General.

Josh and Sandee are absolutely all in. All the resistance they've faced, all the official Philadelphia doors closing in their faces, has only made them stronger in their resolve. Sandee says, "My mission statement, my personal journey, has been and continues to be to clear her name."

And man, are they up against it. Every step of the way, then and now, has been an uphill battle. It was only after a secretive meeting between police, medical examiner's offices, and the District Attorney's Office that Josh and Sandee were finally told about the change in the manner of death ruling. No written record of that meeting exists. "We learned about it from depositions." Can this and so any other discrepancies be explained? Maybe.

Ellen's family is still waiting on that.

* * *

On behalf of the Greenbergs, attorney Joseph Podraza Jr. filed an initial civil lawsuit against both the Philly Medical Examiner's Office and the pathologist who conducted the autopsy. They sought to have the manner of Ellen's death changed back to homicide or "undetermined." Either would allow the investigation to be reopened, paving the way for legal action. "We're asking to change the manner of death and open a new investigation with impartial people and an impartial prosecutor," Josh Greenberg says. "We're not asking for the moon, just justice for our daughter."

The Philadelphia Law Department began ardently defending the suit and the suicide ruling. Even if Osbourne's findings were incorrect, which the city contends they were not, a city attorney wrote in court filings: "…the law makes clear that a medical examiner can be wrong as to the manner of death yet cannot be compelled to change it."

But if the medical examiner's ruling was wrong, why *wouldn't* the city want to change it? It doesn't make sense. They are actually arguing that if the ME is wrong, he/she still doesn't have to correct it? Why?

With this official response, however, something critical was quickly and effectively accomplished. The lawsuit unveiled new information about the bizarre process as to how Ellen's death was classified, and it elicited new testimony about a stab to her neck that, in fact, OCCURRED AFTER HER DEATH. THIS IS A MAJOR DISCOVERY. But would the civil suit be enough to get the manner of death changed back to homicide? Would it provide any additional information about WHAT HAPPENED TO ELLEN?

Even then, Medical Examiner Marlon Osbourne testified at deposition that the case was unusual and that "I did believe I had enough information" to rule the death of Ellen Greenberg a homicide. And he so ruled it.

Then, January 2020, a judge ruled the civil case could move forward. That was at least a step in the right direction, but the court proceedings were put on hold due to the coronavirus pandemic. They finally began moving forward in 2021.

After months of pretrial testimony, depositions, and media coverage, on December 10, 2021, Podraza announced his team provided "numerous additional materials to the AG's Office in response to the AG's statement to the press that the AG would review new material if the material was supplied."

In his deposition, Osbourne, on the subject of a spinal cord finding, which he called "an important question," said he asked Dr. Lucy Rorke-Adams, a renowned neuropathologist, formerly at the Children's Hospital of Philadelphia in 2015, to conduct the exam. Oddly (of course!), instead of having her come to the ME's office, Osbourne reported walking a section of Ellen Greenberg's spinal cord over to Rorke-Adams at CHOP through "very heavy snow" for an informal "curbside exam." I have never heard of delicate human tissue in a potential homicide case being analyzed in a curbside exam conducted by the naked eye. THIS IS HIGHLY INAPPROPRIATE.

Osbourne went on to explain that Rorke-Adams didn't do a microscopic exam yet was still able to tell him that the dura, the sheath covering the spinal cord, had been cut, but not the spinal cord itself. Therefore, according to the curbside exam, there was no indication Ellen lost motor function. They suggest Ellen could have continued stabbing herself with her spinal cord dura sliced.

"I was flabbergasted by the absence of professionalism surrounding that review Dr. Osbourne testified he had Dr. Rorke-Adams do," Podraza said. "Essentially, he's taking a pickle jar with Ellen's spine and brain stem through the piled-up snow, walking with that across the street or a couple of streets…thrusting it into her hands, and saying give me a look-see."

Now, another disturbing aspect of this so-called curbside exam. Rorke-Adams never created notes, records, a phone-call notation, a diary entry, a schedule…nothing to document the curbside exam ever happened. Notably, she also did not create a bill for her work, which was her custom. No such bill has ever been found.

Disturbingly, she told *The Inquirer* in 2018 that she had absolutely no recollection of conducting the exam and that without a report or bill for her services, "I would conclude that I did not see the specimen in question, although there is a remote possibility that it was shown to me."

As a victim of violent crime myself, I cannot imagine how I would feel if my fiancé's autopsy were so incredibly botched. Not to mention the complete disrespect not only to the deceased but to the victim's family as well. The casual, nonchalant handling of Ellen's remains alone proves how little authorities cared about finding the truth as to what happened to Ellen.

From a physiological perspective alone, how can this "test" bear any validity? Rorke-Adams took a gross specimen at best and operated under deeply questionable boundaries, leaving no record it even happened? And now has no recollection of the event? No lab, no microscope, no bright lights over the specimen allowing her to truly see microscopic trauma to the cells? Just looking through murky liquid in a pickle jar?

Let's follow this assertion through to its logical conclusion. That is, that even with twenty stab wounds, including to her liver, her neck, her head, and, importantly, her spinal cord, Ellen still had the strength and mobility to continue stabbing herself deeply with amazing force and accuracy?

In that vein, Rorke-Adams, when pressed, claimed Ellen Greenberg would definitely have had sensory loss, meaning she felt no pain? So she kept stabbing herself in the back of the neck? This far-fetched theory is actually insulting to the intellect of even a casual observer.

In that *Inquirer* article, notice Rorke-Adams did not exclude the fact that there was or could have been a killer. THE EXPERT NEUROPATHOLOGIST DOES NOT EXCLUDE THE POSSI-BILITY ELLEN WAS MURDERED. She states only that Ellen could have continued to move after being severely wounded. Rorke-Adams is now ninety-four years old and no longer involved in these proceedings.

During the deposition, Podraza asked Osbourne if he'd ever been disciplined. "He said, 'No.' The truth is, he had been disciplined," Podraza says now.

This development has far-reaching implications. Other attorneys working other cases likely did not have access to this information when Osbourne testified in court, including in homicide cases. Breaking it down, wouldn't a prosecutor want to know the medical examiner they put on the stand has been professionally reprimanded? Wouldn't a defense attorney in a homicide trial want that information to impeach the credibility of the witness? Cutting corners, claiming collaborations with specialists that neither they nor anyone else recalls, and the list goes on … it reeks. And that stench blankets the manner of death in Ellen's case.

At the time, Philly's chief medical examiner was Sam Gulino. Gulino resigned in 2021 amid controversy over the handling of the remains of MOVE bombing victims. It was after Rorke-Adams's alleged curbside spinal cord exam that Osbourne and then Chief Medical Examiner Gulino were asked to attend a meeting with the Philly District Attorney's Office and Philly police. Gulino states such a meeting was "unusual." Neither pathologist remembered another like it during their time in that city.

"[It's] clear that they were presenting information because they felt that the manner of death was different from what had been ruled," Gulino said.

Later on, at deposition, when Osborne was asked under oath if he would have changed his ruling had he thought there was no witness when the apartment door was entered, Osbourne responded, "No, I would not," but explained he would have been closer to ruling the manner of death as "undetermined."

And what about the sheer weight of additional evidence? Podraza says that includes apartment building surveillance video, declarations of two building employees, and videotaped depositions of Drs. Sam Gulino and Marlon Osbourne.

Additional evidence includes that of Dr. Lyndsey Emery of the Philadelphia Medical Examiner's Office. Dr. Emery previously testified that a specimen of Ellen's cervical spine retained from the original autopsy contained one of Ellen's stab wounds. "According to Dr. Emery [from the Philly Medical Examiner's], the preserved wound … *was administered when Ellen had no pulse—she was already dead,*" Podraza said.

Importantly, the wound to the spine was, without question, not the last stab wound Ellen suffered. Why? Because the knife was still plunged deeply into Ellen's chest when EMTs arrived, meaning that the chest wound was the last.

WHAT? AT LEAST ONE STAB WOUND OCURRED AFTER ELLEN WAS ALREADY DEAD? THIS ACCORDING TO A DOCTOR FROM WITHIN THE PHILADELPHIA MEDICAL EXAMINER'S OFFICE?

How could a dead person stab themselves? They can't. In light of Emery's findings, this had to be murder.

Of course, when pressed under pretrial questioning, Dr. Emery attempted to walk back her explosive ruling. So where were her notes supporting or discrediting her own findings? There are none. Dr. Emery says she was told at the time by her higher-ups (the city solicitor—yes, you heard that right) not to write a formal report.

Why on earth would anyone, much less the city solicitor, vested to do the right thing, tell Dr. Emery not to document what she was analyzing?

According to the *Philadelphia Inquirer*, "A month after her deposition, the city filed a written declaration by Emery, in which she said she didn't fully understand the scope of questions posed to her at deposition, and offered several other possibilities for why the spinal cord cut didn't bleed: (1) that nothing was injured along the wound path (What? There was a STAB.), (2) that bleeding in other areas of the body prevented bleeding at the dura (That's crazy-talk.), or (3) that the injury could have been done at the time of autopsy.

Hold your horses. They now want us to believe Ellen's spinal cord dura was cut during autopsy? That did not happen. No mention of that was made in the autopsy report. None whatsoever.

No backtracking can change Emery's testimony, and it never will. I don't care how they want to restate it, repackage it, or whitewash it—Emery said the wounds were postmortem. They're stuck with it.

Is this more evidence in a disturbing trend? Orders being handed down to medical examiners, investigators, and pathologists, all working on official cases, not to take notes or keep records. This orders them, in effect, to leave no trace of what they find, when those findings run contrary to opinions of those "in charge"? Regardless of the truth?

This is not the justice system to which I have devoted my life.

With the submission of new and additional evidence, the Greenbergs called on then Pennsylvania Attorney General Josh Shapiro, now the state's forty-eighth governor, to reopen their daughter's case. Attorney General Shapiro would not respond to questions regarding Ellen's case.

It was only after local newspapers started beating the drum that a spokesperson for Shapiro confirmed to *Dateline* that they received new evidence and were reviewing it. They would not confirm what evidence they reviewed.

Near the somber anniversary of Ellen's death, the AG's office released the following statement: "Our hearts go out to the Greenberg family on the anniversary of Ellen's traumatic death. At the urging of the family and following a conflict referral from the Philadelphia District Attorney's office in 2018, our office reviewed the case and conducted an extensive investigation that did not uncover evidence to change the medical examiner's finding of suicide. There is no statute of limitation on homicide, however, and if any new evidence is brought forward we believe it should be reviewed by the proper authorities. At this time, no such information has been shared with our office."

"I've never seen anything like it," said Tom Brennan Jr., who at that point had been working Ellen's case for free for the past eight years. "Every time we think we're making headway, something blocks our path—we take two steps forward and one step back…. [T]here is more than enough sufficient evidence to prove our case in court. And that's what we intend to do. Our next step is to get the cause of death changed. Then we can go about the whodunnit."

Ellen's parents agree and note that over 125,000 people have signed a Change.org petition calling on the Pennsylvania Attorney General to revisit the case. That number is ballooning.

But the hits keep coming. Recall Ellen's laptop and phone taken from the apartment by the Goldbergs? The AG's office drops another bombshell obtained by *Dateline* released in January 2021: "The Attorney General's Office conducted its own investigation which resulted in evidence on Ellen's computer and phone that supported the suicide ruling."

Wait! This statement is made despite the fact that the ME's report from 2011 said NOTHING INDICATIVE OF SUICIDE WAS FOUND ON ELLEN'S COMPUTER. ALSO, THE FBI FOUND NOTHING SUPPORTING SUICIDE ON ELLEN'S LAPTOP WHEN CALLED IN BY PHILLY PD AFTER ELLEN'S DEATH. Brennan claims the Pennsylvania AG promised to perform a forensic analysis of Ellen's laptop but never did. The Greenbergs believe it was never done. They do have faith, however, in the FBI analysis, which found zero evidence Ellen was suicidal.

The FBI doesn't have a dog in this fight. The Pennsylvania AG does. I believe the FBI.

CHAPTER TWENTY-TWO

Following depositions, both the city and the Greenbergs filed for summary judgment, where a party asks the judge to throw out the other side's case at the get-go. Both sides were denied, and the case headed to trial in the Philly Court of Common Pleas.

But then, city attorneys, who'd declined to comment on this to the *Philadelphia Inquirer*, through a spokesperson, filed a rare pretrial petition in Commonwealth Court. They actually wanted permission to appeal the judge's ruling allowing the case to move forward. They wanted to appeal, claiming it would be "an egregious abuse of discretion that ignored binding precedent." The city argued that, under the law, a medical examiner's opinion CANNOT BE CHALLENGED, EVEN IF ARBITRARY ON ITS FACE. They insisted that reopening the ruling would "open the door to any party unhappy with the determination of the medical examiner or coroner" and open "floodgates to litigation."

So? What if the challenge is legitimate? What if the medical examiner admits he/she was wrong? What then? Ignore the truth?

"Temple University law professor Mary Levy said government officials can be compelled by law to perform a mandatory duty, such as determining a manner of death, but the law can't be used to force an official to reach a particular conclusion," according to the *Philadelphia Inquirer*. "That finding is subject to the professional's judgment, expertise, and discretion."

I agree in part. The law should not force an ME to reach a certain conclusion. But, when his/her conclusion is so obviously incorrect, that conclusion must be open to question. It must be tested in a court of law, placing the ME and all involved under cross-examination and introducing evidence to debunk the false ruling.

In a shock ruling one month later, the Commonwealth Court granted the city's petition; the order was for the civil trial to be placed on hold, pending a decision in the appeal case. Levy said Podraza and the Greenbergs likely face an uphill battle.

Podraza makes the point. Osbourne must be confronted with all the extrinsic facts he himself claims would make him change his ruling. He must.

Podraza provided the civil case depositions and more to Attorney General Josh Shapiro's office, hoping they would do the right thing and reopen Ellen's case. The AG's office was again intractable, standing by the suicide ruling, citing suicide-related searches they claim existed, contrary to the FBI findings, allegedly found on Ellen's computer and text messages showing she was upset. The Greenbergs knew their daughter had anxiety and wanted to move home, and were also aware her psychiatrist, Dr. Ellen Berman, told police "there was never any feeling of suicidal thoughts," according to the medical examiner's investigation report.

We can't place enough emphasis on that FBI report. The FBI was called in to analyze in 2011, thoroughly reviewed all of Ellen's electronic devices and found no searches related to suicide, painless deaths, or anything else related to how to end your own life.

"The city's of the belief the coroner can do whatever he or she wants," Podraza said. "It's unassailable, according to the city." For Josh and Sandee, the irregularities are glaring; the secrecy around the case is obvious. As of 2022, authorities continued to refuse to even release the police files in Ellen's case. They were not turned over in discovery and were, apparently, not subject to the state's Right-to-Know Law. And if they really did exist, why not share them with Ellen's parents?

"If there are things they don't want revealed, why?" Sandee Greenberg said. "Let the truth set us free."

CHAPTER TWENTY-THREE

I first learned about Ellen Greenberg and this obvious miscarriage of justice in 2022. Compounding the pain her family had already experienced was the trauma of being dismissed, of their girl's life being invalidated. I saw a mom and dad who were not heard, not seen, not treated as grieving parents should be and afforded no closure. They had no light shed on Ellen's case, no how, no why, no who.

From the mishandling of the crime scene, the lack of questioning witnesses, the sidewalk "look-see" of Ellen's spinal dura, the secret meeting, the immunity given to a prosecutor to protect her from prosecution, the broken chain of evidence, the professional cleaning of the death scene, the postmortem stab...it was all bungled *at the least*.

This must be either the sloppiest police work of all time, with one material mistake and failure to follow protocol after another, or, simply put, a cover-up. A cover-up for sloppy police work, a death ruling by police on the spot, lack of luminol testing, limited crime-scene photos and testing, a secret meeting where the ME was pressured to change his ruling, for an incompetent investigation by the ME's office or some alternative.

The list of fails is endless. That night, on the spot, police committed to a suicide MOD before obvious forensic steps were taken. Steps like gathering security footage; speaking to all witnesses (like the building supervisor) and residents, handymen, vendors, delivery guys, co-workers, and more, and then reducing them to witness statements; searching for hair, fiber, DNA, and a requisite search of witnesses' hands, fingers, clothing, and hair; conducting blood pattern analysis; and so much more were never done. Yet, suicide it was, according to them.

Practically speaking, how many stories like this have you heard? Of so brutal a suicide or self-attack? Of anyone who's stabbed themselves twenty times, so barbarically? Not to mention doing so in parts of the body that are impossible to reach even lightly, forget about with such ferocious power. Many women struggle to zip their back zipper, but Ellen Greenberg managed to stab herself multiple times in the back of the neck? At an upward angle?

And somehow, she managed to hack herself to death but leave an incredibly neat scene? Where's the blood spatter? Where is the trail of blood, the spattered counters, the kitchen floor awash with her life's blood? Nowhere.

A woman prepping a salad. A woman planning her wedding. A woman contacting students' parents to check on them. Mid-fruit-salad, she goes suicidal? It didn't happen that way.

* * *

That early morning, I was researching breaking crime to select what cases would appear on our *Crime Stories* telecast when I came across Ellen Greenberg. And that million-dollar smile. And those deep brown eyes, brimming with life. I remember the moment. I was immediately struck, filled with sadness for Ellen and her parents. It never diminishes. I wanted to find them and somehow "fix it."

I was equally transfixed by the manner of death. How could that be? Twenty stabs, including to the back of the neck and head, called suicide? *That can't be right*, I thought then, and still do.

I threw myself into learning everything known about Ellen Greenberg from her family, her schooling, her history, her demeanor, her personality, and her fiancé. I wanted answers, held out hope that I would find that magic fact that explained it all and proved to me there had not been an awful injustice.

I did not and have not found it.

I am saddened to report that the saga is still going on. It is my deepest hope and aim THAT ELLEN'S CASE IS REOPENED AND INDEPENDENT INVESTIGATORS AND AN INDEPENDENT MEDICAL EXAMINER WILL BE NAMED TO THE CASE BY THE STATE. It is my mission.

CHAPTER TWENTY-FOUR

After learning about Ellen Greenberg's death, I brought the story to Fox Nation, my TV home at that time.

August 10, 2022

"Teacher Death Mystery: A Nancy Grace Investigation"

Among our expert guests was Tom Brennan Jr., the veteran Pennsylvania State Police and retired Dauphin County detective, who trained with the FBI's Behavioral Sciences Unit, a private investigator working Ellen's case from the beginning. Next to weigh in, Joseph Scott Morgan, a professor of forensics at Jacksonville State University, author, and death investigator with over one thousand death scenes under his belt.

For the broadcast, we gathered numerous interviews with other experts and key players like Joseph Podraza Jr., the Greenbergs' counsel, and the deeply affected Phil Hanton, from Venice Lofts apartments. Hanton, under oath, denied ever leaving his station or going anywhere near the apartment's front door. He recounted insisting that he in no way could accompany him, as it was against the building's policy.

A visibly choked-up and shaken Phil Hanton asked for a tissue, then said, "I'll never forget that day. It never stopped snowing." He got quiet, then went on. "You know when you make a connection with somebody? She was one of those regulars for me," Hanton said, referring to Ellen. He then disputed Sam's statement. "He said I escorted him. I don't even know where their apartment was."

Hanton's version is corroborated by video evidence. Yes, Sandee and Josh managed to secure possession of camera footage from inside the Venice Lofts building from the evening Ellen was killed. It clearly shows Sam Goldberg leaving the gym area, then heading to and arriving at their front door alone.

* * *

We also spoke to Melissa Ware, the senior property manager at Venice Lofts apartments, who also filed a sworn affidavit. She was on duty for both the afternoon and evening shifts on January 26, 2011, and was present in the building when Ellen's body was found. While the police worked the scene, if you could call it that, Ware was seeing to Sam's family members including Mindy and Richard Goldberg; Goldberg's uncle, James Schwartzman; and friends. All were milling about in the lobby and ultimately gathered in the building's clubroom in the midst of a snowstorm that shut down the city.

You'll recall, between January 26, 2011, when the apartment was investigated, and January 28, 2011, when Medical Examiner Osbourne ruled Ellen Greenberg's death was homicide, Melissa was approached by Richard Goldberg and James Schwartzman. They wanted access to the apartment to get personal items for Ellen's funeral.

Ward wisely contacted Philly PD for permission. She was told by police the apartment was no longer considered a crime scene and there was no problem allowing Goldberg's father and uncle inside. At this critical juncture in time, the apartment was on the cusp of being officially labeled a crime scene. The ME's report was not yet filed, and the investigation was ongoing.

Goldberg and Schwartzman took Ellen and Sam's laptops and Ellen's cell phone. They left behind, however, Ellen's diamond engagement ring, a family heirloom that once belonged to Goldberg's grandmother. The ring was left sitting on the counter.

All related correspondence, texts, phone log, emails, and internet search histories for both Ellen and Josh were taken. An innocent explanation could be that they thought the items were valuable.

Making matters much worse is that Melissa Ware was then given permission by, yes, once again the Philly PD, to have the apartment professionally deep-cleaned and sanitized. This occurred while the investigation was ongoing and just one day before the ME ruled Ellen's death a homicide and the apartment was ruled a crime scene.

Just one day.

This means the crime scene, in one fell swoop, was rendered unusable, any potential evidence gone. This represents a monumental break in the evidence chain of custody. James "Uncle Jimmy" Schwartzman, Goldberg's uncle, was, at that time, a veteran lawyer specializing in ethics. He was later appointed to serve as a judge on the Pennsylvania Court of Judicial Discipline. According to Melissa Ware, he took a cell phone and laptops from the death scene.

One more fact.

"Crime Scene Cleanup," hired by Melissa, was actually recommended to her by…the Philly PD.

CHAPTER TWENTY-FIVE

On *Crime Stories*, Tom Brennan Jr. was as plainspoken as ever: "I don't know how in the hell anyone in their right mind could call this suicide."

Let's review what was happening in Ellen Greenberg's life the day she was killed. A major snowstorm was blanketing the entire region. Ellen spoke to her mom that morning, and she was perfectly fine—happy as a matter of fact. We know the schools closed early and Ellen called every student's family to make sure they arrived home safely.

We know Ellen stopped on the way home to fill up the car with gas, likely planning to be tanked up in case weather got worse and she needed to drive. We know that she was surfing a wedding website, making lesson plans on her laptop, and prepping a fruit salad just before she was stabbed dead.

Ellen was busy working, dreaming of weddings, and prepping lunch when she was overcome with the overwhelming compulsion to violently kill herself, dish towel still in hand? No, according to experts.

Ellen was clearly in a normal state of mind, navigating as a functional person of sound mind. But even more probative, the crime scene does not support suicide. Podraza calls it a "murder that has been covered up."

CHAPTER TWENTY-SIX

From various camps come allegations of a cover-up. By this, they mean that physically, physiologically, scientifically, and forensically, suicide is impossible.

In the 2022 Fox Nation telecast, highly experienced professionals shared deep concerns and profound skepticism. Further, these experts are not simply cold, academic investigators and attorneys. They are also fathers, husbands, uncles, brothers, sons. Their work has serious impact, yet they navigate armed with their training, expertise, and education combined with personal drive to get it right, finally, for Ellen.

* * *

Many facts have been ferreted out that obviously debunk the suicide ruling. On a very basic level, obvious to a casual observer, a layperson untrained in forensics or postmortems, would she really have had that kind of bionic power? Stabbing herself at least twenty times, the wounds both significant and deep? How could this slight first-grade teacher have the power, the stamina, and the will to keep stabbing herself while in intense, maiming pain, twenty times?

When you cut your finger with a knife in the kitchen, you wince and stop for a Band-Aid...not continue slicing yourself. Her wounds were deep, multiple, and disabling, yet the ME would have us accept she could continue her self-mutilation, with a severed spinal dura, culminating with plunging a knife into her own chest with her kitchen dish towel still in her other hand?

That did not happen.

Moreover, the deep stab wound in the heart area would be extremely difficult to manage, for anyone. Analysis from the scene makes it clear that Ellen would have had to use her left hand (she was right-handed). Try simply arranging your hair, putting on makeup, or buttoning your shirt with your nondominant hand. I did for purposes of this case. It did not work.

Among the many stab wounds in Ellen's head was a very substantial, and probative, gash. The wound was deep, which means it required massive force. How did she summon the force or perform the physical gymnastics to inflict such a gash on the back of her head?

She didn't. Philly will have to work really hard to explain this, if there ever is an actual investigation.

On her neck near THE BACK OF HER HEAD, knife patterns show the knife was moving in an UPWARD TRAJECTORY, STABBING UPWARD, in a purposeful, calculated, AND PAINFUL modus operandi.

Again. IMPOSSIBLE. Good luck with that, Philly PD.

Then, there is the stab that went so deep, it actually sliced the spinal dura, the tough, fibrous membrane that protects the spinal cord. Look at the diagram of the stab wounds and their trajectory paths. Who in the world could stab themselves in that spot and with such force? And with the wrong hand?

No one.

Then, the inescapable evidence of bruising across all parts of Ellen's body. I learned from former prosecutor Guy D'Andrea, who was IN THE DISTRICT ATTORNEY'S OFFICE AT THE TIME OF THE INVESTIGATION AND WAS ASKED TO SIFT THROUGH THE CASE WITH A FINE-TOOTH COMB, that the DA's office tried to chalk the bruises up TO PILATES.

PILATES. There's this: Ellen didn't do Pilates.

On our Ellen Greenberg episode, we analyzed the bruising, including bruises UNRELATED TO HER STABBING DEATH. We analyzed the medical examiner's own analysis that the bruises were AT VARIOUS STAGES OF HEALING, occurring at various times. Joseph Scott Morgan observes that many bruises seemingly predated Ellen's death and were "all over her arms." He explained that they should have been investigated and explored as part of the ruling and death analysis.

There is smoke billowing from that secretive and unprecedented meeting between the Philly DA, police reps, and the medical examiners ruling on Ellen's COD. According to witnesses, ME Marlon Osbourne was pressured to change the ruling from homicide to suicide. According to Brennan, who questioned him as to why he changed the ruling, Osbourne states, "I did it at the insistence of Philadelphia police."

Shedding more light, Osbourne told Brennan the whole purpose of the "secret" meeting was to pitch the suicide ruling and convince him to go against his own work and conclusion in order to align with the police, district attorney, and attorney general's offices. And thus, following the meeting and months after Osbourne rules Ellen's death a homicide, he changes it to suicide.

This stinks to high Heaven.

The backdrop? Brennan states that at the get-go, he contacted Dr. Gulino for permission to interview Marlon Osbourne. Gulino refused. Why? What was Gulino's problem with Osbourne discussing his findings? I've worked with countless medical examiners, and I've never had a single one refuse to discuss their findings. Ever.

Months later, Brennan shared Ellen's autopsy report with eminent pathologist Dr. Wayne Ross, a court-certified expert in stab wounds. Dr. Ross stated "this was clearly a homicide we were looking at," said Brennan. Brennan emailed Dr. Gulino a copy of Dr. Ross's report and asked again to speak to Osbourne. This time, Brennan got permission to do a conference call with the medical examiner.

At the Dauphin County Coroner's Office, Brennan had the conference call with Dr. Osbourne. Also on the call were the Dauphin County coroner and Dr. Wayne Ross. "I told Dr. Osbourne who was present and then began asking him questions. I inquired about the bruises on Ellen Greenberg's wrists and the other noted defensive trauma on her body, cuts and scratches, and asked him why he'd changed the manner of death from homicide to suicide," Brennan explains.

Then, BOMBSHELL. Osbourne responded, with multiple experts on the phone listening, that the ruling was changed at the insistence of police during that meeting he'd attended. Brennan pushed back: "Since when does any police officer have a degree in pathology?" Osbourne abruptly ended the call.

Ellen's case was then shut down. Marlon Osbourne is no longer at the Philly Medical Examiner's Office. At last check, he was an associate medical examiner in Palm Beach County, Florida. "It seems like there was an awful lot of shuffling in the department. Many who worked on that case and had their own opinions are no longer working there," says an inside source.

There is a grieving family, literally begging for help and being harshly ignored by those in positions to serve and protect the public. What is standing in the way?

CHAPTER TWENTY-SEVEN

Shortly before the broadcast of "Teacher Death Mystery: A Nancy Grace Investigation," Joseph Scott Morgan, distinguished scholar of applied forensics at Jacksonville State University, board-certified fellow of the American Board of Medicolegal Death Investigators, forensic expert and consultant, author, and professor of investigative forensics, came on board.

After an initial review of the case, Morgan was stunned, certain there was something very wrong with both the case's handling and the MOD conclusion. Of course, he not only studied the facts and reports, he painstakingly re-created the death scene. The two of us then walked through the attack on Ellen, step-by-step.

We discussed the deep wound to Ellen's upper left chest, which JSM described as "very difficult to do." According to the autopsy and medical examiner's report, Ellen had six hundred milliliters of liquid blood in her left pleural cavity, surrounding the lungs, and five hundred milliliters in the right pleural cavity. In effect, she was drowning in her own bodily fluids.

Further, JSM is confident no one could sustain these disabling wounds and not only survive but keep on stabbing themselves or exerting the superpower to do so.

And as JSM points out, why butcher yourself when pills or carbon monoxide poisoning is such a readily accessible, and painless, way to go? He called the largest, most dramatic gash on Ellen's head "bone-deep," the kind of injury requiring enormous strength and aggression to execute. I insisted he show me, using my own head, how it could have happened. He explained the knife would have to be driven along Ellen's scalp, the cut made left to right, leaving wound tracks and "clean margins" found on her.

"How do you take the knife and orient it unless you're a contortionist?" he rightly asks. And again, this would all have been done with her nondominant left hand.

As to the very specific pattern to the wound at the top and back of her neck, he agreed that achieving those stabs would require attention, focus, and the ability to see the area, all lacking here. Again using me as the stunt double, he showed how the knife would have had to move up, up, up, and from back to front.

He turned to the neck wound that sliced Ellen's spinal cord and, according to him, did not bleed. He pointed out the knife cut ten centimeters through first Ellen's clothing then through her skin and muscles. Then he pounced on the most telling piece of evidence that authorities were seemingly determined to ignore.

JSM explains the absence of blood at the wound meant that by the time Ellen was stabbed, at least in that particular spot, her heart had already stopped beating. "By definition," he said, "a postmortem wound means you're dead," which means she no longer had a pulse or an ability to bleed. According to Podraza, Dr. Emery, who'd been retained by the Philly medical examiner to examine a section of Ellen's spinal cord, in her sworn deposition reaches the same conclusion: that Ellen was stabbed postmortem, after death.

Ellen, found clinging to a spotlessly clean white towel in her left hand, a knife still plunged into her upper left chest, had been stabbed, through her clothing, in her heart, her stomach, her liver, her head, her back, and the back of her neck. There were sixteen wounds alone to her head, the back of her neck, and chest. "This was not a quick death. Not a painless death," says JSM, and he adds that the assault went on for an extended period of time. "She did not commit suicide," he said.

Then, there is the position of Ellen's body when she was found and the blood on the scene. I asked Joseph how Ellen could have stabbed herself in her back, given her position. He said she could not have.

Then he shared a finding that is heartbreaking, a fact I had not yet understood. He points out, given contact traces of blood on the lower kitchen cabinets above Ellen's body, the positioning of her head, and the fact that her long, black hair was saturated with blood, Ellen's head was swiped across the cabinets, indicating a struggle.

As you will recall, the police who arrived at the scene used the "lack of a struggle" as a reason to find suicide. More evidence ignored by Philly PD, MEs, and prosecutors in order to uphold a suicide manner of death.

Now to the markings on Ellen's neck. They are significant. JSM points out the clear existence of fingernail marks within the bruising there. "What we see in a classic strangulation are these classic nail marks, like a rake moving through the skin. This indicates a struggle," he said. NOT ONLY THAT, THERE IS BRUISING ALONG THE "STRAP MUSCLES" ON THE FRONT OF ELLEN'S NECK, ANOTHER STRANGULATION RED FLAG. CLASSIC SIGNS OF STRANGULATION.

In agreement, forensic pathologist Dr. Wayne K. Ross observed strap mark bruising to the front of Ellen's throat, unrelated to the stabs. Dr. Ross agrees there is considerable evidence of strangulation and writes that the manner of death is homicide. Bruising to the strap muscles in the neck is classic strangulation. So now I am to believe she stabbed AND strangled herself dead? How could Osbourne look the other way?

Yet, the office of Attorney General Josh Shapiro, in an official statement, said there was "no credible evidence of strangulation."

And now to the door and latch. JSM agrees the latch lock on Ellen and Sam's door was still largely intact and believes no one could open the door without completely breaking it off. Practically speaking, when anyone breaks through a door such as this, evidence of whether it was actually locked is completely destroyed. Is it possible? Is there an explanation, so that all parties speak the truth? Maybe there is. The answer to this will only be determined by a full and independent investigation.

CHAPTER TWENTY-EIGHT

There is another significant point of contention. The stab wounds that penetrated Ellen Greenberg's spinal cord, according to Dr. Wayne K. Ross, "would have caused severe pain, cranial nerve dysfunction, and traumatic brain injuries." According to the original medical report, neuropathologist Dr. Lucy Rorke-Adams had concluded that there was no such wound. When interviewed by the *Philadelphia Inquirer*, however, Rorke-Adams backtracked, stating that it was possible she'd seen the body and commented upon it, as she had "contracts with the medical examiner during the time Greenberg's body was observed." That said, she added, she had no records of the examination and could therefore not confirm any reports in question.

Dr. Henry Lee said with authority that the scene of Ellen's death appeared to have been staged. He said that the body had to have been moved, as evidenced by the dried, coagulated blood that ran straight across Ellen Greenberg's nose horizontally while her body was propped up vertically.

Tom Brennan Jr. insists blood-related aspects of the scene are not consistent with the official finding and more. He explained what is visible, the blood on Ellen's face ran straight across from her nose to her ear. If she were sitting up, even propped up as she was found, her head cast to the left, the blood wouldn't have run horizontally. It would have traveled vertically. "The scene just doesn't jibe," he said.

Ignoring the obvious, Attorney General Josh Shapiro hit back, stating there was no evidence of staging. Of course, Shapiro's office also made official statements denying any evidence existed of strangulation or postmortem wounds. The AG also foreclosed on the possibility of tampering with the scene or contamination. And so on.

Brennan goes on. "When you put politics…ahead of a human life, what the hell have we become? This is about arrogance [and] unethical behavior." Podraza takes it a step further, stating it's "a homicide that has been covered up."

CHAPTER TWENTY-NINE

There is another pressing matter here. The knife found embedded in Ellen Greenberg's upper left chest was never fingerprinted. How is this even possible? This is a keystone, a basic, a fundamental of police work. It didn't happen that night or ever. Yes, Ellen's DNA was on the knife. It was plunged into her chest near the heart. Of course her DNA is on the knife.

And as to claims there is no proof of a struggle, two knives had skittered into the sink, there is blood on the kitchen cabinet indicating her head was swiped against it, as well as bruising to the wrists, and there was bruising to the strap muscles on Ellen's neck. All of this and more are huge signs a struggle ensued.

Podraza began working with the Greenbergs in 2019 and knew from the start that something was seriously wrong with this case. "The investigation had been absolutely atrocious. But for the media, this case would have been over long ago. If we had to depend on the courts and the justice system in general, we'd be nowhere. We would not have learned half of what we now know," he insists.

Podraza recounts how supportive the newspapers, TV personalities and newscasters, reporters, and podcasters have been. It's been powerful and is very much appreciated. Now, the case is being championed by throngs of listeners and viewers who can see what the Philly ME's office, prosecutors, and even the AG ignore.

"Kudos to Sandee and Josh. Kudos to a few great judges. Judge Hill and Judge Carpenter. Both have been so supportive in helping us to get to the truth. They have allowed access to police files when nobody else would," Podraza says.

So, what have we learned from those police files, you ask?

"You know," Podraza goes on, "sometimes the cover-up is more lethal than the crime. There was one mishap after another. Have they been trying to cover up terrible police work, or is this much darker?"

That night, in the middle of a storm, four foot patrol officers arrive, see the scene, and immediately know they were dealing with something sinister. They call in the Northwest detectives. "You don't go up the chain asking for more sophisticated officers if you don't think it's serious," Podraza says. Then the Northwest officers call in homicide. They show up with their supervisor in tow, ready to deal with a dramatic scene.

"We see the progression over a three-hour period," Podraza explains. This is how long it took for all of the police officers and detectives to get to and work the scene. "There was a strong belief that this was a homicide," Podraza declares.

"Then we started hearing nonsense from the city after we got the deposition from Philip Hanton, the security official on duty at Venice Lofts apartments, who denied all of it. They're trying to say like maybe it wasn't the security guy from Venice Lofts apartments but someone else who escorted and witnessed him."

What is the truth? We cannot decide; this book cannot decide. Only a full, fair and impartial investigation can determine the truth.

In addition to not printing the knife, another and possibly one of the most egregious "mistakes" made by the police relates to essential video recordings. Two of the most pertinent recordings, both of them invaluable evidence, have vanished without a trace FROM POLICE CUSTODY.

First. Venice Lofts apartments has a steady surveillance video running at all times inside and outside of the complex. It just so happens that on the day of the incident, the only recording that can now be found covers the hours between 3:00 and 7:00 PM. All that precious coverage, gone. No one can explain, and no one has been pressed very hard, or at all, to do so. If we could see who was there that night, riding the elevator, moving through the building, we could identify a potential suspect and rule out others.

Second. Vital evidence was recorded by Melissa Ware, who took a video of the apartment before and after the ill-advised crime scene cleanup was okayed by Philly PD. Recall, one day before Ellen's death was ruled a homicide, rendering the apartment an official crime scene, Philly PD gave Ware authorization for a professional cleanup and she did just that.

Ware recorded the apartment BEFORE AND AFTER THE PRO-CLEANUP, to protect the complex from responsibility, should the cleaning crew steal anything. NOW, BOTH RECORDINGS, TURNED OVER TO THE PHILLY PD, HAVE VANISHED.

"This is why an independent prosecutor needs to be brought in," Podraza says. "This case is bigger than Ellen. It is a picture of operations in the Philadelphia Police Department."

CHAPTER THIRTY

I personally interviewed Guy D'Andrea, a felony prosecutor in the Philly DA's office who was tasked with combing through the Ellen Greenberg evidence. He testified under oath that the investigation was shocking. He, an experienced criminal homicide prosecutor, was taken aback by the mishandling of the case and how quickly it had been squelched.

D'Andrea was so concerned, he approached Dr. Samuel Gulino, the former Philly medical examiner who supervised Osbourne on Ellen's autopsy. Gulino stated Ellen Greenberg's body was moved between her death and the arrival of the police to the scene. To be clear, this would mean the scene was tampered with and that someone else would have been in that apartment with her.

Dr. Gulino told D'Andrea, "This is a homicide."

D'Andrea rang a bell of alarm to his supervisors and others within the DA's office. Nothing was done. Instead, the office decided to "wait" for the ME to amend the manner of death back to homicide. That never happened, so in effect, the office did nothing even though D'Andrea, a veteran prosecutor, flagged the evidence.

CHAPTER THIRTY-ONE

Death investigator Morgan says Ellen's death was "overkill." "When you have this many stab wounds, generally this is an indication of extreme anger, rage." His analysis says many of the injuries Ellen sustained were not compatible with human anatomy. "No way she would have been able to do this, again and again and again, all while suffering horrific pain. Not possible," he insists.

"I have worked cases where individuals have self-inflicted injuries. I had one where someone drove a knife into their heart and stomach. So I have seen, studied, and worked my share of suicides. I am quite familiar with how that looks, with the physicality of it, with what it does to a human body and how that body reacts. One of the basic things we look for as death investigators, and this cannot be dismissed. The body is telling you a story. This is not a debate. It should be pretty open-and-shut. But this situation really baffles the mind. How do prosecutors worth their salt go along with the suicide ruling?" Joseph demands.

* * *

"First off," Joseph starts, "self-inflicted stab wounds cases are rare. When you come across them, you have someone who is psychotic.

Your pain centers scream out. Not like shooting yourself; this would be massively painful. Unbearable. Excruciating."

Joseph noted Ellen had a history of anxiety, which is not uncommon, but also, would not change the impossibility of the wounds being self-inflicted.

Considering Ellen Greenberg's case, Joseph wondered how in the world could this young woman have inflicted this many painful injuries on her own body, even striking bone?

"Unlike with a burn, you don't get desensitized to the pain."

"These stab wounds cover so many areas of Ellen's body," Morgan says. "Anteriorly, on the front on the body, posteriorly, the back of the body. If all the injuries were on the front, I might, maybe, maybe, be inclined to buy in. But when you're talking about injuries on the back, which are much more difficult to inflict anatomically…I cannot overly emphasize how painful this would have been, and we're to believe that she would have had to keep going."

Morgan sighs heavily and says, "Doesn't take a rocket scientist. Gunshot wounds are dispassionate."

He goes on to explain that this fits into a category "we call *overkill*," not just an attempt to kill someone but an attempt to inflict as much pain as possible, "wanting to rip them to shreds." There is a hell of a lot of anger involved here.

Morgan asserts it is highly unlikely when compared to other cases he's worked on. "I have worked on cases with people who've cut their own throats. With people who have driven knives into their own bodies. But twenty times?! Well, that defies logic."

Morgan found Ellen's case to be open-and-shut. He said there is no doubt about this: "This is homicide."

That said, he believes it will be difficult to get turned around, the longer it goes on. "I have recollections of things turning around, but it requires such a change of heart and mind. Public officials have to step up and say they were wrong, or new people have to be brought in. The state attorney general or governor; you hope that with every new administration, someone's going to be moved by conscience and be willing to take a look at it. But then, of course, it opens a huge can of worms when they admit a case was mishandled."

CHAPTER THIRTY-TWO

D r. Michelle P. DuPre is a forensic pathologist and served as
a highly respected medical examiner for years, with literally
thousands of autopsies and death investigations to her credit. Her
illustrious career began in law enforcement; she walked the beat
in the mid-1970s with the Columbia, South Carolina, police, was
promoted to detective with the Lexington County Sheriff's Department, and later worked undercover operations. After medical school,
she completed her residency in pathology at Duke University Medical
Center and went on to complete a forensic fellowship in San Antonio,
Texas, with Dr. Vincent Di Maio (known as a "father of forensic
pathology"). She went on to work in the Miami Dade Medical Examiner's Office, which never has a lack of business at the morgue.

For nearly twenty years, Dr. DuPre worked for the US and British
governments and the Department of Justice. She has acted as a trusted
medical examiner in seven states and two foreign jurisdictions. An
expert witness in numerous cases, she has presented at state, regional,
and national law enforcement and medical conferences.

Dr. DuPre is also a respected author and forensic consultant for
Merit Street Media (Dr. Phil's new network), CNN, HLN, and Fox,
among others. I have been privileged to join forces with Dr. DuPre on

multiple crime investigations over the years. I asked Dr. DuPre to review Ellen's case. After intense scrutiny of the case, she has much to share.

She started out by saying there is a "very, very slim chance that Ellen could have done this to herself." Interestingly, she was shocked by all that was missing, by all that had not been done, by how many questions were left unanswered and unexplored.

Dr. DuPre points out that the order in which the wounds were captured in the crime scene report and autopsy is not necessarily the order in which they occurred. On another point, Dr. DuPre said: "In [the] description, he (the medical examiner) mentions bruising, a chronic pattern of abuse. Any time we see something like this, a kit should be done, including scraping the fingernails. This was, according to these city documents, not done."

Dr. DuPre found glaring omissions on the medical examiner's, police, and EMS reports—for example, how long Ellen had been deceased before she was found and if her body was warm to the touch. She also notes that nothing was ostensibly captured, questioned, or noted about the fact Ellen's hands weren't cut up, considering the ruling that she'd brutally stabbed herself twenty times. Dr. DuPre also noted the toxicology report, which revealed very little and seems to have been oddly processed.

DuPre was intrigued by all that had not been determined about or examined regarding the "suicide" weapon. "How did the knife stay in the chest at such a shallow depth?" she inquired. She said that if she were handling the autopsy or doing the crime scene investigation, she'd have "taken something the same length as the knife, put it in her hand, and then seen if she could have stabbed herself." If the knife were ten inches, the blade accounting for half of that (five inches) and the handle accounting for the other five inches, and it were anchored ten centimeters (less than four inches) into Ellen's chest when she was found, how would it have stayed put? That, she explains, could have been simulated. It wasn't.

DuPre noted some stab wounds were superficial, while others were substantial and fatal. The orientation of the wounds stood out for her. "They were all over the place. Left to right, back to front." That piece of the evidence is highly significant. How could Ellen have committed wounds from so many, varying angles? She couldn't.

Here is another extremely troubling and deeply telling piece of scientific evidence Dr. DuPre noted: "At least three of the wounds would have relatively been quickly fatal."

This leads me to ask: How many times can one person die? How many wounds, each one fatal in their own right, can one person inflict upon themselves? And why was this seemingly not considered or explained when the ruling was changed from homicide to suicide?

The following are a few specific details from Dr. DuPre about the wounds as they were labeled and captured in the autopsy:

- Stab wound E would be certainly near fatal.
- Stab wound H—also fatal.
- Stab wound #2—very likely fatal.
- Stab wound K had to have been inflicted with serrated abrasion with this wound, yet it says the wound edges were sharp.
- Wound J—this one was at the scalp. This is not a stab wound but a deep cut.

How could Ellen possibly self-inflict multiple *deadly* stab wounds and continue stabbing herself...and with such ferocious force?

More questions arose from the autopsy report for Dr. DuPre:

1. Was Ellen right- or left-handed? And why wasn't this captured on the autopsy or taken into consideration? This very much matters and even holds the answer to whether any of these wounds could have been self-inflicted.
2. The wounds are oriented in three different directions, some vertical, some horizontal, some oblique [at a slant]. Again, it very much matters how Ellen would have held a knife.
3. The blade of the knife was noted as being 12.5 centimeters. What were the exact dimensions of the knife? The handle, the blade? Once that has been ascertained, one can tell, beyond the shadow of a doubt, if Ellen would possibly have been able to stab herself in the back.
4. This is a bit unusual; Ellen has wounds at the level of C-2 and C-3. A neuropathologist looked at it grossly, not under the microscope, and concluded that it would not have incapacitated her. But anything from C-1 to C-4 would necessarily mean she wouldn't have been able to do more.
5. The knife was found in the chest wound—that would definitely be the last wound. But that was not affirmed or mentioned in the report, which is sloppy on the part of the pathologist.

While so many highly respected forensic experts weigh in, attesting to their certainty Ellen Greenberg could not possibly perpetrate this series of stabbings upon herself, Dr. DuPre, too, adds how the handling of this forensic and crime scene examination leaves gaping holes. It highlights how many steps, impossible to miss after she points them out for us, were overlooked.

Let me just add that Dr. DuPre was able to get this very detailed sense of all that appears to have been mishandled by simply studying the official documents. How can she have zeroed in on these basic facts and those involved, officially, did not?

CHAPTER THIRTY-THREE

Now, let's "unleash the lawyers."

First in October 2019, Podraza filed suit against the City of Philadelphia to have the manner of Ellen's death changed back to homicide or undetermined. This move would allow for an investigation to be reopened, paving the way for a possible wrongful death or misconduct result.

The Commonwealth Appellate Court decision of 2023 is thirty-three pages long. "For the vast majority of it, thirty-one pages, it seems like we are going to win," Podraza says. "It's in those final pages that the judges assert that we don't have authority to challenge an opinion.

"While they agreed that we raised very serious questions, they found that we lacked standing to bring our claim, that we are not allowed to compel an investigation to be done; that has to come from the medical examiner, police department, or District Attorney's Office." That said, it was made clear, by a three-judge panel, in a two-to-one decision, that they strongly believe that this should be done, but they can't be compelled to do it.

The favoring judge said that the Greenbergs should be able to make the challenge, that nobody (a medical examiner) has absolute power, and warrants a court to get involved. According to Philly's CBSNews.com, "The court also indicated it 'had no choice' but to rule against the Greenbergs in their quest to change the death certificate due to procedural restrictions."

In its opinion, the court did raise questions about the authorities who'd first investigated Ellen's death. "They have blatantly said the investigation was faulty on the part of the police, on the part of the medical examiner, on the part of the district attorney," Joshua Greenberg said.

Podraza was stunned by the court's ruling. He said it seemed to side with Ellen's parents but then ruled against them. "Three judges say there is a completely flawed investigation, and it goes across three parts of our government—the Medical Examiner's Office, the District Attorney's Office, and the Philadelphia Police Department," Podraza said.

The CBS reporter asked if someone was obstructing this investigation. Podraza's reply: "There's something going on here plainly interfering with it. I don't know what it is."

The City of Philadelphia provided a statement, saying they were "pleased" the court agreed with them. It's more like the court disagreed with them and held their noses when they signed the opinion. Philly added: "If Mr. and Mrs. Greenberg have new evidence about their daughter's death, we urge them to present it to the investigators in Chester County, as they have the authority to reopen the investigation in this case."

An appeal has been filed with the Pennsylvania Supreme Court and is pending.

* * *

The second lawsuit was also filed in October 2019.

"We filed for conspiracy; we had really strong suspicions. Dr. Emery said there was no hemorrhage, Dr. Gulino knew it all, what was transpiring back in 2011, and kept quiet until now. We assert that Marlon Osbourne, and Drs. Gulino and Emery became aware that Ellen couldn't commit suicide because of at least one postmortem wound."

The Greenbergs are demanding answers. Why did the city solicitor, for example, instruct the pathologist not to document her findings in writing? And that secret meeting, which was handled like a "Star Chamber," according to Podraza, was highly suspicious. "And where is the search for a hard drive? And for those missing video recordings?"

"They refused to change the manner of death. It is our position that they have a motive, that they are continuing to punish these innocent parents with emotional distress. They should be held accountable. We believe that the police used false information and pressured ME Osbourne to change the manner of death. He deferred to the police rather than exercising his judgment," an incensed Podraza argues.

And then there is the false claim of Dr. Rorke-Adams's involvement, lingering questions surrounding the apartment door, and so much more. "It is intentional misconduct because Osbourne is intentionally not doing his job," Podraza concludes.

Then there was the Philadelphia Police Department quickly and aggressively pushing suicide as a ruling. Then they put pressure on ME Marlon Osbourne, to, as Podraza puts it, "cover their asses."

This all culminated with Dr. Emery saying it was a postmortem wound. That, by its very nature, requires a change to the established manner of death. "This is a conspiracy to prevent the case from being viewed as it is," says Podraza.

The Greenbergs believe that the Chester County District Attorney's Office, with its small budget and intractable view of Ellen's case, is not the appropriate venue. Podraza, on their behalf, is appealing for the appointment of a special prosecutor with a team to investigate. They want an impartial prosecutor. They want fresh eyes on this. Podraza argues, "They don't want to do it right. Clearly they have something to hide. Too many questions that need answers."

A new complaint was filed in 2022 because of new information, including the Philadelphia Police Department providing and pushing false information and the medical examiner giving in to the police, not exercising independent judgment.

AMAZINGLY, DR. GULINO SAYS HE WOULD CHANGE THE MANNER OF DEATH.

CHAPTER THIRTY-FOUR

I do not condone conspiracy theories, yet many speculate there is a deep-seated conspiracy here that goes right to the top (the Pennsylvania Attorney General's Office). Fingers have been pointed everywhere. There is ample reason to be suspicious. I rarely believe multiple parties can keep their traps shut this long. I believe gross mistakes were made on the night of the murder at the scene and it was then, a sloppy coverup ensued, and once started, it snowballed, furthering the initial suicide claim.

There's a lot at stake for any law enforcement or judicial agency when they go wrong, make mistakes, or have bad apples among them. When you pull back the curtain and expose wrongdoings on the level of the police, for example, of a district attorney's office, you not only create an explosive scandal, but you also expose all the other cases before and after Ellen's to appeals and suspicion.

It feels elementary to Podraza that this all started with subpar policing and then mushroomed, taking on a life of its own. We all know that in order to protect and foster even one small lie, a forest of them grows. One lie begets another to cover up the first lie and so on.

Who killed Ellen? We don't know that, but we do know she was murdered. The facts leave no alternative.

CHAPTER THIRTY-FIVE

It took me a while ... it took some digging. But, as is so often the case, the truth has a way of making itself known. We finally uncovered the sworn deposition of Medical Examiner Marlon Osbourne, the doctor who performed the autopsy on Ellen Greenberg, the medical examiner who changed his ruling after a secret meeting with law enforcement. After seeing and examining Ellen's body, Osbourne absolutely ruled Ellen's manner of death was homicide the very day after she died. Inexplicably, after meeting with members of the Philadelphia Police Department and District Attorney's Office, he changed his ruling to suicide.

We learned that Osbourne, in an interview with former FBI agent Tom Brennan Jr. and others, admitted that he'd changed his finding at the "insistence" of the police. That admission led to Osbourne being called to give his testimony under oath, during deposition.

On the morning of April 22, 2021, Osbourne was questioned under oath. Osbourne testified from his location in West Palm Beach, Florida, and was duly recorded by a registered professional reporter, approved by the United States District Court.

What I learned from reading the deposition both shocked and sickened me. At several points, chills literally went down my body.

There is so much within the pages of this depo, I hardly know where to start, so I will just dive in with what I consider to be one of the most fatal errors. Osbourne did not render a true and factual time of death.

Let that sink in. We do not have an accurate time of death. This is the keystone, the first building block for every murder case I have ever investigated, prosecuted, or covered. The time of death is absolutely essential. What does this mean? It means we don't know how long Ellen was dead before her body was found. It means that if and when this case ever goes to a jury trial, any persons of interest would be either included or excluded as suspects in her murder based on their ability or inability to provide a verifiable alibi.

Understand that time of death is *absolutely essential in a murder prosecution*. In cases where time of death is in a "window," difficulties of proof rear their ugly heads. How would it affect our view of the facts as we know them? The reverberations from this single flaw are incalculable. In fact, on page 97 of Osbourne's sworn deposition, he tries to insist that "time of death" was at 6:40 PM on the evening of January 26, when Ellen was pronounced dead at the scene. Ludicrous! Her time of death could not possibly have been when an investigator saw her, determined she had no pulse, and filled out a written report. No! She'd been dead prior to that.

The autopsy report is reported to be devoid of any reference to rigor or livor mortis, the stiffening of the limbs that sets in after death and the settling of the blood to the lowest point of the body postmortem (i.e., if you fall on your back dead from a gunshot wound and lie undisturbed, your blood, no longer being pumped through your body, will "settle," or pool along your back, backside, and the back of your legs). Based on the ambient temperature of the room, rigor stiffening sets in, and based on the degree of rigor, a time of death can be better established.

As previously discussed, none of that was done here, and no mention of either rigor or livor mortis was alluded to in Osbourne's deposition. This determination *could have changed everything*.

But it didn't happen.

Another bombshell appears on pages 105–119, where I learn about extensive injuries across Ellen's body—her legs, thigh, knee, right forearm, and upper arm. On page 115, Osbourne states that Ellen's pattern of bruising across her body *is caused by "blunt trauma"* in varied states of healing. Blunt trauma often results from forceful impact.

Osbourne specifically notes bruises on Ellen's palm and fingertips. How did they happen? He says one bruise in particular is more recent than others and questions whether this one bruise could be a thumb-print or indicate "restraint," describing it as a "round bruise." He says, "Upon reflection," the bruise "might have been involved in some sort of restraint outside that day," and that the bruising pattern on her palm could indicate "restraint."

Astoundingly, Osbourne says all the bruising "did not factor into" his ruling of homicide. It didn't?

Then, there is the neck hemorrhage. Yes, Ellen had bruising on her anterior, or front, part of her neck, *not where she was stabbed*. Again, it took me a moment to understand that and let it sink in. Once Ellen was autopsied, and the skin pulled back from her neck (commonly referred to as "neck dissection"), her neck muscles revealed bruising. The significance of this anterior neck bruising is that it was not a result of the multiple stabs to the neck, most of which were "posterior" stabs to the back of her neck (page 120). Why did Ellen Greenberg have bruising to the neck not connected to the stabs? Osbourne says he "considered" the bruising to the neck muscles *could have been strangulation*" (page 121)!

Could have been strangulation? How could she strangle herself? Was she strangled in order to subdue or restrain her in some way? Was she fighting wildly and suffocated in order to control and kill her? There is no discussion whatsoever of this in his report. It is glossed over. He then goes on to state (on page 129) that the bruises on her arms and across her body are not signs of restraint—but why? He earlier stated they were the result of "blunt trauma."

Osbourne then admits error in the autopsy report. Did he not review possibly the single most important document relating to the death of a beautiful young schoolteacher? Really? Astoundingly, he admits that the bizarre wound to her head, "Wound J," is, in fact, a traumatic injury. Moreover, a careful look at the location of Wound J, located at the top-right back of her scalp, seems impossible for her to have done herself. We know Ellen was right-handed…how is this wound possibly self-inflicted? It's not.

I tried to act out this scenario as if I were Ellen. It's like a deadly game of Twister, contorting yourself into impossible positions to what…stab yourself repeatedly? This did not happen.

Then there is the stab to the spinal cord dura, the protective sheath around the spine that connects your body to your brain and controls much of human function by carrying nerve signals from the brain to the body and vice versa. On page 155, Osbourne confesses that he "did not think it was possible" for Ellen to stab herself in the back of the neck. This is a bombshell! If he didn't think it was possible, why change his ruling to a suicide? And if he "didn't think it was possible" to stab herself once in the back of the neck…how about stabbing herself *ten times* in the back of the neck and elsewhere?

In fact, Osbourne states that there was, among so many others, a stab to the spinal cord and one stab that went "into the cranium" (page 154). He says (also on page 154) the "more concerning" stabs were to the spinal cord and the two to the posterior torso. In other words, her back. In simple terms, she stabbed herself in her back. Yes, Dr. Osbourne, I too am concerned about your claim Ellen stabbed herself in her back.

Osbourne says his "main concern" was whether Ellen could continue stabbing herself *after* the stab to the spinal cord dura (page 155). How about admitting she could not have stabbed herself in the back of the head and neck *at all*? But instead, Osbourne tries his best to push this particular point onto another doctor, Dr. Lucy Rorke-Adams, who denies knowledge of this and did not submit a written report, nor did she bill anyone for a consult (page 23). That said, Osbourne swears that after consulting with "other associates" about the possibility that Ellen would have been completely incapacitated once her spinal sheath was cut, whomever those associates might be, he could not remember. Osbourne then decided to consult with a specialist (pages 22–23).

Enter neuropathologist Dr. Lucy Rorke-Adams, who now denies any such consult ever occurred. Osbourne himself states that a cut to the spinal cord dura could cause "unrelenting, intense pain" (page 48) and could absolutely "incapacitate" a person (page 49). Keep in mind, the stab to her spinal cord was not her last injury.

Even so, whether intentionally or by old-fashioned sloppy work, he admits that he never performed a reenactment (I did) nor did he measure and/or determine angles of knife wounds or the length of Ellen's fingers and arms to determine if there were any way Ellen could have self-administered the twenty wounds to herself.

In a shocking moment of the deposition, Osbourne states that if he were shown a wound or wounds that Ellen "could not have performed," then her death "is not a suicide." Repeat: Medical Examiner Marlon Osbourne says if there were a single wound or wounds Ellen could not have physically self-administered, then her death is not a suicide.

Is he blind? Or does he just not care about her savage stabbing death or her parents' suffering? Or was he "persuaded" to change his ruling? And also…why has this miscarriage been allowed to fester for years on end? There have been so many opportunities for the medical examiner, investigators, prosecutors, the state's attorney general, or the appellate courts to fix this. Why not?

Speaking of sloppy, the so-called consult with Rorke-Adams? Osbourne admits that all "prior interactions" with Rorke-Adams were in an office setting and on every occasion, *except this one*, Rorke-Adams generated a written report (page 59). But not this time (page 60).

Osbourne testifies that he *walked* through the snow, carrying Ellen's spine, I guess in a jar, for a "curb-side look-see" (pages 58, 60). What? What, even, is that? No microscope, no white jackets, no plastic gloves or footies, no face covering to protect the specimen? They just, what? Looked in the jar like they were shopping for pickles at Kroger? That is, if the meeting ever happened.

Rorke-Adams did *not* perform a histologic (examination of cells and/or tissue under a microscope) or microscopic (exam whereby the image or item is enlarged so as to notice detail not visible to the naked eye) examination of Ellen's dura. Isn't that what pathologists are supposed to do? According to the dictionary, a pathologist is a scientist who examines laboratory samples of body tissue for a diagnostic or forensic purpose.

That does not mean slogging through the snow with Ellen's dura in what, a pickle jar in a grocery bag? That does not mean taking a gander at extremely delicate human tissue in natural daylight, without use of medical instruments, laboratory conditions, according to scientific protocol, but instead, opting for a "curb-side look-see."

For this reason alone, Osbourne's ruling must be vacated. All trust is gone.

According to Osbourne, who at this point has lost all credibility, Rorke-Adams's exam of Ellen's dura lasted anywhere between five minutes to an hour and a half (page 61). The delicate and precise examination of a human dura in order to determine whether the spine itself had been sliced down to the very cells of the tissue could have taken…five minutes?

This scenario would be laughable if it weren't for the fact that I've seen the crime scene photos, the blood, the knife, the kitchen. I've seen the angles of the twenty stab wounds that took Ellen's life. I've seen Sandee and Josh Greenberg crying tears of anguish over her murder. That's why I cannot dismiss this gross incompetence with any semblance of a smile.

As to Osbourne's conjecture the exam lasted up to an hour and a half…in the snow? Outdoors? By the curb?

Not true.

Incompetence…or intentional obfuscation of the truth?

Osbourne goes on to say that, in his professional opinion, a "full exam" of Ellen's dura was not necessary. Shocking as all this is, Osbourne states that he had *no DNA findings at the time he changed his ruling to suicide* (page 75) and that his so-called meeting with Rorke-Adams occurred *before* his secret meeting with the Philadelphia PD and at least one prosecutor at which he changed his ruling to suicide (page 71).

Speaking of the secret meeting, Osbourne says that the meeting was very important but he took zero notes on it, cannot remember who was present, did not add the meeting's information into his findings, and can remember nothing "specific" that was new that he was told. Yet, he did a 180 and changed his ruling (page 76).

Osbourne concedes he ruled Ellen's death a homicide based on "all he observed at autopsy" and all the notes from the Philadelphia

PD detectives and Detective Olszewski regarding the scene. He was initially told all and ruled the case a homicide (page 57).

Then we have the warnings; some may call it intimidation. Osbourne swears his boss, Dr. Gulino, warned him that if Osbourne's ruling remained "homicide," and I quote, "Someone could be unduly incarcerated and/or wrongful charges adjudicated against them."

I had to reread this. Since when is a medical examiner warned his ruling could result in legal accountability for an alleged killer? They have their MD, not their JD. A medical examiner does not sit as judge and jury. Have they all lost their minds? Osbourne had been warned about potential repercussions stemming from his ruling that Ellen was killed? And then... he changed his ruling?

Police earlier "asked" Osbourne to leave the manner of death as "pending" while the Philadelphia PD "investigated" (page 41). Osbourne states that in all his time as a medical examiner, he had never once had a meeting to discuss changing his ruling on mode of death (page 28)—until this. And after the meeting, during which no notes were taken and no new information was presented, he changed his ruling to forever damn Ellen and her family.

How can we let this stand? We cannot. Join us.

EPILOGUE

In the early morning hours of July 30, 2024, I woke up thinking about Josh and Sandee. Josh estimates that this battle has already cost them $700,000. Their life savings has been ravaged, and they recently sold their home. Some wonder if the City of Philadelphia is either waiting for Josh and Sandee to die or go completely broke and go away. Yet, they say they'll never give up.

What woke me up was them saying that they don't get to the cemetery too often because it's so excruciatingly painful. "I think of her under there. She shouldn't be there. It bothers me physically, emotionally, mentally," Josh told me. "This is not where she belongs."

A few short hours later, I was in studio recording our daily program, *Crime Stories*. Mid-sentence, from the corner of my eye, I saw my cell phone screen light up, indicating an incoming message. As our producer played part of a statement for the viewers, I glanced down to check if my children, the twins, were trying to reach me. I saw the text was not from John David or Lucy...it was from Sandee Greenberg.

I saw from the digital clock running at the bottom of my screen that I had eleven seconds left before we came out of sound. I had time to check Sandee's message. When the sound ended, the camera came to me. Our producer in New York immediately saw my face and urgently asked in my ear, "What is it?"

"The courts agreed to hear Ellen's case!" The words rushed out in a torrent. I could hear producers on set and in the New York control room clapping and cheering. I couldn't see them. My eyes were closed. In prayer. Thanking Heaven for this moment and for granting what seemed for so long a near-impossible miracle. For over thirteen years, this had been the prayer of so many…for a chance, just a chance, an opportunity for Ellen's case to be heard. Dare we hope and pray now for justice?

The taping was delayed while I immediately began calling various people who have worked so hard on the case and invested so much in the endeavor. Even now, retelling that moment, I am overwhelmed by what I consider to be a miracle, against all odds.

I saved the text and still look back at it. Sandee wrote, very simply, "PA Supreme Court took our case!"

The issue soon to be before the Pennsylvania Supreme Court is very narrow in scope: whether Sandee and Josh have the right, on behalf of Ellen's estate, to challenge the cause of death ruling. If successful, the ruling could forge a way to reopen her case.

But on November 8, 2024, the Chester County D.A.'s Office, in a public press conference, announced it is "unable to move forward" with Ellen's case. Why? They say they "cannot prove Ellen's case beyond a reasonable doubt." They certainly can't, if they refuse to try. But why this? Why now? Why is the burden of proving Ellen was murdered on Ellen's own parents? They have dedicated years and years of their lives and their life savings to doing just that… Isn't it time for local law enforcement and prosecutors to finally step up and do the right thing?

Given appellate rulings, however, is there a sliver of a light at the end of the dark tunnel? It has been a heartbreaking journey for the

Greenbergs, who spent all of their life savings and recently put their beloved home up for sale, and who never backed off from a single court battle. All while still mourning the murder of their only child, their precious pearl.

There is a very long and rocky road ahead. We begin. And we wait…as justice unfolds, as we determine once and for all, God willing, what happened to Ellen.

ng

On November 7, 2024, the Chester County District Attorney's Office announced that they'd be holding a press conference the next day. On November 8, they released the following devastating bombshell: Related to the death of Ellen Greenberg, the office "is currently unable to move forward with criminal charges and is placing the investigation into an inactive status." They also said that they would not officially be closing the case. "Therefore, we will not be answering any questions about this matter."

NANCY GRACE

DISTRICT ATTORNEY'S OFFICE OF CHESTER COUNTY
201 WEST MARKET STREET, SUITE 4450
WEST CHESTER, PENNSYLVANIA 19380-0989
TELEPHONE: (610) 344-6801

CHRISTOPHER DE BARRENA-SAROBE
DISTRICT ATTORNEY

ERIN O'BRIEN
FIRST ASSISTANT DISTRICT ATTORNEY

DAVID SASSA
CHIEF, COUNTY DETECTIVES

MAURICE NADACHOWSKI
LIEUTENANT, COUNTY DETECTIVES

For more information contact Dana Moore, Director of Communications, at dtmoore@chesco.org or 610-344-4415

November 8, 2024

NEWS RELEASE: UPDATE TO ELLEN GREENBERG INVESTIGATION

The Chester County District Attorney's Office announces an update in the investigation related to the death of Ellen Greenberg. As discussed below, the office is currently unable to move forward with criminal charges and is placing the investigation into an inactive status.

The details of the investigation into the cause of Ellen Greenberg's death, which have been widely reported, are briefly summarized here. On January 26, 2011, Ms. Greenberg, then 27 years old, was found dead by her fiancé in the kitchen of her residence at 5601 Flat Rock Road, Apartment 603, in Philadelphia. The Philadelphia Police Department (PPD) investigated the case in coordination with the Philadelphia District Attorney's Office. After an autopsy on January 27, 2011, Ms. Greenberg's death was ruled a homicide. That initial determination was later changed to a suicide by the Philadelphia Medical Examiner's Office.

In 2018, the investigation was turned over to the Pennsylvania Attorney General's Office (OAG) for review. In order to avoid the appearance of a conflict of interest, in August of 2022, the investigation was turned over to the Chester County Detectives.

After receiving the case, Chester County investigators worked to determine whether sufficient evidence existed to reopen the investigation. Detectives first conducted a thorough review of the PPD and OAG investigations. They then pursued additional investigative steps, including but not limited to, conducting new interviews and consulting with an independent forensic expert.

After this review, the investigative team determined that, based on the current state of the evidence, we cannot prove beyond a reasonable doubt that a crime was committed. This standard of proof—beyond a reasonable doubt—makes the criminal investigation different than other legal cases or issues that surround Ms. Greenberg's death. Because we cannot meet our burden of proof with the information and evidence presently available, we placed this investigation in an inactive status.

There is no statute of limitations for criminal homicide in Pennsylvania, and because investigations can take new directions, we are not closing the case. Therefore, we will not be answering any questions about this matter.

Approved for release by Christopher L. de Barrena-Sarobe, District Attorney

APPENDIX A

City of Philadelphia
Office of the Medical Examiner
321 University Avenue
Philadelphia, PA 19104

Case Number : **11-00420**
Date of Death : **Jan 26 2011**

REPORT OF EXAMINATION

DECEDENT'S NAME
ELLEN R. GREENBERG

An autopsy was performed on the body of the decedent at the Philadelphia Medical Examiner's Office on January 27, 2011. The external examination was started at approximately 9AM. The internal examination was started at approximately 11AM.

Clothing: The clothing that accompanies the decedent consists of grey/purple hooded sweatshirt, grey sweat pants, and brown boots.

EXTERNAL EXAMINATION:

The body is that of a 5 foot 7 inch, 136 pound, white female who appears compatible with reported age of 27 years. The atraumatic scalp is covered by brown hair. The facial bones have no palpable fractures. The irides are brown. The sclerae are white. The conjunctivae have no petechiae. The external auditory meatuses have no discharge. The nares are patent. The nasal bones and nasal septum are intact. The lips are atraumatic. The oral cavity has no injuries. The tongue has no injuries. The teeth are natural and in good repair. The neck is symmetric. The chest is symmetric. The abdomen is flat. The body habitus is mesomorphic. The back is symmetric. The upper and lower extremities have no deformities or fractures. The external genitalia are those of an adult female. The anus and perineum have no trauma or abnormalities.

STAB WOUND "A" OF CHEST:

An elliptical, horizontally oriented 0.4 x 0.2 centimeter stab wound is centered 30 centimeters below the top of the head in the midline of the chest. The medial end of the wound is sharp. The lateral end is blunt. The edges of the wound are smooth. The wound is approximately 0.4 centimeters when reapproximated. The wound extends through the skin of the chest for a depth of 0.2 centimeters.

Associated with the wound track are hemorrhages in the adjacent soft tissues of the chest

The pathway of the wound with the body in the normal anatomic position is front to back.

STAB WOUND "B" OF CHEST:

An elliptical, horizontally oriented 0.3 x 0.1 centimeter stab wound is centered 31 centimeters below the top of the head in the midline of the chest. The ends of the wound are sharp. The edges of the wound are smooth. The wound is approximately 0.3 centimeters when reapproximated. The wound extends through the skin of the chest for a depth of 0.2 centimeters.

Associated with the wound track are hemorrhages in the adjacent soft tissues of the chest

The pathway of the wound with the body in the normal anatomic position is front to back.

STAB WOUND "C" OF CHEST:

An elliptical, obliquely oriented 2 x 0.6 centimeter stab wound is centered 29 centimeters below the top of the head, and 4.5 centimeters to the right of midline. The sharp end is in the 5 o'clock position. The blunt end is in the 10 o'clock position. The edges of the wound are smooth. The wound is approximately 1.7 centimeters when reapproximated. The wound extends through the skin and muscles of the right side of the chest and the right clavicle for a depth of 1.4 centimeters.

Associated with the wound track are hemorrhages in the adjacent soft tissues and muscles of the right side of the chest and beneath the right clavicle.

Printed on: 4/4/2011

133

The pathway of the wound with the body in the normal anatomic position is slightly right to left, front to back and slightly upward.

STAB WOUND "D" OF CHEST:

An elliptical, horizontally oriented 0.3 x 0.1 centimeter stab wound is centered 33 centimeters below the top of the head and 2.7 to the right of midline. The ends of the wound are sharp. The edges of the wound are smooth. The wound is approximately 0.3 centimeters when reapproximated. The wound extends through the skin of the chest for a depth of 0.2 centimeters.

Associated with the wound track are hemorrhages in the adjacent soft tissues of the chest

The pathway of the wound with the body in the normal anatomic position is front to back.

STAB WOUND "E" OF CHEST:

An elliptical, horizontally oriented 1.7 x 0.5 centimeter stab wound is centered 33 centimeters below the top of the head, and 2.5 centimeters to the left of midline. The sharp end is in the 3 o'clock position. The blunt end is in the 9 o'clock position. The edges of the wound are smooth. The wound is approximately 1.6 centimeters when reapproximated. The wound extends for a depth of 10 centimeters through the skin and muscles of the left side of the chest, the left second intercostal space, into the superior mediastinum.

Associated with the wound track are hemorrhages in the adjacent soft tissues and muscles of the left side of the chest, creates a 2.4 centimeter incised defect to the aortic arch, and a incises the upper lobe of the left lung. The pericardial sac contains 120 milliliters of liquid and clotted blood. The left pleural cavity contains 600 milliliters of liquid blood. The right pleural cavity contains 500 milliliters of liquid blood. .

The pathway of the wound with the body in the normal anatomic position is left to right, front to back and slightly downward.

STAB WOUND "F" OF CHEST:

An elliptical, vertically oriented 0.6 x 0.2 centimeter stab wound is centered 34.5 centimeters below the top of the head and 0.8 to the left of midline. The ends of the wound are sharp. The edges of the wound are smooth. The wound is approximately 0.5 centimeters when reapproximated. The wound extends through the skin of the chest for a depth of 0.2 centimeters.

Associated with the wound track are hemorrhages in the adjacent soft tissues of the chest

The pathway of the wound with the body in the normal anatomic position is front to back.

STAB WOUND "G" OF CHEST:

An elliptical, vertically oriented 0.6 x 0.2 centimeter stab wound is centered 34.5 centimeters below the top of the head in the midline. The ends of the wound are sharp. The edges of the wound are smooth. The wound is approximately 0.5 centimeters when reapproximated. The wound extends through the skin of the chest for a depth of 0.2 centimeters.

Associated with the wound track are hemorrhages in the adjacent soft tissues of the chest

The pathway of the wound with the body in the normal anatomic position is front to back.

STAB WOUND "H" OF CHEST:

An elliptical, vertically oriented 1.5 x 0.5 centimeter stab wound is centered 42 centimeters below the top of the head in the midline. The sharp end is in the 6 o'clock position. The blunt end is in the 12 o'clock position. The edges of the wound are smooth. The wound is approximately 1.5 centimeters when reapproximated. The wound extends for a depth of 4 centimeters through the skin and muscles chest, through the right sixth intercostal space, and 2.3 centimeter into the liver.

Associated with the wound track are hemorrhages in the adjacent soft tissues and muscles of the right side of the chest a 2.3

APPENDIX A

:entimeter deep liver defect, and intraabdominal blood.

The pathway of the wound with the body in the normal anatomic position is slightly left to right, front to back.

STAB WOUND "I" OF ABDOMEN:

An elliptical, vertically oriented 2 x 0.8 centimeter stab wound is centered 46 centimeters below the top of the head in the midline. The sharp end is in the 6 o'clock position. The blunt end is in the 12 o'clock position. The edges of the wound are smooth. The wound is approximately 1.9 centimeters when reapproximated. The wound extends for a depth of 6 centimeters through the skin and muscles of the abdominal wall.

Associated with the wound track are hemorrhages in the adjacent soft tissues and muscles of the abdominal, intramesentric hemorrhage and intraabdominal blood.

The pathway of the wound with the body in the normal anatomic position is slightly left to right, front to back.

INCISED WOUND "J" OF SCALP:

An obliquely oriented 6.5 x 1.1 centimeter wound is centered 8 centimeters above the right external auditory meatus, and 6 centimeters to the right of midline. The ends of the wound are sharp. The edges of the wound are smooth. The wound is approximately 6.5 centimeters when reapproximated. The wound extends through the skin and the scalp.

STAB WOUND "K" OF NECK:

An elliptical, vertically oriented 2 x 0.2 centimeter stab wound is centered 9 centimeters below the top of the head, and 2 centimeters to the left of midline. A 1 x 0.2 centimeter serrated abrasion is associated with the wound. The ends of the wound are sharp. The edges of the wound are smooth. The wound is approximately 1 centimeter when reapproximated. The 0.3 centimeter deep wound extends through the skin of the posterior neck.

Associated with the wound track are hemorrhages in the adjacent soft tissues of the posterior neck.

The pathway of the wound with the body in the normal anatomic position is slightly left to right, back to front.

STAB WOUND "L" OF NECK:

An elliptical, vertically oriented 1.1 x 0.6 centimeter stab wound is centered 14 centimeters below the top of the head, and 4 centimeters to the left of midline. The ends of the wound are sharp. The edges of the wound are smooth. The wound is approximately 1.1 centimeter when reapproximated. The 0.2 centimeter deep wound extends through the skin of the posterior neck.

Associated with the wound track are hemorrhages in the adjacent soft tissues of the posterior neck.

The pathway of the wound with the body in the normal anatomic position is slightly left to right back to front.

STAB WOUND "M" OF NECK:

An elliptical, vertically oriented 0.2 x 0.1 centimeter stab wound is centered 11 centimeters below the top of the head in the midline. The ends of the wound are sharp. The edges of the wound are smooth. The wound is approximately 0.2 centimeter when reapproximated. The 0.3 centimeter deep wound extends through the skin of the posterior neck.

Associated with the wound track are hemorrhages in the adjacent soft tissues of the posterior neck.

The pathway of the wound with the body in the normal anatomic position is back to front.

STAB WOUND "N" OF NECK:

An elliptical, vertically oriented 1.1 x 0.4 centimeter stab wound is centered 13 centimeters below the top of the head, and 0.5 centimeters to the left of midline. The ends of the wound are sharp. The edges of the wound are smooth. The wound is approximately 1.2 centimeter when reapproximated. The 8 centimeter deep wound extends through the skin and muscles of the posterior neck through the occipital triangle and into the ligamentum nuchae.

Associated with the wound track are hemorrhages in the adjacent soft tissues and muscles of the posterior neck, a defect in the ligamentum nuchae, incises small vessels overlying the cerebellum, creating a subarachnoid hemorrhage over the vermis, the caudal aspect of the right cerebellar hemisphere.

The pathway of the wound with the body in the normal anatomic position is left to right, back to front and upward.

STAB WOUND "O" OF NECK:

An elliptical, horizontally oriented 1.2 x 0.6 centimeter stab wound is centered 14 centimeters below the top of the head, and 6.8 centimeters below the right external auditory meatus. The ends of the wound are sharp. The edges of the wound are smooth. The wound is approximately 1.4 centimeter when reapproximated. The 3 centimeter deep wound extends through the skin and muscles of the posterior neck.

Associated with the wound track are hemorrhages in the adjacent soft tissues and muscles of the posterior neck.

The pathway of the wound with the body in the normal anatomic position is right to left, back to front.

STAB WOUND "P" OF NECK:

An elliptical, vertically oriented 1 x 0.3 centimeter stab wound is centered 13.5 centimeters below the top of the head, and 2 centimeters to the right of midline. The ends of the wound are sharp. The edges of the wound are smooth. The wound is approximately 1 centimeter when reapproximated. The 2.1 centimeter deep wound extends through the skin and muscles of the posterior neck.

Associated with the wound track are hemorrhages in the adjacent soft tissues and muscles of the posterior neck.

The pathway of the wound with the body in the normal anatomic position is right to left, back to front.

STAB WOUND "Q" OF NECK:

An elliptical, vertically oriented 0.6 x 0.3 centimeter stab wound is centered 15 centimeters below the top of the head, and 3 centimeters to the left of midline. The ends of the wound are sharp. The edges of the wound are smooth. The wound is approximately 0.6 centimeters when reapproximated. The 2 centimeter deep wound extends through the skin and muscles of the posterior neck.

Associated with the wound track are hemorrhages in the adjacent soft tissues and muscles of the posterior neck.

The pathway of the wound with the body in the normal anatomic position is slightly left to right, back to front.

STAB WOUND "R" OF NECK:

An elliptical, vertically oriented 0.9 x 0.6 centimeter stab wound is centered 16 centimeters below the top of the head, and 3 centimeters to the left of midline. The ends of the wound are sharp. The edges of the wound are smooth. The wound is approximately 0.9centimeters when reapproximated. The 1.9 centimeter deep wound extends through the skin and muscles of the posterior neck.

Associated with the wound track are hemorrhages in the adjacent soft tissues and muscles of the posterior neck.

APPENDIX A

The pathway of the wound with the body in the normal anatomic position is slightly left to right, back to front.

STAB WOUND "S" OF NECK:

An elliptical, vertically oriented 0.5 x 0.1 centimeter stab wound is centered 16.5 centimeters below the top of the head, and 1.1 centimeters to the left of midline. The ends of the wound are sharp. The edges of the wound are smooth. The wound is approximately 0.5 centimeters when reapproximated. The 2.1 centimeter deep wound extends through the skin and muscles of the posterior neck.

Associated with the wound track are hemorrhages in the adjacent soft tissues and muscles of the posterior neck.

The pathway of the wound with the body in the normal anatomic position is slightly left to right, back to front.

STAB WOUND "T" OF NECK:

An elliptical, horizontally oriented 1.5 x 0.3 centimeter stab wound is centered 16.5 centimeters below the top of the head, and 4.5 centimeters to the right of midline. The medial end of the wound is sharp. The lateral end is blunt. The edges of the wound are smooth. The wound is approximately 1.5 centimeters when reapproximated. The 7 centimeter deep wound extends through the skin, and muscles of the back, between the second and third cervical vertebra laterally, and incises the dura covering the subjacent spinal cord.

Associated with the wound track are hemorrhages in the adjacent soft tissues and muscles of the left side of the back, a defect of the dura and focal epidural hemorrhage. Grossly there is bulging of the cervical cord subjacent to the dural defect.

Note: Neuropathologist Dr. Lucy Rouke examined the spinal cord and concluded that there is no defect of the spinal cord.

The pathway of the wound with the body in the normal anatomic position is right to left, back to front.

OTHER INJURIES:

The right upper arm has a round 3 x 4 centimeter contusion. The right forearm has a 3 x 1.5 centimeter area of three round contusions. The right lower quadrant of the abdomen has a 3 x 3.5 centimeter contusion. The right thigh has vertical row of round contusions that are a 2.5 x 3 centimeter, 4.5 x 3 centimeter, and 5 x 6 centimeters. Above the right knee is a 4.5 x 3 centimeter area of three round contusions.

INTERNAL EXAMINATION:

The firm, brown, muscles of the anterior neck, have no hemorrhage or injuries. The adjacent connective tissue and vessels of the anterior aspect of the cervical spine are unremarkable. The clavicles, sternum, and pelvic bones have no fractures. The hyoid bone and thyroid cartilage are intact. The peritoneal cavity has no adhesions. The intrathoracic and intraabdominal organs are in their normal positions.

The smooth epicardium has a normal amount of subepicardial adipose tissue in a normal distribution. The heart is 230 grams. The right coronary artery supplies the posterior interventricular septum. The coronary arteries have no atherosclerosis. The chambers of the heart contain no mural thrombi. The atrioventricular and semilunar valves are normally formed and have no calcifications, nodularity, or vegetations. The coronary arteries arise normally from the sinuses of Valsalva. The firm, red-brown, homogenous myocardium has no areas of fibrosis or necrosis. Injuries to the aorta are as previously described. The aorta arises from its usual position, has a normal branching pattern and no atherosclerosis. The pulmonary arteries have no thromboemboli.

The larynx and trachea have no foreign objects or mucous plugs. The right and left lungs are 220 grams and 200 grams, respectively. Injuries to the right lung are as previously described. The smooth pink-tan to purple visceral pleural surfaces have mild anthracosis. The red-maroon and congested lung parenchyma has no areas of consolidation, granulomata or masses. The tracheobronchial tree has no mucous plugs or foreign objects.

The pathway of the wound with the body in the normal anatomic position is slightly left to right, back to front.

STAB WOUND "S" OF NECK:

An elliptical, vertically oriented 0.5 x 0.1 centimeter stab wound is centered 16.5 centimeters below the top of the head, and 1.1 centimeters to the left of midline. The ends of the wound are sharp. The edges of the wound are smooth. The wound is approximately 0.5 centimeters when reapproximated. The 2.1 centimeter deep wound extends through the skin and muscles of the posterior neck.

Associated with the wound track are hemorrhages in the adjacent soft tissues and muscles of the posterior neck.

The pathway of the wound with the body in the normal anatomic position is slightly left to right, back to front.

STAB WOUND "T" OF NECK:

An elliptical, horizontally oriented 1.5 x 0.3 centimeter stab wound is centered 16.5 centimeters below the top of the head, and 4.5 centimeters to the right of midline. The medial end of the wound is sharp. The lateral end is blunt. The edges of the wound are smooth. The wound is approximately 1.5 centimeters when reapproximated. The 7 centimeter deep wound extends through the skin, and muscles of the back, between the second and third cervical vertebra laterally, and incises the dura covering the subjacent spinal cord.

Associated with the wound track are hemorrhages in the adjacent soft tissues and muscles of the left side of the back, a defect of the dura and focal epidural hemorrhage. Grossly there is bulging of the cervical cord subjacent to the dural defect.

Note: Neuropathologist Dr. Lucy Rouke examined the spinal cord and concluded that there is no defect of the spinal cord.

The pathway of the wound with the body in the normal anatomic position is right to left, back to front.

OTHER INJURIES:

The right upper arm has a round 3 x 4 centimeter contusion. The right forearm has a 3 x 1.5 centimeter area of three round contusions. The right lower quadrant of the abdomen has a 3 x 3.5 centimeter contusion. The right thigh has vertical row of round contusions that are a 2.5 x 3 centimeter, 4.5 x 3 centimeter, and 5 x 6 centimeters. Above the right knee is a 4.5 x 3 centimeter area of three round contusions.

INTERNAL EXAMINATION:

The firm, brown, muscles of the anterior neck, have no hemorrhage or injuries. The adjacent connective tissue and vessels of the anterior aspect of the cervical spine are unremarkable. The clavicles, sternum, and pelvic bones have no fractures. The hyoid bone and thyroid cartilage are intact. The peritoneal cavity has no adhesions. The intrathoracic and intrabdominal organs are in their normal positions.

The smooth epicardium has a normal amount of subepicardial adipose tissue in a normal distribution. The heart is 230 grams. The right coronary artery supplies the posterior interventricular septum. The coronary arteries have no atherosclerosis. The chambers of the heart contain no mural thrombi. The atrioventricular and semilunar valves are normally formed and have no calcifications, nodularity, or vegetations. The coronary arteries arise normally from the sinuses of Valsalva. The firm, red-brown, homogenous myocardium has no areas of fibrosis or necrosis. Injuries to the aorta are as previously described. The aorta arises from its usual position, has a normal branching pattern and no atherosclerosis. The pulmonary arteries have no thromboemboli.

The larynx and trachea have no foreign objects or mucous plugs. The right and left lungs are 220 grams and 200 grams, respectively. Injuries to the right lung are as previously described. The smooth pink-tan to purple visceral pleural surfaces have mild anthracosis. The red-maroon and congested lung parenchyma has no areas of consolidation, granulomata or masses. The tracheobronchial tree has no mucous plugs or foreign objects.

APPENDIX A

The esophagus has a white-tan, longitudinally folded mucosa and no varices. The empty stomach has a pink smooth serosa. The tan gastric mucosa has rugal folds and no erosions or ulcers. The small and large intestines have tan, smooth serosa and no perforation, obstruction, masses or ischemic injuries. The appendix is normal. The rectum is filled with green stool.

The 1160 gram liver has an intact capsule, red-brown congested parenchyma and no masses or cysts. The gallbladder is empty. The tan, lobulated pancreas has no masses or cysts.

The 100 gram spleen has a lavender intact capsule, red-maroon parenchyma and inconspicuous Malpighian corpuscles. The paraaortic, paratracheal, and mediastinal lymph nodes are inconspicuous.

The right and left kidneys are 110 grams and 140 grams, respectively. The cortical surfaces are smooth. The renal parenchyma has pale cortices and distinct and prominent medullary pyramids. The calyces and pelves are not dilated and have no masses or calculi. The ureters are unobstructed and normal in course and caliber to the urinary bladder. The urinary bladder contains 100 milliliters of yellow urine.

The vagina has a smooth mucosa and no lesions. The cervix is normal. The uterus has a normal shape and normal myometrial thickness. The endometrium is smooth and has no lesions. The ovaries are normal. The fallopian tubes have normal caliber.

The brown, bilobed thyroid gland has no masses or cysts. The parathyroid glands are inconspicuous. The adrenal glands have thin yellow cortices and brown medullae.

The reflected scalp has no subgaleal hemorrhages. The calvarium and skull base are intact. The epidural and subdural spaces have no liquid accumulations. A small amount of subarachnoid blood covers the rostral surface of the vermis, right cerebellar hemisphere, and the basal cisterns. No gross parenchymal defects are identified in theses areas. The leptomeninges are thin and translucent. The brain is 1440 grams. The cerebral hemispheres are symmetric. The corpus callosum is intact. The basilar artery, its tributaries and branches have no atherosclerosis or aneurysms. The cingulate gyri, unci and cerebellar tonsils are not herniated.

Marlon Osbourne, M.D.
Assistant Medical Examiner

(End of Report)

139

APPENDIX B

Toxicology Report

City of Philadelphia
Office of the Medical Examiner

CASE NO. 11-00420
Name: ELLEN R. GREENBERG
Age: 27 Years **Sex:** Female **Race:** White
Pathologist: Marlon Osbourne

ELISA - Enzyme Immunoassay

BENZODIAZEPINES	Blood, Cardiac (F)	Negative
FENTANYL	Blood, Cardiac (F)	Negative
OPIATES	Blood, Cardiac (F)	Negative
OPIATES	Urine	Negative

Wet Chemical Tests - Colorimetry

VOLATILES	Blood, Cardiac (F)	Negative

Drug Screen - SPE, GC/MSD

ZOLPIDEM	Urine	Trace
ZOLPIDEM	Blood, Cardiac (F)	Trace

Benzodiazepine Confirmation/Quantitation - SPE, GC/MSD

CLONAZEPAM	Blood, Cardiac (F)	Present	<7.5 µg/L

Analysis Notes

Volatiles analysis is a colorimetric method that screens for low molecular weight organic volatile reducing agents such as ethanol, methanol, isopropanol, acetaldehyde, and formaldehyde.

Drug Screen by GC/MSD includes screening for the following drug(s) and class of drugs: anticonvulsants, antidepressants, antihistamines, anticholinergics, barbiturates, muscle relaxants and non-steriodal anti-inflammatory agents (excluding salicylates), non-benzodiazepine sedative-hypnotics. Detection of specific compounds of each class is concentration dependent and not all drugs of each class are detected. Certain compounds outside of these classes are also detected. Common incidental findings such as caffeine and metabolites or nicotine and metabolites are not reported.

Benzodiazepine Confirmation/Quantitation is a GC/MSD screen/quantitation for: diazepam, nordiazepam, oxazepam, temazepam, alprazolam, triazolam, estazolam, midazolam, lorazepam, clonazepam, 7-aminoclonazepam.

Enzyme immunoassay testing results are preliminary. Any positive results must be confirmed by another technique.

Toxicologist: Lisa A. Mundy **Date:** 2/8/2011

APPENDIX C

IN THE SUPREME COURT OF PENNSYLVANIA
EASTERN DISTRICT

MARLON OSBOURNE, M.D. AND THE
CITY OF PHILADELPHIA OFFICE OF THE
MEDICAL EXAMINER,

               Respondents

               v.

: No. 332 EAL 2023
:
:
:
: Petition for Allowance of Appeal
: from the Order of the
: Commonwealth Court
:
:
: JOSHUA M. GREENBERG AND SANDRA
: GREENBERG, ADMINISTRATORS OF
: THE ESTATE OF MS. ELLEN R.
: GREENBERG,   :
:
               Petitioners

ORDER

PER CURIAM

     AND NOW, this 30th day of July, 2024, the Petition for Allowance of Appeal is

GRANTED. The issue, as stated by Petitioners is:

> Whether, as an issue of statewide importance, executors and administrators of an estate have standing to challenge an erroneous finding recorded on the decedent's death certificate where that finding constitutes a bar or material impediment to recovery of victim's compensation, restitution or for wrongful death, as well as private criminal complaints.

Justice Wecht did not participate in the consideration or decision of this matter.

You can join the fight to get justice for Ellen Greenberg.

Change.org: Justice for Ellen Rae Greenberg. Please sign this petition.

https://www.change.org/p/justice-for-ellen-rae-greenberg-justiceforellen

Facebook: Justice for Ellen

https://www.facebook.com/JusticeForEllen2019/

Instagram: Justice for Ellen

https://www.instagram.com/justiceforellen/?hl=en

Audioboom: Sign this petition to reopen this case and get justice for Ellen.

https://audioboom.com/posts/8331166-what-will-it-take-to-re-open-the-murder-case-of-ellen-greenbergPodcasts

APPENDIX D

Commonwealth Court of Pennsylvania

Docket Number: 1461 CD 2021

Page 1 of 8

December 9, 2024

CAPTION

Marlon Osbourne, M.D. and the
City of Philadelphia Office of the
Medical Examiner,
Appellants

v.

Joshua M. Greenberg and Sandra
Greenberg, Administrators of the
Estate of Ms. Ellen R. Greenberg

CASE INFORMATION

Initiating Document:	Petition for Permission to Appeal	
Case Status:	Decided/Active	
Case Processing Status:	September 13, 2023	Filing of Decision or Opinion
Journal Number:	31-11-2022	
Case Category:	Civil	Case Type(s): Mandamus

CONSOLIDATED CASES   RELATED CASES

COUNSEL INFORMATION

Appellant   Osbourne, Marlon
Pro Se: No
IFP Status:

Attorney:	Diffily, Kelly Susan	
Law Firm:	City of Philadelphia	
Address:	City Of Phila Law Dept	
	1515 Arch St Fl 17	
	Philadelphia, PA 19143	
Phone No:	(215) 683-5010	Fax No:

Appellant   City of Philadelphia Office of the Medical Examiner
Pro Se: No
IFP Status:

Attorney:	Diffily, Kelly Susan	
Law Firm:	City of Philadelphia	
Address:	City Of Phila Law Dept	
	1515 Arch St Fl 17	
	Philadelphia, PA 19143	
Phone No:	(215) 683-5010	Fax No:

Commonwealth Docket Sheet

Commonwealth Court of Pennsylvania

Docket Number: 1461 CD 2021

Page 2 of 8

December 9, 2024

COUNSEL INFORMATION

Amicus Curiae   **National Association of Medical Examiners (NAME)**

Pro Se: No

IFP Status:

Attorney:	Menendez, Mary Jo	
Law Firm:	NMS Labs, Inc.	
Address:	Nms Labs	
	200 Welsh Rd	
	Horsham, PA 19044	
Phone No:	(215) 366-1513	Fax No:

Appellee   **Greenberg, Sandra**

Pro Se: No

IFP Status:

Attorney:	Podraza, Joseph R.	
Law Firm:	Lamb McErlane, PC	
Address:	1 S Broad St Ste 1500	
	Philadelphia, PA 19107	
Phone No:	(610) 701-4405	Fax No:

Attorney:	Trask, William Howard	
Law Firm:	Lamb McErlane, PC	
Address:	Lamb Mcerlane Pc	
	1 S Broad St Ste 1500	
	Philadelphia, PA 19107	
Phone No:	(215) 609-3148	Fax No:

Appellee   **Greenberg, Joshua M.**

Pro Se: No

IFP Status:

Attorney:	Podraza, Joseph R.	
Law Firm:	Lamb McErlane, PC	
Address:	1 S Broad St Ste 1500	
	Philadelphia, PA 19107	
Phone No:	(610) 701-4405	Fax No:

Attorney:	Trask, William Howard	
Law Firm:	Lamb McErlane, PC	
Address:	Lamb Mcerlane Pc	
	1 S Broad St Ste 1500	
	Philadelphia, PA 19107	
Phone No:	(215) 609-3148	Fax No:

APPENDIX D

COUNSEL INFORMATION

Appellee   Estate of Ms. Ellen R. Greenberg

Pro Se: No

IFP Status:

Attorney:	Podraza, Joseph R.
Law Firm:	Lamb McErlane, PC
Address:	1 S Broad St Ste 1500
	Philadelphia, PA 19107
Phone No:	(610) 701-4405 Fax No:

Attorney:	Trask, William Howard
Law Firm:	Lamb McErlane, PC
Address:	Lamb Mcerlane Pc
	1 S Broad St Ste 1500
	Philadelphia, PA 19107
Phone No:	(215) 609-3148 Fax No:

FEE INFORMATION

Fee Dt	Fee Name	Fee Amt	Receipt Dt	Receipt No	Receipt Amt
12/23/2021	Petition for Review - Appellate	90.25	01/03/2022	2022-CMW-H-000006	90.25

AGENCY/TRIAL COURT INFORMATION

Order Appealed From:	October 21, 2021	Notice of Appeal Filed:	
Order Type:	Order Entered		
Documents Received:	December 23, 2021		

Court Below:	Philadelphia County Court of Common Pleas		
County:	Philadelphia	Division:	Philadelphia County Civil Division
Judge:	Hill, Glynnis D.	OTN:	
Docket Number:	191001241	Judicial District:	01

ORIGINAL RECORD CONTENT

Original Record Item	Filed Date	Content Description
Trial Court Record	May 19, 2022	
Trial Court Opinion	May 19, 2022	
Testimony	June 09, 2022	
Trial Court Opinion	June 10, 2022	

Date of Remand of Record:

BRIEFING SCHEDULE

Amicus Curiae
National Association of Medical Examiners (NAME)
  Brief
Due: Filed: May 2, 2022

Appellee
Estate of Ms. Ellen R. Greenberg
  Brief
Due: July 6, 2022   Filed: July 6, 2022

Appellant
City of Philadelphia Office of the Medical Examiner
  Brief
Due: May 4, 2022   Filed: May 4, 2022

Greenberg, Joshua M.
  Brief
Due: July 6, 2022   Filed: July 6, 2022

Greenberg, Sandra
  Brief

Reply Brief

Commonwealth Docket Sheet

Commonwealth Court of Pennsylvania

Docket Number: 1461 CD 2021

Page 4 of 8

December 9, 2024

Appellant		Appellee	
City of Philadelphia Office of the Medical Examiner		Greenberg, Sandra	
Reply Brief		**Brief**	
Due: August 5, 2022	Filed: August 5, 2022	Due: July 6, 2022	Filed: July 6, 2022

Reproduced Record	
Due: May 4, 2022	Filed: May 4, 2022

DOCKET ENTRY

Filed Date	Docket Entry / Filer	Representing	Participant Type	Exit Date
December 23, 2021	Petition for Permission to Appeal Filed			
	Osborne, Marlon		Appellant	
	City of Philadelphia Office of the Medical Examiner		Appellant	
January 6, 2022	Answer Filed			
	Podraza, Joseph R.	Greenberg, Joshua M.	Appellee	
	Podraza, Joseph R.	Greenberg, Sandra	Appellee	
	Podraza, Joseph R.	Estate of Ms. Ellen R. Greenberg	Appellee	
	Document Name: Answer in Opposition to PPA			
January 6, 2022	Filed - Other			
	Podraza, Joseph R.	Greenberg, Joshua M.	Appellee	
	Podraza, Joseph R.	Greenberg, Sandra	Appellee	
	Podraza, Joseph R.	Estate of Ms. Ellen R. Greenberg	Appellee	
	Document Name: Appendix to Answer in Opposition to PPA			
February 4, 2022	Order Granting Petition for Permission to Appeal			02/04/2022
	Per Curiam			
	Document Name: Petition for Permission to Appeal is Granted			

APPENDIX D

Commonwealth Court of Pennsylvania

Filed Date	Docket Entry / Filer	Representing	Participant Type	Exit Date
	Comment: Now, February 4, 2022, upon consideration of the Petition for Permission to Appeal (Petition) filed by Marlon Osbourne, M.D. and the City of Philadelphia Office of the Medical Examiner (Appellants), which was filed pursuant to Pa.R.A.P. 1311(a)(1) as the Court of Common Pleas of Philadelphia County (trial court) denied Appellants' motion to certify its order pursuant to 42 Pa.C.S. § 702(b), and the Answer in opposition thereto by Joshua M. Greenberg and Sandra Greenberg, Administrators of the Estate of Ms. Ellen R. Greenberg (Appellees), the Petition is GRANTED. Appeal is permitted from the October 21, 2021 Order of the trial court at Docket No. 191001241. The Court will consider the following issues: Do parents as administrators of the estate have standing to seek court-ordered revision of the manner of their adult child's death where the harm they identify is the alleged stigma of suicide, the forestalling of any further investigation into the death, and the effective bar to bringing a potential lawsuit including a wrongful death action? Is mandamus and/or declaratory relief available to compel revision of a medical examiner's opinion as to the manner of death stated on a death certificate? The Prothonotary of the Commonwealth Court shall amend the caption as indicated above and shall list this appeal on the next appropriate argument list. The Office of Judicial Records - Civil of the Court of Common Pleas of Philadelphia County shall certify the record in this matter to this Court on or before March 4, 2022. Appellants shall file and serve their brief (4 copies) and the reproduced record (4 copies) on or before April 4, 2022. Subsequent briefs shall be filed in accordance with the schedule set in Pa.R.A.P. 2185. All proceedings in this matter before the trial court are stayed pending resolution of this appeal. In addition to sending copies of this Order to counsel of record, the Prothonotary of the Commonwealth Court shall send a copy to the Honorable Glynnis D. Hill of the trial court, and a copy to the Office of Judicial Records - Civil of that court.			
March 14, 2022	Application for Extension of Time to File Brief - First Request Diffily, Kelly Susan City of Philadelphia Office of the Medical Examiner	City of Philadelphia Office of the Med	Appellant Appellant	
March 16, 2022	Order Granting Application for Extension of Time to File Per Curiam			03/17/2022
	Document Name: Appellant's brief and reproduced record due May 4, 2022			
	Comment: NOW, March 16, 2022, upon consideration of Appellants' First Unopposed Application for a 30-Day Extension of Time to File Brief (Application), the Application is GRANTED. Appellants shall file and serve their brief (4 copies) and the reproduced record (4 copies) on or before May 4, 2022.			
May 2, 2022	Amicus Curiae Brief National Association of Medical Examiners (NAME)		Amicus Curiae	
May 4, 2022	Appellant's Reproduced Record Filed Diffily, Kelly Susan	City of Philadelphia Office of the Med	Appellant	
May 4, 2022	Appellant's Brief Filed City of Philadelphia Office of the Medical Examiner		Appellant	

Commonwealth Docket Sheet

Commonwealth Court of Pennsylvania

Docket Number: 1461 CD 2021

Page 6 of 8

December 9, 2024

DOCKET ENTRY				
Filed Date	Docket Entry / Filer	Representing	Participant Type	Exit Date
May 10, 2022	Application for Extension of Time to File Brief - First Request			
	Podraza, Joseph R.	Greenberg, Joshua M.	Appellee	
	Podraza, Joseph R.	Greenberg, Sandra	Appellee	
	Podraza, Joseph R.	Estate of Ms. Ellen R. Greenberg	Appellee	
	Greenberg, Joshua M.		Appellee	
	Greenberg, Sandra		Appellee	
	Estate of Ms. Ellen R. Greenberg		Appellee	
May 12, 2022	Order Granting Application for Extension of Time to File			05/13/2022
	Per Curiam			
	Document Name: Appellee's brief due July 6, 2022			
	Comment: NOW, May 12, 2022, upon consideration of Appellees' "First Unopposed Application for a 30-Day Extension of Time to File Brief" (Application), the Application is GRANTED. Appellees shall file and serve their brief (4 copies) and any supplemental reproduced record (4 copies) on or before July 6, 2022.			
May 19, 2022	Trial Court Record Received			
	Philadelphia County Civil Division			
May 19, 2022	Trial Court Opinion Received			
	Philadelphia County Civil Division			
	Document Name: Trial Court Record - 3 (Commonwealth Court Order)			
June 9, 2022	Transcripts of Testimony			
	Court Reporters, Digital Recording, and Interpreters Administration - First Judicial District of Pennsylvania			
June 10, 2022	Trial Court Opinion Received			
	Philadelphia County Civil Division			
July 6, 2022	Tentative Session Date			
	Krimmel, Michael			
	Document Name: November 2022			
July 6, 2022	Appellee's Brief Filed			
	Greenberg, Joshua M.		Appellee	
	Greenberg, Sandra		Appellee	
	Estate of Ms. Ellen R. Greenberg		Appellee	
July 18, 2022	Application for Extension of Time to File Brief - First Request			
	Diffily, Kelly Susan	City of Philadelphia Office of the Mec	Appellant	
	City of Philadelphia Office of the Medical Examiner		Appellant	
July 20, 2022	Order Granting Application for Extension of Time to File Appellant Paperbook			07/21/2022
	Per Curiam			
	Document Name: due August 5, 2022			
	Comment: NOW, July 20, 2021, upon consideration of Appellants' Unopposed Application for a 14-day Extension of Time to File Reply Brief, the Application is GRANTED. Appellants' reply brief (4 copies) shall be filed and served no later that August 5, 2022.			

APPENDIX D

Commonwealth Docket Sheet			**Commonwealth Court of Pennsylvania**	

Docket Number: 1461 CD 2021

Page 7 of 8

December 9, 2024

DOCKET ENTRY				
Filed Date	Docket Entry / Filer	Representing	Participant Type	Exit Date
August 5, 2022	Appellant's Reply Brief			
	City of Philadelphia Office of the Medical Examiner		Appellant	
October 12, 2022	Argument Scheduled			
	Krimmel, Michael			
	Document Name: TUESDAY, November 15, 2022 @ 1:00 p.m. (Panel), Court Room 1, Ninth Floor, Widener Building,			
	Comment: 1339 Chestnut Street, Philadelphia, PA			
	No. 31 on the list.			
November 14, 2022	Order Filed			11/14/2022
	Per Curiam			
	Document Name: This case shall be the head of the list of cases			
	Comment: The above-captioned matter, scheduled for oral argument before a panel of judges on November 15, 2022 in Courtroom No. 1, 9th Floor, Widener Building, 1339 Chestnut Street, One South Penn Square, Philadelphia, Pennsylvania, shall be called at the head of the list of cases to be heard on that same day and location. The argument session commences at 1:00 p.m.			
September 13, 2023	Reversed/Remanded			09/13/2023
	Ceisler, Ellen			
	Document Name: Memorandum Opinion: Order of Phila. Co. CCP is REVERSED / Case remanded / Jurisdiction relinquished.			
	Comment: AND NOW, this 13th day of September, 2023, the October 21, 2021 Order of the Court of Common Pleas of Philadelphia County (Trial Court) in the above-captioned matter is hereby REVERSED. The case is remanded to the Trial Court for the entry of judgment in favor of Marlon Osbourne, M.D., and the City of Philadelphia Office of the Medical Examiner. Jurisdiction relinquished.			
	Judge Wallace did not participate in the decision of this case.			
October 13, 2023	Petition for Allowance of Appeal to PA Supreme Court Filed			
	Greenberg, Joshua M.		Appellee	
	Greenberg, Sandra		Appellee	
	Estate of Ms. Ellen R. Greenberg		Appellee	
	Document Name: 55 EAP 2024			
	Comment: 332 EAL 2023			

SESSION INFORMATION	
Journal Number:	31-11-2022
Consideration Type:	Oral Argument - Panel
Listed/Submitted Date:	November 15, 2022

Panel Composition:

The Honorable Patricia A. McCullough	Judge
The Honorable Ellen Ceisler	Judge
The Honorable Lori A. Dumas	Judge

DISPOSITION INFORMATION

Neither the Appellate Courts nor the Administrative Office of Pennsylvania Courts assumes any liability
for inaccurate or delayed data, errors or omissions on the docket sheets.

Commonwealth Docket Sheet

Commonwealth Court of Pennsylvania

Docket Number: 1461 CD 2021

Page 8 of 8

December 9, 2024

DISPOSITION INFORMATION

Final Disposition:	Yes		
Related Journal No:		Judgment Date:	
Category:	Decided	Disposition Author:	Ceisler, Ellen
Disposition:	Reversed/Remanded	Disposition Date:	September 13, 2023

Disposition Comment: AND NOW, this 13th day of September, 2023, the October 21, 2021 Order of the Court of Common Pleas of Philadelphia County (Trial Court) in the above-captioned matter is hereby REVERSED. The case is remanded to the Trial Court for the entry of judgment in favor of Marlon Osbourne, M.D., and the City of Philadelphia Office of the Medical Examiner.
Jurisdiction relinquished.

Judge Wallace did not participate in the decision of this case.

Dispositional Filing:	**Memorandum Opinion**	Filing Author:	Ceisler, Ellen
Filed Date:	9/13/2023 12:00:00AM		
Dispositional Filing:	**Dissenting Opinion**	Filing Author:	McCullough, Patricia A.
Filed Date:	9/13/2023 12:00:00AM		

APPENDIX E

A $5 Convenience fee will be added to the transaction at checkout.

Case Description

Case ID:	191001241
Case Caption:	GREENBERG VS OSBOURNE
Filing Date:	Tuesday , October 15th, 2019
Court:	MAJOR NON JURY STANDARD
Location:	CITY HALL
Jury:	NON JURY
Case Type:	EQUITY - NO REAL ESTATE
Status:	DEFERRED - ON APPEAL

Related Cases

No related cases were found.

Case Event Schedule

No case events were found.

Case motions

No case motions were found.

Case Parties

Seq #	Assoc	Expn Date	Type	Name
1			ATTORNEY FOR PLAINTIFF	PODRAZA JR, JOSEPH R
Address:	1601 MARKET STREET SUITE 2560 PHILADELPHIA PA 19103 (215)609-3170 jpodraza@lambmcerlane.com	**Aliases:**	*none*	
2	1		ADMINISTRATOR - PLAINTIFF	GREENBERG ADMINISTRATOR ESTATE OF ELLEN R GREENBERG DECEASED, JOSHUA M
Address:	4408 SAYBROOK LANE HARRISBURG PA 17110	**Aliases:**	*none*	

3		1		ADMINISTRATOR - PLAINTIFF	GREENBERG ADMINISTRATRIX ESTATE OF ELLEN R GREENBERG DECEASE, SANDRA
Address:	4408 SAYBROOK LANE HARRISBURG PA 17110		**Aliases:**	*none*	

4		7		DEFENDANT	OSBOURNE MD, MARLON
Address:	5301 SW 31ST AVENUE FORT LAUDERDALE FL 33312		**Aliases:**	*none*	

5		7		DEFENDANT	PHILADELPHIA COUNTY MEDICAL EXAMINER'S OFFICE
Address:	321 UNIVERSITY AVENUE PHILADELPHIA PA 19104		**Aliases:**	*none*	

6			06-OCT-2020	TEAM LEADER	SHIRDAN-HARRIS, LISETTE
Address:	516 CITY HALL PHILADELPHIA PA 19107		**Aliases:**	*none*	

7				ATTORNEY FOR DEFENDANT	BERKOWITZ, ELLEN
Address:	1515 ARCH STREET 17TH FLOOR PHILADELPHIA PA 19102 (215)683-5253 ellen.berkowitz@phila.gov		**Aliases:**	*none*	

8		1		ATTORNEY FOR PLAINTIFF	TRASK, WILLIAM H
Address:	1601 MARKET STREET SUITE 2560 PHILADELPHIA PA 19103 (215)609-3148 wtrask@lambmcerlane.com		**Aliases:**	*none*	

9			JUDGE	PATRICK, PAULA
Address:	CITY HALL RM 510 PHILADELPHIA PA 19107 (215)686-8338	**Aliases:**	*none*	

10		04-JUL-2021	TEAM LEADER	SHREEVES-JOHNS, K
Address:	364 CITY HALL PHILADELPHIA PA 19107	**Aliases:**	*none*	

11		18-JAN-2022	MOTION ASSIGMENT JUDGE	HILL, GLYNNIS
Address:	1416 STOUT CENTER FOR CJ 1301 FILBERT ST PHILADELPHIA PA 19107	**Aliases:**	*none*	

12		31-OCT-2023	TEAM LEADER	FLETMAN, ABBE F
Address:	606 CITY HALL PHILADELPHIA PA 19107	**Aliases:**	*none*	

13			JUDGE	EMERGENCY JUDGE, JUDGE
Address:	ROOM 280 CITY HALL PHILADELPHIA PA 19107	**Aliases:**	*none*	

14			MOTION ASSIGMENT JUDGE	HANGLEY, MICHELE D
Address:	CITY HALL PHILADELPHIA PA 19107	**Aliases:**	*none*	

15			JUDGE PRO TEMPORE	CHARAMELLA, REBECCA
Address:	SETTLEMENT OFFICER 691 E CITY HALL PHILADELPHIA PA 19107	**Aliases:**	*none*	

16	7		ATTORNEY FOR DEFENDANT	KIRBY, AMY MARIE

Address:	1515 ARCH ST PHILADELPHIA PA 19102 (215)683-3566 Amy.Kirby@phila.gov	Aliases:	*none*	

17			TEAM LEADER	ROBERTS, JOSHUA
Address:	538 CITY HALL PHILADELPHIA PA 19107	**Aliases:**	*none*	

Docket Entries

Filing Date/Time	Docket Type	Filing Party	Disposition Amount
15-OCT-2019 11:08 AM	ACTIVE CASE		
Docket Entry:	E-Filing Number: 1910034385		
15-OCT-2019 11:08 AM	COMMENCEMENT OF CIVIL ACTION	PODRAZA JR, JOSEPH R	
Documents:	⚲ Click link(s) to preview/purchase the documents Final Cover	🛒 **Click HERE to purchase all documents related to this one docket entry**	
Docket Entry:	*none.*		
15-OCT-2019 11:08 AM	COMPLAINT FILED NOTICE GIVEN	PODRAZA JR, JOSEPH R	
Documents:	⚲ Click link(s) to preview/purchase the documents 2019 10 14 Complaint - FINAL.pdf EXH A.pdf EXH B.pdf EXH C.pdf EXH D.pdf EXH E.pdf EXH F.pdf EXH G.pdf EXH H.pdf EXH I.pdf EXH J.pdf	🛒 **Click HERE to purchase all documents related to this one docket entry**	
Docket Entry:	COMPLAINT WITH NOTICE TO DEFEND WITHIN TWENTY (20) DAYS AFTER SERVICE IN ACCORDANCE WITH RULE 1018.1 FILED.		
15-OCT-2019 11:08 AM	WAITING TO LIST CASE MGMT CONF	PODRAZA JR, JOSEPH R	

154

APPENDIX E

Docket Entry:	none.		

29-OCT-2019 12:06 PM	AFFIDAVIT OF SERVICE FILED	PODRAZA JR, JOSEPH R	
Documents:	🔗 Click link(s) to preview/purchase the documents 2019 10 29 Praecipe to File AOS - Med Examiner Office.pdf	🛒 Click HERE to purchase all documents related to this one docket entry	
Docket Entry:	AFFIDAVIT OF SERVICE OF PLAINTIFF'S COMPLAINT UPON PHILADELPHIA COUNTY MEDICAL EXAMINER'S OFFICE BY PERSONAL SERVICE ON 10/21/2019 FILED. (FILED ON BEHALF OF SANDRA GREENBERG ADMINISTRATRIX ESTATE OF ELLEN R GREENBERG DECEASE AND JOSHUA M GREENBERG ADMINISTRATOR ESTATE OF ELLEN R GREENBERG DECEASED)		

06-NOV-2019 03:01 PM	PRAECIPE TO REINSTATE CMPLT	PODRAZA JR, JOSEPH R	
Documents:	🔗 Click link(s) to preview/purchase the documents 2019 11 06 Praecipe to Reinstate Complaint.pdf 2019 10 15 Complaint.pdf	🛒 Click HERE to purchase all documents related to this one docket entry	
Docket Entry:	COMPLAINT WITH NOTICE TO DEFEND WITHIN TWENTY (20) DAYS AFTER SERVICE IN ACCORDANCE WITH RULE 1018.1 REINSTATED. (FILED ON BEHALF OF SANDRA GREENBERG ADMINISTRATRIX ESTATE OF ELLEN R GREENBERG DECEASE AND JOSHUA M GREENBERG ADMINISTRATOR ESTATE OF ELLEN R GREENBERG DECEASED)		

12-NOV-2019 01:20 PM	ENTRY OF APPEARANCE	BERKOWITZ, ELLEN	
Documents:	🔗 Click link(s) to preview/purchase the documents Entry of Appearance.pdf	🛒 Click HERE to purchase all documents related to this one docket entry	
Docket Entry:	ENTRY OF APPEARANCE OF ELLEN BERKOWITZ FILED. (FILED ON BEHALF OF PHILADELPHIA COUNTY MEDICAL EXAMINER'S OFFICE AND MARLON OSBOURNE)		

12-NOV-2019 01:20 PM	CITY CHARGE SUBSEQUENT FILINGS	BERKOWITZ, ELLEN	
Docket Entry:	none.		

12-NOV-2019 03:55 PM	ENTRY OF APPEARANCE	TRASK, WILLIAM H	
Documents:	🔗 Click link(s) to preview/purchase the documents 2019 11 12 EOA - WRT.pdf	🛒 Click HERE to purchase all documents related to this one docket entry	

Docket Entry	ENTRY OF APPEARANCE OF WILLIAM H TRASK FILED. (FILED ON BEHALF OF SANDRA GREENBERG ADMINISTRATRIX ESTATE OF ELLEN R GREENBERG DECEASE AND JOSHUA M GREENBERG ADMINISTRATOR ESTATE OF ELLEN R GREENBERG DECEASED)		
12-NOV-2019 05:59 PM	PRELIMINARY OBJECTIONS	BERKOWITZ, ELLEN	
Documents:	⚖ Click link(s) to preview/purchase the documents Defendants Preliminary Objections.pdf Memo of Law - POs.pdf	🛒 **Click HERE to purchase all documents related to this one docket entry**	
Docket Entry	53-19111653 PRELIMINARY OBJECTIONS TO PLAINTIFF'S INITIAL COMPLAINT FILED. RESPONSE DATE: 12/03/2019 (FILED ON BEHALF OF PHILADELPHIA COUNTY MEDICAL EXAMINER'S OFFICE AND MARLON OSBOURNE)		
18-NOV-2019 03:13 PM	AFFIDAVIT OF SERVICE FILED	PODRAZA JR, JOSEPH R	
Documents:	⚖ Click link(s) to preview/purchase the documents 2019 11 18 Praecipe to File AOS - Osbourne.pdf	🛒 **Click HERE to purchase all documents related to this one docket entry**	
Docket Entry:	AFFIDAVIT OF SERVICE OF PLAINTIFF'S COMPLAINT UPON MARLON OSBOURNE BY CERTIFIED MAIL ON 11/12/2019 FILED. (FILED ON BEHALF OF SANDRA GREENBERG ADMINISTRATRIX ESTATE OF ELLEN R GREENBERG DECEASE AND JOSHUA M GREENBERG ADMINISTRATOR ESTATE OF ELLEN R GREENBERG DECEASED)		
03-DEC-2019 04:02 PM	ANSWER TO PRELIMINARY OBJCTNS	PODRAZA JR, JOSEPH R	
Documents:	⚖ Click link(s) to preview/purchase the documents 2019 12 03 Ps Answer to Ds POs.pdf 2019 12 03 MOL - Ps Answer to Ds POs - FINAL.pdf	🛒 **Click HERE to purchase all documents related to this one docket entry**	
Docket Entry:	53-19111653 ANSWER IN OPPOSITION OF PRELIMINARY OBJECTIONS FILED. (FILED ON BEHALF OF SANDRA GREENBERG ADMINISTRATRIX ESTATE OF ELLEN R GREENBERG DECEASE AND JOSHUA M GREENBERG ADMINISTRATOR ESTATE OF ELLEN R GREENBERG DECEASED)		
05-DEC-2019 11:18 AM	PRELIM OBJECTIONS ASSIGNED		
Docket Entry:	53-19111653 PRELIMINARY OBJECTIONS ASSIGNED TO JUDGE: PATRICK, PAULA . ON DATE: DECEMBER 05, 2019		
07-JAN-2020 02:45 PM	ORDER ENTERED/236 NOTICE GIVEN	PATRICK, PAULA	

APPENDIX E

Documents:	✎ Click link(s) to preview/purchase the documents ORDER_14.pdf	🛒 **Click HERE to purchase all documents related to this one docket entry**
Docket Entry:	53-19111653 AND NOW, THIS 7TH DAY OF JANUARY, 2020, UPON CONSIDERATION OF THE DEFENDANTS' PRELIMINARY OBJECTIONS TO PLAINTIFFS' COMPLAINT, AND THE RESPONSE, IT IS HEREBY ORDERED AND DECREED THAT THE OBJECTIONS ARE OVERRULED. IT IS FURTHER ORDERED AND DECREED THAT DEFENDANTS ARE GRANTED LEAVE OF 20 DAYS FROM THE DATE THIS ORDER IS DOCKETED TO ANSWER PLAINTIFF'S COMPLAINT. ...BY THE COURT: PATRICK, J., 1/7/20	

07-JAN-2020 02:45 PM	NOTICE GIVEN UNDER RULE 236		
Docket Entry:	NOTICE GIVEN ON 08-JAN-2020 OF ORDER ENTERED/236 NOTICE GIVEN ENTERED ON 07-JAN-2020.		

08-JAN-2020 12:04 PM	LISTED FOR CASE MGMT CONF		
Docket Entry:	*none.*		

10-JAN-2020 12:30 AM	NOTICE GIVEN		
Docket Entry:	*none.*		

27-JAN-2020 10:24 AM	CASE MGMT CONFERENCE COMPLETED	ORVIK, ERIK	
Docket Entry:	*none.*		

27-JAN-2020 10:24 AM	CASE MANAGEMENT ORDER ISSUED		
Documents:	✎ Click link(s) to preview/purchase the documents CMOIS_19.pdf	🛒 **Click HERE to purchase all documents related to this one docket entry**	
Docket Entry:	IT IS ORDERED THAT THE ABOVE CAPTIONED MATTER IS HEREBY ASSIGNED TO THE MAY_POOL TRIAL POOL AND COUNSEL SHOULD ANTICIPATE TRIAL TO BEGIN EXPEDITIOUSLY THEREAFTER. COUNSEL AND PARTIES WILL BE NOTICED FOR TRIAL TO TAKE PLACE DURING THE DESIGNATED TRIAL POOL MONTH. ALL COUNSEL AND PARTIES MUST IMMEDIATELY NOTIFY THE COURT IN WRITING OF ANY SCHEDULING CONFLICTS, INCLUDING TRIAL ATTACHMENTS AND PRE-PAID VACATIONS BY ELECTRONICALLY FILING A TRIAL POOL CONFLICT LETTER AND ARE UNDER A CONTINUING OBLIGATION TO NOTIFY THE COURT OF ANY SUBSEQUESNT TRIAL ATTACHMENTS		

DURING THE TRIAL POOL MONTH. THE COURT WILL NOT RECOGNIZE ANY UNTIMELY CONFLICT NOTIFICTIONS. FAILURE TO NOTIFY COURT OF SCHEDULING CONFLICTS WILL RESULT IN THE IMPOSITION OF APPROPRIATE SANCTIONS. TO ELECTRONICALLY FILE A TRIAL POOL CONFLICT LETTER, ACCESS THE "EXISTING CASE" SECTION OF THE COURT'S ELECTRONIC FILING SYSTEM. SELECT " CONFERENCE SUBMISSIONS" AS THE FILING CATEGORY. SELECT "TRIAL POOL CONFLICT LETTER" AS THE DOCUMENT TYPE AND NOW, 27-JAN-2020, IT IS ORDERED THAT: 1. THE CASE MANAGEMENT AND TIME STANDARDS ADOPTED FOR STANDARD TRACK CASES SHALL BE APPLICABLE TO THIS CASE AND ARE HEREBY INCORPORATED INTO THIS ORDER. 2. ALL DISCOVERY IN THE ABOVE MATTER SHALL BE COMPLETED NOT LATER THAN 04-JAN-2021. 3. PLAINTIFF'S EXPERT REPORT, IF APPLICABLE, INCLUDING ANY SUPPLEMENTAL REPORT, IS TO BE SERVED ON OPPOSING COUNSEL AND/OR OPPOSING PARTY ON OR BEFORE 04-JAN-2021. 4. DEFENDANT'S AND ANY ADDITIONAL DEFENDANTS' EXPERT REPORT IS TO BE SERVED ON OPPOSING COUNSEL AND/OR OPPOSING PARTY ON OR BEFORE 01-FEB-2021. 5. ALL PRE-TRIAL AND DISPOSITIVE MOTIONS MUST BE FILED NO LATER THAN 01-FEB-2021. 6. A MANDATORY PRE-TRIAL SETTLEMENT CONFERENCE WILL BE SCHEDULED ANY TIME AFTER 05-APR-2021. EARLIER LISTINGS WILL BE SCHEDULED AT THE DISCRETION OF THE COURT. COUNSEL MUST APPEAR AT THE MANDATORY PRE-TRIAL SETTLEMENT CONFERENCE WITH KNOWLEDGE OF THE CASE AND SETTLEMENT AUTHORITY. FAILURE TO COMPLY WITH THIS DIRECTIVE WILL RESULT IN SANCTIONS IN THE AMOUNT OF $100.00. NOTICE WILL BE SENT TO ALL PARTIES AT LEAST THIRTY (30) DAYS IN ADVANCE OF THE CONFERENCE. TEN (10) DAYS PRIOR TO THE CONFERENCE, ALL COUNSEL SHALL SERVE UPON ALL OPPOSING COUNSEL AND/OR OPPOSING PARTIES AND FILE WITH THE COURT A PRE-TRIAL SETTLEMENT MEMORANDUM CONTAINING THE FOLLOWING: (a) A CONCISE SUMMARY OF THE NATURE OF THE CASE IF PLAINTIFF OR THE DEFENSE IF DEFENDANT OR ADDITIONAL DEFENDANT; (b) A LIST OF ALL WITNESSES WHO MAY BE CALLED TO TESTIFY AT TRIAL BY NAME AND ADDRESS. COUNSEL SHOULD EXPECT WITNESSES NOT LISTED TO BE PRECLUDED FROM TESTIFYING AT TRIAL; (c) A LIST OF ALL EXHIBITS THE PARTY INTENDS TO OFFER INTO EVIDENCE. ALL EXHIBITS SHALL BE PRE-NUMBERED AND SHALL BE EXCHANGED AMONG COUNSEL PRIOR TO THE CONFERENCE. COUNSEL SHOULD EXPECT ANY EXHIBIT NOT LISTED TO BE PRECLUDED AT TRIAL; (d) PLAINTIFF SHALL LIST AN ITEMIZATION OF INJURIES OR DAMAGES SUSTAINED TOGETHER WITH ALL SPECIAL DAMAGES CLAIMED BY CATEGORY AND AMOUNT. THIS LIST SHALL INCLUDE AS APPROPRIATE, COMPUTATIONS OF ALL PAST LOST EARNINGS AND FUTURE LOST EARNING CAPACITY OR MEDICAL EXPENSES TOGETHER WITH ANY OTHER UNLIQUIDATED DAMAGES CLAIMED; AND (e) DEFENDANT SHALL STATE ITS POSITION REGARDING DAMAGES AND SHALL IDENTIFY ALL APPLICABLE INSURANCE CARRIERS, TOGETHER WITH APPLICABLE LIMITS OF LIABILITY; AND (f) EACH COUNSEL SHALL PROVIDE AN ESTIMATE OF THE ANTICIPATED LENGTH OF TRIAL. FAILURE TO TIMELY FILE A PRE-TRIAL SETTLEMENT CONFERENCE MEMORANDUM MAY RESULT IN THE IMPOSITION OF MONETARY SANCTIONS. ALL MOTIONS IN LIMINE SHALL BE FILED IN ACCORDANCE WITH ELECTRONIC FILING PROCEDURES NOT LATER THAN FIFTEEN (15) DAYS PRIOR TO THE START OF TRIAL. RESPONDING COUNSEL SHALL HAVE TEN (10) DAYS THEREAFTER TO FILE ANY RESPONSE. FOR POOL CASES, THE

	START OF THE TRIAL IS DEFINED AS THE FIRST DAY OF THE TRIAL POOL LISTING. REQUESTS TO EXTEND ANY CASE MANAGEMENT DEADLINE OR FOR TRIAL CONTINUANCE MUST BE SUBMITTED BY FILING A MOTION FOR EXTRAORDINARY RELIEF AND FILED PRIOR TO THE EXPIRATION OF THE DEADLINE IN QUESTION. ANY REQUESTS FOR A DATE-CERTAIN TRIAL LISTING MUST BE SUBMITTED IN WRITING WITH SPECIFICITY, WITH A COPY TO OPPOSING PARTY, AND DIRECTED TO THE HONORABLE LISETTE SHIRDAN-HARRIS, TEAM LEADER, VIA FACSIMILE (215-686-5137) OR US MAIL (622 CITY HALL, PHILADELPHIA, PA 19107). HOWEVER, SAID REQUESTS MAY BE MADE ONLY UNDER EXIGENT CIRCUMSTANCES. COUNSEL SHOULD HAVE SUBSTITUTE COUNSEL PREPARED TO CONDUCT SETTLEMENT CONFERENCE AND/OR TRIAL WHERE PRACTICABLE. ALL COUNSEL ARE UNDER A CONTINUING OBLIGATION AND ARE HEREBY ORDERED TO SERVE A COPY OF THIS ORDER UPON ALL UNREPRESENTED PARTIES AND UPON ALL COUNSEL ENTERING AN APPEARANCE SUBSEQUENT TO THE ENTRY OF THIS ORDER. ...BY THE COURT: LISETTE SHIRDAN-HARRIS, J.		
27-JAN-2020 10:24 AM	LISTED-PROJ. PRE-TRIAL CONF		
Docket Entry:	none.		
27-JAN-2020 10:24 AM	LISTED IN TRIAL READY POOL		
Docket Entry:	none.		
27-JAN-2020 10:24 AM	NOTICE GIVEN UNDER RULE 236		
Docket Entry:	NOTICE GIVEN ON 27-JAN-2020 OF CASE MANAGEMENT ORDER ISSUED ENTERED ON 27-JAN-2020.		
27-JAN-2020 02:52 PM	ANSWER TO COMPLAINT FILED	BERKOWITZ, ELLEN	
Documents:	Click link(s) to preview/purchase the documents Answer of Defendants City of Philadelphia MEO and Marlon Osbourne _.pdf	Click HERE to purchase all documents related to this one docket entry	
Docket Entry:	ANSWER WITH NEW MATTER TO PLAINTIFF'S COMPLAINT FILED. (FILED ON BEHALF OF PHILADELPHIA COUNTY MEDICAL EXAMINER'S OFFICE AND MARLON OSBOURNE)		
14-FEB-2020 04:35 PM	REPLY TO NEW MATTER	PODRAZA JR, JOSEPH R	

Documents:	⚲ Click link(s) to preview/purchase the documents 2020 02 14 Reply to NM - FINAL.pdf	🛒 Click HERE to purchase all documents related to this one docket entry
Docket Entry:	REPLY TO NEW MATTER OF PHILADELPHIA COUNTY MEDICAL EXAMINER'S OFFICE AND MARLON OSBOURNE FILED. (FILED ON BEHALF OF SANDRA GREENBERG ADMINISTRATRIX ESTATE OF ELLEN R GREENBERG DECEASE AND JOSHUA M GREENBERG ADMINISTRATOR ESTATE OF ELLEN R GREENBERG DECEASED)	

28-DEC-2020 09:53 AM	MOT-FOR EXTRAORDINARY RELIEF	PODRAZA JR, JOSEPH R	
Documents:	⚲ Click link(s) to preview/purchase the documents 2020 12 28 Mot for Extraordinary Relief.pdf Motion CoverSheet Form	🛒 Click HERE to purchase all documents related to this one docket entry	
Docket Entry:	26-20122626 MOTION SUBMITTED JOINTLY (FILED ON BEHALF OF SANDRA GREENBERG ADMINISTRATRIX ESTATE OF ELLEN R GREENBERG DECEASE AND JOSHUA M GREENBERG ADMINISTRATOR ESTATE OF ELLEN R GREENBERG DECEASED)		

28-DEC-2020 10:01 AM	MOTION ASSIGNED		
Docket Entry:	26-20122626 MOT-FOR EXTRAORDINARY RELIEF ASSIGNED TO JUDGE: SHREEVES-JOHNS, KAREN . ON DATE: DECEMBER 28, 2020		

19-JAN-2021 01:59 PM	ORDER ENTERED/236 NOTICE GIVEN	SHREEVES-JOHNS, K	
Documents:	⚲ Click link(s) to preview/purchase the documents ORDER_27.pdf	🛒 Click HERE to purchase all documents related to this one docket entry	
Docket Entry:	26-20122626 IT IS ORDERED THAT ALL DEADLINES ARE EXTENDED 60 DAYS. BY THE COURT ...SHREEVES-JOHNS,J 1/19/21		

19-JAN-2021 01:59 PM	NOTICE GIVEN UNDER RULE 236		
Docket Entry:	NOTICE GIVEN ON 20-JAN-2021 OF ORDER ENTERED/236 NOTICE GIVEN ENTERED ON 19-JAN-2021.		

19-JAN-2021 02:00 PM	CASE RESCHEDULED BY COURT		
Docket Entry:	*none.*		

19-JAN-2021 02:00 PM	CASE RESCHEDULED BY COURT		

Docket Entry:	*none.*		
19-JAN-2021 02:00 PM	LISTED FOR PRE-TRIAL CONF		
Docket Entry:	*none.*		
19-JAN-2021 02:01 PM	LISTED IN TRIAL READY POOL		
Docket Entry:	*none.*		
19-JAN-2021 02:19 PM	REVISED CASE MGMT ORDER ISSUED		
Documents:	⚖ Click link(s) to preview/purchase the documents RVCMO_32.pdf	🛒 Click HERE to purchase all documents related to this one docket entry	
Docket Entry:	REVISED CASE MANAGEMENT ORDER - Be advised that the Case Management Order issued for the above-captioned action has been revised as follows: 1. All discovery shall be completed not later than 01-MAR-2021. 2. Plaintiff shall submit expert reports not later than 01-MAR-2021. 3. Defendant shall submit expert reports not later than 05-APR-2021. 4. All pre-trial motions other than motions in limine shall be filed not later than 05-APR-2021. 5. A settlement conference will be scheduled any time after 07-JUN-2021. 6. It is expected that this case shall be ready for trial by 06-JUL-2021. All other terms and conditions on the original Case Management Order will remain in full force and effect. ...BY THE COURT: KAREN SHREEVES-JOHNS, J., 19-JAN-2021		
19-JAN-2021 02:19 PM	NOTICE GIVEN UNDER RULE 236		
Docket Entry:	NOTICE GIVEN ON 20-JAN-2021 OF REVISED CASE MGMT ORDER ISSUED ENTERED ON 19-JAN-2021.		
26-FEB-2021 03:08 PM	MOT-FOR EXTRAORDINARY RELIEF	BERKOWITZ, ELLEN	
Documents:	⚖ Click link(s) to preview/purchase the documents Greenberg Joint Motion For Extraordinary Relief Feb 26 2021.pdf Motion CoverSheet Form	🛒 Click HERE to purchase all documents related to this one docket entry	
Docket Entry:	78-21022778 MOTION SUBMITTED JOINTLY (FILED ON BEHALF OF PHILADELPHIA COUNTY MEDICAL EXAMINER'S OFFICE AND MARLON OSBOURNE)		

26-FEB-2021 03:08 PM	CITY CHARGE SUBSEQUENT FILINGS	BERKOWITZ, ELLEN	
Docket Entry:	*none.*		

01-MAR-2021 09:22 AM	MOTION ASSIGNED		
Docket Entry:	78-21022778 MOT-FOR EXTRAORDINARY RELIEF ASSIGNED TO JUDGE: SHREEVES-JOHNS, KAREN . ON DATE: MARCH 01, 2021		

19-MAR-2021 10:23 AM	ORDER ENTERED/236 NOTICE GIVEN	SHREEVES-JOHNS, K	
Documents:	⚲ Click link(s) to preview/purchase the documents ORDER_38.pdf	🛒 **Click HERE to purchase all documents** related to this one docket entry	
Docket Entry:	78-21022778 IT IS HEREBY ORDERED THAT DEFENDANT'S MOTION FOR EXTRAORDINARY RELIEF IS GRANTED. ALL CASE MANAGEMENT ORDER DEADLINES ARE EXTENDED BY SIXTY (60) DAYS. ...BY THE COURT: SHREEVES-JOHNS, J. 3/18/2021		

19-MAR-2021 10:23 AM	NOTICE GIVEN UNDER RULE 236		
Docket Entry:	NOTICE GIVEN ON 19-MAR-2021 OF ORDER ENTERED/236 NOTICE GIVEN ENTERED ON 19-MAR-2021.		

19-MAR-2021 11:13 AM	REVISED CASE MGMT ORDER ISSUED		
Documents:	⚲ Click link(s) to preview/purchase the documents RVCMO_39.pdf	🛒 **Click HERE to purchase all documents** related to this one docket entry	
Docket Entry:	REVISED CASE MANAGEMENT ORDER - Be advised that the Case Management Order issued for the above-captioned action has been revised as follows: 1. All discovery shall be completed not later than 03-MAY-2021. 2. Plaintiff shall submit expert reports not later than 03-MAY-2021. 3. Defendant shall submit expert reports not later than 07-JUN-2021. 4. All pre-trial motions other than motions in limine shall be filed not later than 07-JUN-2021. 5. A settlement conference will be scheduled any time after 02-AUG-2021. 6. It is expected that this case shall be ready for trial by 06-SEP-2021. All other terms and conditions on the original Case Management Order will remain in full force and effect. ...BY THE COURT: KAREN SHREEVES-JOHNS, J., 19-MAR-2021		

19-MAR-2021 11:13 AM	NOTICE GIVEN UNDER RULE 236		
Docket Entry:	NOTICE GIVEN ON 19-MAR-2021 OF REVISED CASE MGMT ORDER ISSUED ENTERED ON 19-MAR-2021.		

162

19-MAR-2021 11:14 AM	WAITING TO LIST PRE-TRIAL CONF		
Docket Entry:	*none.*		

19-MAR-2021 11:14 AM	WAITING TO LIST FOR TRIAL		
Docket Entry:	*none.*		

19-MAR-2021 11:14 AM	LISTED FOR PRE-TRIAL CONF		
Docket Entry:	*none.*		

19-MAR-2021 11:15 AM	LISTED IN TRIAL READY POOL		
Docket Entry:	*none.*		

28-APR-2021 04:32 PM	MOT-FOR EXTRAORDINARY RELIEF	PODRAZA JR, JOSEPH R	
Documents:	Click link(s) to preview/purchase the documents 2021 04 28 Mot for Extraordinary Relie.pdf proposed revised order.pdf Motion CoverSheet Form	Click HERE to purchase all documents related to this one docket entry	
Docket Entry:	05-21044805 MOTION SUBMITTED JOINTLY (FILED ON BEHALF OF SANDRA GREENBERG ADMINISTRATRIX ESTATE OF ELLEN R GREENBERG DECEASE AND JOSHUA M GREENBERG ADMINISTRATOR ESTATE OF ELLEN R GREENBERG DECEASED)		

29-APR-2021 08:58 AM	MOTION ASSIGNED		
Docket Entry:	05-21044805 MOT-FOR EXTRAORDINARY RELIEF ASSIGNED TO JUDGE: SHREEVES-JOHNS, KAREN . ON DATE: APRIL 29, 2021		

25-MAY-2021 05:05 PM	MOTION ASSIGNMENT UPDATED		
Docket Entry:	05-21044805 REASSIGNED TO JUDGE ANDERS, DANIEL J ON 25-MAY-21		

27-MAY-2021 01:13 PM	MOTION ASSIGNMENT UPDATED		
Docket Entry:	05-21044805 REASSIGNED TO JUDGE SHREEVES-JOHNS, KAREN ON 28-MAY-21		

04-JUN-2021 09:48 AM	ORDER ENTERED/236 NOTICE GIVEN	SHREEVES-JOHNS, K	
Documents:	⚖ Click link(s) to preview/purchase the documents ORDER_50.pdf	🛒 **Click HERE to purchase all documents related to this one docket entry**	
Docket Entry:	05-21044805 AND NOW, THIS 3RD DAY OF JUNE, 2021, UPON CONSIDERATION OF THE PARTIES' JOINT MOTION FOR EXTRAORDINARY RELIEF, IT IS HEREBY ORDERED AND DECREED THAT THE MOTION IS GRANTED. IT IS HEREBY FURTHER ORDERED THAT THE DEADLINES SET FORTH IN THE CASE MANAGMENT ORDER OF MARCH 19, 2021 ARE EXTENDED BY 30 DAYS. BY THE COURT: JUDGE KAREN SHREEVES-JOHNS		

04-JUN-2021 09:48 AM	NOTICE GIVEN UNDER RULE 236		
Docket Entry:	NOTICE GIVEN ON 07-JUN-2021 OF ORDER ENTERED/236 NOTICE GIVEN ENTERED ON 04-JUN-2021.		

04-JUN-2021 04:53 PM	DISCOVERY MOTION FILED	PODRAZA JR, JOSEPH R	
Documents:	⚖ Click link(s) to preview/purchase the documents 2021 06 04 Motion to Compel Ware Video- for filing.pdf	🛒 **Click HERE to purchase all documents related to this one docket entry**	
Docket Entry:	25-21061025 MOTION TO COMPEL DEFENDANTS TO PRODUCE VIDEO RECORDING. CERTIFICATION DUE DATE: 06/14/2021. RESPONSE DATE: 06/21/2021. (FILED ON BEHALF OF SANDRA GREENBERG ADMINISTRATRIX ESTATE OF ELLEN R GREENBERG DECEASE AND JOSHUA M GREENBERG ADMINISTRATOR ESTATE OF ELLEN R GREENBERG DECEASED)		

07-JUN-2021 11:43 AM	CASE RESCHEDULED BY COURT		
Docket Entry:	*none.*		

07-JUN-2021 11:43 AM	CASE RESCHEDULED BY COURT		
Docket Entry:	*none.*		

07-JUN-2021 11:46 AM	LISTED FOR PRE-TRIAL CONF		
Docket Entry:	*none.*		

07-JUN-2021 11:46 AM	LISTED IN TRIAL READY POOL		
Docket Entry:	*none.*		

07-JUN-2021 11:52 AM	REVISED CASE MGMT ORDER ISSUED		
Documents:	⚲ Click link(s) to preview/purchase the documents RVCMO_57.pdf	🛒 **Click HERE to purchase all documents related to this one docket entry**	
Docket Entry:	REVISED CASE MANAGEMENT ORDER - Be advised that the Case Management Order issued for the above-captioned action has been revised as follows: 1. All discovery shall be completed not later than 07-JUN-2021. 2. Plaintiff shall submit expert reports not later than 07-JUN-2021. 3. Defendant shall submit expert reports not later than 05-JUL-2021. 4. All pre-trial motions other than motions in limine shall be filed not later than 05-JUL-2021. 5. A settlement conference will be scheduled any time after 07-SEP-2021. 6. It is expected that this case shall be ready for trial by 04-OCT-2021. All other terms and conditions on the original Case Management Order will remain in full force and effect. ...BY THE COURT: KAREN SHREEVES-JOHNS, J., 07-JUN-2021		

07-JUN-2021 11:52 AM	NOTICE GIVEN UNDER RULE 236		
Docket Entry:	NOTICE GIVEN ON 09-JUN-2021 OF REVISED CASE MGMT ORDER ISSUED ENTERED ON 07-JUN-2021.		

07-JUN-2021 03:58 PM	DISCOVERY MOTION FILED	PODRAZA JR, JOSEPH R	
Documents:	⚲ Click link(s) to preview/purchase the documents 2021 06 07 Final MTC Osborne Records FOR FILING.pdf	🛒 **Click HERE to purchase all documents related to this one docket entry**	
Docket Entry:	57-21061357 MOTION TO COMPEL DEFENDANTS TO PRODUCE DOCUMENTATION. CERTIFICATION DUE DATE: 06/14/2021. RESPONSE DATE: 06/21/2021. (FILED ON BEHALF OF SANDRA GREENBERG ADMINISTRATRIX ESTATE OF ELLEN R GREENBERG DECEASE AND JOSHUA M GREENBERG ADMINISTRATOR ESTATE OF ELLEN R GREENBERG DECEASED)		

11-JUN-2021 03:23 PM	CERT MOTION IS CONTESTED	TRASK, WILLIAM H	

Documents:	⚲ Click link(s) to preview/purchase the documents Praecipe for Contested Motion Osbourne Disciplinary Records.pdf	🛒 Click HERE to purchase all documents related to this one docket entry
Docket Entry:	57-21061357 MOTION IS CONTESTED. (FILED ON BEHALF OF SANDRA GREENBERG ADMINISTRATRIX ESTATE OF ELLEN R GREENBERG DECEASE AND JOSHUA M GREENBERG ADMINISTRATOR ESTATE OF ELLEN R GREENBERG DECEASED)	

11-JUN-2021 03:24 PM	CERT MOTION IS CONTESTED	TRASK, WILLIAM H	
Documents:	⚲ Click link(s) to preview/purchase the documents Praecipe for Contested Motion Ware Video.pdf	🛒 Click HERE to purchase all documents related to this one docket entry	
Docket Entry:	25-21061025 MOTION IS CONTESTED. (FILED ON BEHALF OF SANDRA GREENBERG ADMINISTRATRIX ESTATE OF ELLEN R GREENBERG DECEASE AND JOSHUA M GREENBERG ADMINISTRATOR ESTATE OF ELLEN R GREENBERG DECEASED)		

21-JUN-2021 09:53 AM	MOTION FOR SUMMARY JUDGMENT	BERKOWITZ, ELLEN	
Documents:	⚲ Click link(s) to preview/purchase the documents Exh binder 2 of 8.pdf Exh binder 1 of 8.pdf Exh binder 3 of 8.pdf Exh binder 4 of 8.pdf Exh binder 5 of 8.pdf Exh binder 6 of 8.pdf Exh binder 7 of 8.pdf Exh binder 8 of 8.pdf Greenberg Defendants MSJ.pdf Motion CoverSheet Form	🛒 Click HERE to purchase all documents related to this one docket entry	
Docket Entry:	11-21063511 RESPONSE DATE 07/21/2021. (FILED ON BEHALF OF PHILADELPHIA COUNTY MEDICAL EXAMINER'S OFFICE AND MARLON OSBOURNE)		

21-JUN-2021 09:53 AM	CITY CHARGE SUBSEQUENT FILINGS	BERKOWITZ, ELLEN	
Docket Entry:	none.		

21-JUN-2021 02:11 PM	ANSWER (MOTION/PETITION) FILED	BERKOWITZ, ELLEN	
Documents:	⚲ Click link(s) to preview/purchase the documents Greenberg Defendants Opposition to MTC Purported Ware Video.pdf Defendants Exhibits Opp MTC Purported Ware Video.pdf	🛒 Click HERE to purchase all documents related to this one docket entry	
Docket Entry:	25-21061025 ANSWER/RESPONSE IN OPPOSITION TO MOTION/PETITION. (FILED ON BEHALF OF PHILADELPHIA COUNTY		

APPENDIX E

	MEDICAL EXAMINER'S OFFICE AND MARLON OSBOURNE)		
21-JUN-2021 02:44 PM	ANSWER (MOTION/PETITION) FILED	BERKOWITZ, ELLEN	
Documents:	⚖ Click link(s) to preview/purchase the documents Def Opp to MTC Disciplinary Records as Moot.pdf Defendants Exhibits Opposition to MTC Disciplinary Records as MOOT.pdf	🛒 **Click HERE to purchase all documents** **related to this one docket entry**	
Docket Entry:	57-21061357 ANSWER/RESPONSE IN OPPOSITION TO MOTION/PETITION. (FILED ON BEHALF OF PHILADELPHIA COUNTY MEDICAL EXAMINER'S OFFICE AND MARLON OSBOURNE)		
24-JUN-2021 01:06 PM	LISTED FOR DISCOVERY HEARING		
Docket Entry:	57-21061357 DISCOVERY MOTION FILED SCHEDULED FOR A HEARING ON JULY 08, 2021 AT 09:00 AM IN REMOTE HEARING VIA ADVANCED COMMUN. TECH.		
24-JUN-2021 01:06 PM	LISTED FOR DISCOVERY HEARING		
Docket Entry:	25-21061025 DISCOVERY MOTION FILED SCHEDULED FOR A HEARING ON JULY 08, 2021 AT 09:00 AM IN REMOTE HEARING VIA ADVANCED COMMUN. TECH.		
26-JUN-2021 12:30 AM	NOTICE GIVEN-DISCOVERY HEARING		
Docket Entry:	*none.*		
26-JUN-2021 12:30 AM	NOTICE GIVEN-DISCOVERY HEARING		
Docket Entry:	*none.*		
02-JUL-2021 04:45 PM	MOTION FOR SUMMARY JUDGMENT	PODRAZA JR, JOSEPH R	
Documents:	⚖ Click link(s) to preview/purchase the documents 2021 07 02 Ps Motion for Summary Judgment.pdf Motion CoverSheet Form	🛒 **Click HERE to purchase all documents** **related to this one docket entry**	
Docket Entry:	59-21070559 RESPONSE DATE 08/02/2021. (FILED ON BEHALF OF SANDRA GREENBERG ADMINISTRATRIX ESTATE OF ELLEN R GREENBERG DECEASE AND JOSHUA M GREENBERG ADMINISTRATOR ESTATE OF ELLEN R GREENBERG DECEASED)		

06-JUL-2021 02:31 PM	MOTION/PETITION REPLY FILED	PODRAZA JR, JOSEPH R	
Documents:	✒ Click link(s) to preview/purchase the documents _2021 07 06 Reply iso MTC Osbourne Docs w. Exhs and COS.pdf	🛒 **Click HERE to purchase all documents** related to this one docket entry	
Docket Entry:	57-21061357 REPLY IN SUPPORT/OPPOSITION TO MOTION/PEITION. (FILED ON BEHALF OF SANDRA GREENBERG ADMINISTRATRIX ESTATE OF ELLEN R GREENBERG DECEASE AND JOSHUA M GREENBERG ADMINISTRATOR ESTATE OF ELLEN R GREENBERG DECEASED)		

06-JUL-2021 02:33 PM	MOTION/PETITION REPLY FILED	PODRAZA JR, JOSEPH R	
Documents:	✒ Click link(s) to preview/purchase the documents _2021 Reply iso MTC Ware Video w. Exh and COS.pdf	🛒 **Click HERE to purchase all documents** related to this one docket entry	
Docket Entry:	25-21061025 REPLY IN SUPPORT/OPPOSITION TO MOTION/PEITION. (FILED ON BEHALF OF SANDRA GREENBERG ADMINISTRATRIX ESTATE OF ELLEN R GREENBERG DECEASE AND JOSHUA M GREENBERG ADMINISTRATOR ESTATE OF ELLEN R GREENBERG DECEASED)		

07-JUL-2021 10:38 AM	MOTION/PETITION MARKED MOOT	SHREEVES-JOHNS, K	
Docket Entry:	25-21061025		

07-JUL-2021 10:39 AM	MOTION/PETITION MARKED MOOT	SHREEVES-JOHNS, K	
Docket Entry:	57-21061357		

21-JUL-2021 05:04 PM	ANSWER (MOTION/PETITION) FILED	PODRAZA JR, JOSEPH R	
Documents:	✒ Click link(s) to preview/purchase the documents 2021 07 21 Ps Response to Defs MSJ (reduced).pdf Motion CoverSheet Form	🛒 **Click HERE to purchase all documents** related to this one docket entry	
Docket Entry:	11-21063511 ANSWER IN OPPOSITION OF MOTION FOR SUMMARY JUDGMENT FILED. (FILED ON BEHALF OF SANDRA GREENBERG ADMINISTRATRIX ESTATE OF ELLEN R GREENBERG DECEASE AND JOSHUA M GREENBERG ADMINISTRATOR ESTATE OF ELLEN R GREENBERG DECEASED)		

23-JUL-2021 11:28 AM	MOTION RESPONSE DATE UPDATED		

APPENDIX E

Docket Entry:	11-21063511 MOTION FOR SUMMARY JUDGMENT MOTION RESPONSE DATE UPDATED TO 08/02/2021.

23-JUL-2021 02:03 PM	WAITING TO LIST PRE-TRIAL CONF		
Docket Entry:	*none.*		

23-JUL-2021 02:03 PM	LISTED-PROJ. PRE-TRIAL CONF		
Docket Entry:	*none.*		

27-JUL-2021 12:30 AM	NOTICE GIVEN		
Docket Entry:	OF PRE TRIAL CONFERENCE SCHEDULED FOR 24-AUG-2021.		

28-JUL-2021 04:16 PM	MOTION/PETITION REPLY FILED	BERKOWITZ, ELLEN	
Documents:	Click link(s) to preview/purchase the documents Greenberg Defendants Reply Memorandum FIN.pdf Motion CoverSheet Form	Click HERE to purchase all documents related to this one docket entry	
Docket Entry:	11-21063511 REPLY IN SUPPORT OF MOTION FOR SUMMARY JUDGMENT FILED. (FILED ON BEHALF OF PHILADELPHIA COUNTY MEDICAL EXAMINER'S OFFICE AND MARLON OSBOURNE)		

02-AUG-2021 07:58 PM	MEMORANDUM FILED	BERKOWITZ, ELLEN	
Documents:	Click link(s) to preview/purchase the documents Greenberg Defendants Opp to Plaintiffs MSJ and Memorandum of Law.pdf Motion CoverSheet Form	Click HERE to purchase all documents related to this one docket entry	
Docket Entry:	59-21070559 MEMORANDUM IN OPPOSITION OF MOTION FOR SUMMARY JUDGMENT FILED. (FILED ON BEHALF OF PHILADELPHIA COUNTY MEDICAL EXAMINER'S OFFICE AND MARLON OSBOURNE)		

04-AUG-2021 09:29 AM	MOTION ASSIGNED		
Docket Entry:	59-21070559 MOTION FOR SUMMARY JUDGMENT ASSIGNED TO JUDGE: HILL, GLYNNIS . ON DATE: AUGUST 04, 2021		

04-AUG-2021 09:29 AM	MOTION ASSIGNED		

Docket Entry:	11-21063511 MOTION FOR SUMMARY JUDGMENT ASSIGNED TO JUDGE: HILL, GLYNNIS . ON DATE: AUGUST 04, 2021		
17-AUG-2021 11:05 AM	MOTION/PETITION REPLY FILED	PODRAZA JR, JOSEPH R	
Documents:	⚲ Click link(s) to preview/purchase the documents 2021 08 17 Reply iso MSJ.pdf Motion CoverSheet Form	🛒 Click HERE to purchase all documents related to this one docket entry	
Docket Entry:	59-21070559 REPLY IN SUPPORT OF MOTION FOR SUMMARY JUDGMENT FILED. (FILED ON BEHALF OF SANDRA GREENBERG ADMINISTRATRIX ESTATE OF ELLEN R GREENBERG DECEASE AND JOSHUA M GREENBERG ADMINISTRATOR ESTATE OF ELLEN R GREENBERG DECEASED)		
27-SEP-2021 02:39 PM	LETTER SENT FROM COURT	FLETMAN, ABBE F	
Documents:	⚲ Click link(s) to preview/purchase the documents LETRS_85.pdf	🛒 Click HERE to purchase all documents related to this one docket entry	
Docket Entry:	none.		
27-SEP-2021 02:39 PM	NOTICE GIVEN UNDER RULE 236		
Docket Entry:	NOTICE GIVEN ON 27-SEP-2021 OF LETTER SENT FROM COURT ENTERED ON 27-SEP-2021.		
21-OCT-2021 10:20 AM	ORDER ENTERED/236 NOTICE GIVEN	HILL, GLYNNIS	
Documents:	⚲ Click link(s) to preview/purchase the documents ORDER_87.pdf	🛒 Click HERE to purchase all documents related to this one docket entry	
Docket Entry:	59-21070559 AND NOW, THIS 20TH DAY OF OCTOBER, 2021, UPON CONSIDERATION OF PLAINTIFFS' MOTION FOR SUMMARY JUDGMENT, THE DEFENDANTS' RESPONSE THERETO, AND THE EVIDENCE PRESENTED AT THE OCTOBER 15, 2021 HEARING, IT IS HEREBY ORDERED AND DECREED THAT SAID MOTION IS DENIED. BY THE COURT: JUDGE GLYNNIS D. HILL		
21-OCT-2021 10:20 AM	NOTICE GIVEN UNDER RULE 236		
Docket Entry:	NOTICE GIVEN ON 21-OCT-2021 OF ORDER ENTERED/236 NOTICE GIVEN ENTERED ON 21-OCT-2021.		

21-OCT-2021 10:22 AM	ORDER ENTERED/236 NOTICE GIVEN	HILL, GLYNNIS	
Documents:	✄ Click link(s) to preview/purchase the documents ORDER_88.pdf	🛒 **Click HERE to purchase all documents** **related to this one docket entry**	
Docket Entry:	11-21063511 AND NOW, THIS 20TH DAY OF OCTOBER, 2021, UPON CONSIDERATION OF DEFENDANTS' MOTION FOR SUMMARY JUDGMENT, THE PLAINTIFF'S RESPONSE THERETO, AND THE EVIDENCE PRESENTED AT THE OCTOBER 15, 2021 HEARING, IT IS HEREBY ORDERED AND DECREED THAT SAID MOTION IS DENIED. BY THE COURT: JUDGE GLYNNIS D. HILL		
21-OCT-2021 10:22 AM	NOTICE GIVEN UNDER RULE 236		
Docket Entry:	NOTICE GIVEN ON 21-OCT-2021 OF ORDER ENTERED/236 NOTICE GIVEN ENTERED ON 21-OCT-2021.		
19-NOV-2021 10:06 PM	MOT-CERTIFY ORDER INTERLOC APPL	BERKOWITZ, ELLEN	
Documents:	✄ Click link(s) to preview/purchase the documents Defendants Motion to Amend an Interlocutory Order.pdf Exh A Oct 2021 MSJ.pdf Motion CoverSheet Form	🛒 **Click HERE to purchase all documents** **related to this one docket entry**	
Docket Entry:	98-21113998 MOT-CERTIFY ORDER INTERLOC APPL (FILED ON BEHALF OF PHILADELPHIA COUNTY MEDICAL EXAMINER'S OFFICE AND MARLON OSBOURNE)		
19-NOV-2021 10:06 PM	CITY CHARGE SUBSEQUENT FILINGS	BERKOWITZ, ELLEN	
Docket Entry:	*none.*		
22-NOV-2021 10:24 AM	OTHER EVENT CANCELLED		
Docket Entry:	*none.*		
22-NOV-2021 10:24 AM	WAITING TO LIST FOR TRIAL		
Docket Entry:	*none.*		
22-NOV-2021 10:25 AM	LISTED FOR TRIAL		

29-NOV-2021 11:21 AM	NOTICE GIVEN UNDER RULE 236		
Docket Entry:	NOTICE GIVEN ON 30-NOV-2021 OF ORDER ENTERED/236 NOTICE GIVEN ENTERED ON 29-NOV-2021.		

15-DEC-2021 10:36 AM	LISTED-PROJ. PRE-TRIAL CONF		
Docket Entry:	PRE-TRIAL CONFERENCE WILL PROCEED VIRTUALLY ON DECEMBER 29, 2022 AT 1:30 P.M.		

17-DEC-2021 12:29 AM	NOTICE GIVEN		
Docket Entry:	OF PRE TRIAL CONFERENCE SCHEDULED FOR 29-DEC-2021.		

23-DEC-2021 09:45 PM	MOTION TO STAY PROCEEDINGS	BERKOWITZ, ELLEN	
Documents:	⚖ Click link(s) to preview/purchase the documents Greenberg Motion for Stay of Trial FIN.pdf Exhibit A Denial of 702 Motion to Amend Interlocutory Order Nov 29 2021.pdf EXHIBIT B 2021.12.23 Greenberg, Pet Interlocutory Appeal FINAL.pdf Motion CoverSheet Form	🛒 **Click HERE to purchase all documents related to this one docket entry**	
Docket Entry:	73-21124673 (FILED ON BEHALF OF PHILADELPHIA COUNTY MEDICAL EXAMINER'S OFFICE AND MARLON OSBOURNE)		

23-DEC-2021 09:45 PM	CITY CHARGE SUBSEQUENT FILINGS	BERKOWITZ, ELLEN	
Docket Entry:	*none.*		

27-DEC-2021 09:42 AM	MOTION ASSIGNED		
Docket Entry:	73-21124673 MOTION TO STAY PROCEEDINGS ASSIGNED TO JUDGE: JUDGE, EMERGENCY . ON DATE: DECEMBER 27, 2021		

27-DEC-2021 10:12 AM	ORDER ENTERED/236 NOTICE GIVEN		
Documents:	⚖ Click link(s) to preview/purchase the documents ORDER_108.pdf	🛒 **Click HERE to purchase all documents related to this one docket entry**	
Docket Entry:	73-21124673 UPON CONSIDERATION OF DEFENDANTS? EMERGENCY PETITION FOR STAY OF PROCEEDINGS FILED UNDER CONTROL NUMBER 21124673, IT IS HEREBY ORDERED AND DECREED THAT THE		

	MOTION SHALL PROCEED THROUGH THE NORMAL COURT PROCESS. ...BY THE COURT: PATRICK, J. 12/27/2021		
27-DEC-2021 10:12 AM	NOTICE GIVEN UNDER RULE 236		
Docket Entry:	NOTICE GIVEN ON 27-DEC-2021 OF ORDER ENTERED/236 NOTICE GIVEN ENTERED ON 27-DEC-2021.		
27-DEC-2021 10:12 AM	MOTION ASSIGNED		
Docket Entry:	73-21124673 MOTION TO STAY PROCEEDINGS ASSIGNED TO JUDGE: FLETMAN, ABBE F. ON DATE: DECEMBER 27, 2021		
27-DEC-2021 11:23 AM	MOTION RESPONSE DATE UPDATED		
Docket Entry:	73-21124673 MOTION TO STAY PROCEEDINGS MOTION RESPONSE DATE UPDATED TO 01/12/2022.		
29-DEC-2021 02:38 PM	CASE RESCHEDULED BY COURT	CHARAMELLA, REBECCA	
Docket Entry:	SCHEDULED FOR A FOLLOW UP CONFERENCE.		
29-DEC-2021 02:39 PM	LISTED-PROJ. PRE-TRIAL CONF		
Docket Entry:	none.		
31-DEC-2021 12:30 AM	NOTICE GIVEN		
Docket Entry:	OF PRE TRIAL CONFERENCE SCHEDULED FOR 13-JAN-2022.		
11-JAN-2022 09:20 AM	ANSWER (MOTION/PETITION) FILED	PODRAZA JR, JOSEPH R	
Documents:	⚸ Click link(s) to preview/purchase the documents 🛒 **Click HERE to purchase all documents** **related to this one docket entry** Opposition to Motion to Stay in Greenberg - FOR FILING.pdf Motion CoverSheet Form		
Docket Entry:	73-21124673 ANSWER IN OPPOSITION OF MOTION TO STAY PROCEEDINGS FILED. (FILED ON BEHALF OF SANDRA GREENBERG ADMINISTRATRIX ESTATE OF ELLEN R GREENBERG DECEASE AND JOSHUA M GREENBERG ADMINISTRATOR ESTATE OF ELLEN R GREENBERG DECEASED)		

14-JAN-2022 09:24 AM	LISTED-PROJ. PRE-TRIAL CONF		
Docket Entry:	*none.*		

14-JAN-2022 01:25 PM	MOTION ASSIGNED		
Docket Entry:	73-21124673 MOTION TO STAY PROCEEDINGS ASSIGNED TO JUDGE: FLETMAN, ABBE F. ON DATE: JANUARY 14, 2022		

18-JAN-2022 12:28 AM	NOTICE GIVEN		
Docket Entry:	OF PRE TRIAL CONFERENCE SCHEDULED FOR 24-JAN-2022.		

28-JAN-2022 11:20 AM	MOTION ASSIGNMENT UPDATED		
Docket Entry:	73-21124673 REASSIGNED TO JUDGE HILL, GLYNNIS ON 27-JAN-22		

31-JAN-2022 11:54 AM	ORDER ENTERED/236 NOTICE GIVEN	HILL, GLYNNIS	
Documents:	⚖ Click link(s) to preview/purchase the documents ORDER_120.pdf	🛒 **Click HERE to purchase all documents related to this one docket entry**	
Docket Entry:	73-21124673 IT IS ORDERED THAT DEFTS' MOTION TO STAY IS DENIED. BY THE COURT ...HILL,J 1/28/22		

31-JAN-2022 11:54 AM	NOTICE GIVEN UNDER RULE 236		
Docket Entry:	NOTICE GIVEN ON 01-FEB-2022 OF ORDER ENTERED/236 NOTICE GIVEN ENTERED ON 31-JAN-2022.		

09-FEB-2022 02:46 PM	ORDER OF THE APPELLATE COURT		
Documents:	⚖ Click link(s) to preview/purchase the documents APGEN_122.pdf	🛒 **Click HERE to purchase all documents related to this one docket entry**	
Docket Entry:	IN RE: 1461 CD 2021 ORDER ENTERED - UPON CONSIDERATION OF THE PETITION FOR PERMISSION TO APPEAL FILED BY MARLON OSBOURNE, M.D. AND THE CITY OF PHILADELPHIA OFFICE OF THE MEDICAL EXAMINER, WHICH WAS FILED AS THE COURT OF COMMON PLEAS OF PHILADELPHIA COUNTY DENIED APPELLANTS' MOTION TO		

174

APPENDIX E

	CERTIFY ITS ORDER AND THE ANSWER IN OPPOSITION THERETO BY JOSHUA M. GREENBERG AND SANDRA GREENBERG, ADMINISTRATORS OF THE ESTATE OF MS. ELLEN R. GREENBERG, THE PETITION IS GRANTED. APPEAL IS PERMITTED FROM THE OCTOBER 21, 2021 ORDER OF THE TRIAL COURT AT DOCKET NO. 191001241. 02/04/22		
19-MAY-2022 01:41 PM	APPEAL INVENTORY RECORD SENT		
Documents:	Click link(s) to preview/purchase the documents APILM_123.pdf	Click HERE to purchase all documents related to this one docket entry	
Docket Entry:	PURSUANT TO PA. R.A.P. 1931 (d) APPEAL INVENTORY SENT.		
19-MAY-2022 01:41 PM	RECORD MAILED/TRANSMITTED		
Docket Entry:	RECORD SENT TO COMMONWEALTH COURT ELECTRONICALLY VIA PACFILE UNDER 1461 CD 2021.		
19-MAY-2022 01:41 PM	NOTICE GIVEN UNDER RULE 236		
Docket Entry:	NOTICE GIVEN ON 19-MAY-2022 OF APPEAL INVENTORY RECORD SENT ENTERED ON 19-MAY-2022.		
08-JUN-2022 04:18 PM	OPINION FILED/236 NOTICE GIVEN		
Documents:	Click link(s) to preview/purchase the documents OPFLD_126.pdf	Click HERE to purchase all documents related to this one docket entry	
Docket Entry:	1461 CD 2021 OPINION FILED ON 6/8/22 BY J. HILL		
08-JUN-2022 04:18 PM	NOTICE GIVEN UNDER RULE 236		
Docket Entry:	NOTICE GIVEN ON 09-JUN-2022 OF OPINION FILED/236 NOTICE GIVEN ENTERED ON 08-JUN-2022.		
17-JUN-2022 10:36 AM	OTHER EVENT CANCELLED		
Docket Entry:	*none.*		

175

17-JUN-2022 10:36 AM	OTHER EVENT CANCELLED		
Docket Entry:	*none.*		

27-JUL-2022 03:02 PM	LETTER SENT FROM COURT	FLETMAN, ABBE F	
Documents:	✂ Click link(s) to preview/purchase the documents LETRS_130.pdf	🛒 **Click HERE to purchase all documents** related to this one docket entry	
Docket Entry:	*none.*		

27-JUL-2022 03:02 PM	NOTICE GIVEN UNDER RULE 236		
Docket Entry:	NOTICE GIVEN ON 28-JUL-2022 OF LETTER SENT FROM COURT ENTERED ON 27-JUL-2022.		

28-JUL-2022 01:25 PM	ENTRY OF APPEARANCE	KIRBY, AMY MARIE	
Documents:	✂ Click link(s) to preview/purchase the documents EOA-Kirby.pdf	🛒 **Click HERE to purchase all documents** related to this one docket entry	
Docket Entry:	ENTRY OF APPEARANCE OF AMY MARIE KIRBY FILED. (FILED ON BEHALF OF PHILADELPHIA COUNTY MEDICAL EXAMINER'S OFFICE AND MARLON OSBOURNE)		

29-JUL-2022 12:00 PM	DEFERRED - ON APPEAL		
Docket Entry:	*none.*		

19-SEP-2023 04:19 PM	ORDER REVERSED BY APPELLATE CT		
Documents:	✂ Click link(s) to preview/purchase the documents APORR_134.pdf	🛒 **Click HERE to purchase all documents** related to this one docket entry	
Docket Entry:	IN RE: 1461 CD 2021 - THE OCTOBER 21, 2021 ORDER OF THE COURT OF COMMON PLEAS OF PHILADELPHIA COUNTY (TRIAL COURT) IN THE BAOVE-CAPTIONED MATTER IS HEREBY REVERSED. THE CASE IS REMANDED TO THE TRIAL COURT FOR THE ENTRY OF JUDGMENT IN FAVOR OF MARLON OSBOURNE, M.D., AND THE CITY OF PHILADELPHIA OFFICE OF THE MEDICAL EXAMINER. JURISDICTION RELINQUISHED. SEE ORDER FOR FULL TERMS. 9/13/23		

19-OCT-2023 09:34 AM	NOTICE GIVEN		
Documents:	Click link(s) to preview/purchase the documents CLNGV_135.pdf	Click HERE to purchase all documents related to this one docket entry	
Docket Entry:	IN RE: 332 EAL 2023 AND 1461 CD 2021 PETITION FOR ALLOWANCE OF APPEAL TO SUPREME COURT FILED 10/13/23		

01-AUG-2024 04:16 PM	ORDER OF THE APPELLATE COURT		
Documents:	Click link(s) to preview/purchase the documents APGEN_136.pdf	Click HERE to purchase all documents related to this one docket entry	
Docket Entry:	IN RE: 332 EAL 2023, 1461 CD 2021 AND 55 EAP 2024 THE PETITION FOR ALLOWANCE OF APPEAL IS GRANTED. 07/30/24		

APPENDIX F

The Philadelphia Courts
Civil Docket Access

No Items in Cart   LOGIN
Civil Docket Report
A $5 Convenience fee will be added to the transaction at checkout.

Case Description

Case ID:	221002308
Case Caption:	GREENBERG ETAL VS GULINO ETAL
Filing Date:	Wednesday, October 26th, 2022
Court:	MAJOR JURY-COMPLEX
Location:	CITY HALL
Jury:	JURY
Case Type:	FRAUD
Status:	LISTED FOR STATUS CONFERENCE

Related Cases

No related cases were found.

Case Event Schedule

Event	Date/Time	Room	Location	Judge
MOTION HEARING	11-DEC-2024 10:00 AM	CITY HALL	COURTROOM 646	ERDOS, MICHAEL
STATUS CONFERENCE	21-JAN-2025 12:00 PM	VIA ADVANCED COMMUN. TECH.	REMOTE HEARING	CARPENTER, LINDA
JURY SELECTION	30-JAN-2025 09:00 AM	CITY HALL	COURTROOM 653	ANDERS, DANIEL J
TRIAL DATE CERTAIN	03-FEB-2025 09:00 AM	CITY HALL	COURTROOM 653	ANDERS, DANIEL J

Case motions

Motion	Assign/Date	Control No	Date/Received	Judge
MOTION FOR SUMMARY JUDGMENT	20-AUG-2024	24070549	02-JUL-2024	ERDOS, MICHAEL
MOTION FOR SUMMARY JUDGMENT	20-AUG-2024	24070593	02-JUL-2024	ERDOS, MICHAEL
MOTION FOR SUMMARY JUDGMENT	20-AUG-2024	24070627	02-JUL-2024	ERDOS, MICHAEL

APPENDIX F

Case Parties

Seq #		Assoc	Expn Date	Type	Name
1				ATTORNEY FOR PLAINTIFF	PODRAZA JR, JOSEPH R
Address:	1601 MARKET STREET SUITE 2560 PHILADELPHIA PA 19103 (215)609-3170 jpodraza@lambmcerlane.com		**Aliases:** *none*		
2		1		PLAINTIFF	GREENBERG DMD, JOSHUA M
Address:	4076 GREYSTONE DRIVE HARRISBURG PA 17112		**Aliases:** *none*		
3		1		PLAINTIFF	GREENBERG, SANDRA
Address:	4076 GREYSTONE DRIVE HARRISBURG PA 17112		**Aliases:** *none*		
4		1		PLAINTIFF	JOSHUA AND SANDRA GREENBERG ADMIN OF THE ESTATE OF ELLEN GR
Address:	4076 GREYSTONE DRIVE HARRISBURG PA 17112		**Aliases:** *none*		
5		27		DEFENDANT	GULINO MD, SAMUEL P
Address:	2200 ARCH STREET UNIT 901 PHILADELPHIA PA 19103		**Aliases:** *none*		
6		23		DEFENDANT	OSBOURNE MD, MARLON
Address:	3126 GUN CLUB ROAD WEST PALM BEACH FL 33406		**Aliases:** *none*		

7	20		DEFENDANT	EMERY MD, LYNDSEY
Address:	234 EAST SECOND AVENUE COLUMBUS OH 43201	**Aliases:**	*none*	

8	27		DEFENDANT	COONEY, TIM
Address:	750 RACE STREET PHILADELPHIA PA 19106	**Aliases:**	*none*	

9	27		DEFENDANT	MCNAMEE, JOHN
Address:	750 RACE STREET PHILADELPHIA PA 19106	**Aliases:**	*none*	

10	12		DEFENDANT	PONTERIO ESQ, ANN
Address:	8412 SHAWNEE STREET PHILADELPHIA PA 19118	**Aliases:**	*none*	

11			TEAM LEADER	CARPENTER, LINDA
Address:	294 CITY HALL PHILADELPHIA PA 19107	**Aliases:**	*none*	

12			ATTORNEY FOR DEFENDANT	DESIDERATO, JERRY R
Address:	DILWORTH PAXSON LLP 1650 MARKET STREET SUITE 1200 PHILADELPHIA PA 19102 (215)575-7290 jdesiderato@dilworthlaw.com	**Aliases:**	*none*	

13		17-MAR-2023	ATTORNEY FOR DEFENDANT	KIRBY, AMY MARIE
Address:	1515 ARCH ST PHILADELPHIA PA 19102 (215)683-3566 Amy.Kirby@phila.gov	**Aliases:**	*none*	

14		12		ATTORNEY FOR DEFENDANT	WECK JR, DOUGLAS M
Address:	DILWORTH PAXSON LLP 1500 MARKET STREET SUITE 3500E PHILADELPHIA PA 19102 (856)317-3665 dweck@dilworthlaw.com		**Aliases:**	*none*	

15		20-AUG-2024	MOTION ASSIGMENT JUDGE	CUNNINGHAM III, CHARLES J
Address:	1411 STOUT CENTER FOR CJ 1301 FILBERT ST PHILADELPHIA PA 19103 (215)683-7130	**Aliases:**	*none*	

16		12-JAN-2024	ATTORNEY FOR DEFENDANT	THOMSON, AIMEE D
Address:	333 MARKET ST. 17TH FLOOR HARRISBURG PA 17101 (223)234-4986 aimeethomson@pa.gov	**Aliases:**	*none*	

17			JUDGE	CARPENTER, LINDA
Address:	294 CITY HALL PHILADELPHIA PA 19107	**Aliases:**	*none*	

18		18-NOV-2024	ATTORNEY FOR DEFENDANT	SHUEY ESQ, WILLIAM B
Address:	ONE PARKWAY BUILDING 1515 ARCH STREET, 15TH FLOOR PHILADELPHIA PA 19102 (267)357-3168 william.shuey@phila.gov	**Aliases:**	*none*	

19		13-MAY-2024	ATTORNEY FOR DEFENDANT	MEDINA, MELISSA

Address:	1515 ARCH ST. 15TH FL. PHILADELPHIA PA 19102 (215)683-2970 melissa.medina@phila.gov	Aliases:	*none*	

20				ATTORNEY FOR DEFENDANT	SORATHIA, ALEENA Y
Address:	AHMAD ZAFFARESE LLC 1 SOUTH BROAD STREET SUITE 1910 PHILADELPHIA PA 19107 (215)496-9373 asorathia@azlawllc.com	Aliases:	*none*		

21		20		ATTORNEY FOR DEFENDANT	ZAFFARESE, JOSEPH
Address:	AHMAD ZAFFARESE LLC ONE SOUTH BROAD STREET SUITE 1910 PHILADELPHIA PA 19107 (267)242-8917 jzaffarese@azlawllc.com	Aliases:	*none*		

22		20		ATTORNEY FOR DEFENDANT	MAYS, KATELYN L
Address:	ONE SOUTH BROAD STREET SUITE 1910 PHILADELPHIA PA 19107 (215)496-9373 kmays@azlawllc.com	Aliases:	*none*		

23				ATTORNEY FOR DEFENDANT	BAILKIN, MARC B
Address:	BENNETT, BRICKLIN & SALTZBURG CENTRE SQUARE WEST TOWER 1500 MARKET STREET, 32ND FLOOR PHILADELPHIA PA 19102 (215)665-3403 bailkin@bbs-law.com	Aliases:	*none*		

APPENDIX F

24			18-NOV-2024	ATTORNEY FOR DEFENDANT	AXE, BAILEY E
Address:	CITY OF PHILADELPHIA LAW DEPARTMENT 1515 ARCH STREET, 15TH FLOOR PHILADELPHIA PA 19102 (215)683-5024 bailey.axe@phila.gov		**Aliases:**	*none*	

25		23		ATTORNEY FOR DEFENDANT	BRAINARD, ALESSANDRA
Address:	1500 MARKET STREET 32ND FL PHILADELPHIA PA 19120 (215)665-3406 ALESSANDRA.BRAINARD@BBS-LAW.COM		**Aliases:**	*none*	

26				MOTION ASSIGMENT JUDGE	ERDOS, MICHAEL
Address:	532A CITY HALL PHILADELPHIA PA 19148		**Aliases:**	*none*	

27				ATTORNEY FOR DEFENDANT	ESCOBAR, RAYMOND EDWARD
Address:	1515 ARCH STREET PHILADELPHIA PA 19102 (215)683-5000 raymond.escobar@phila.gov		**Aliases:**	*none*	

28		27		ATTORNEY FOR DEFENDANT	PESTRAK, MICHAEL
Address:	1515 ARCH ST. PHILADELPHIA PA 19102 (215)683-5387 michael.pestrak@phila.gov		**Aliases:**	*none*	

29		27		ATTORNEY FOR DEFENDANT	SHUEY ESQ, WILLIAM B
Address:	ONE PARKWAY BUILDING 1515 ARCH STREET, 15TH FLOOR PHILADELPHIA PA 19102 (267)357-3168 william.shuey@phila.gov		**Aliases:**	*none*	

Docket Entries

Filing Date/Time	Docket Type	Filing Party	Disposition Amount
26-OCT-2022 01:26 PM	ACTIVE CASE		
Docket Entry:	E-Filing Number: 2210051656		
26-OCT-2022 01:26 PM	COMMENCEMENT CIVIL ACTION JURY	PODRAZA JR, JOSEPH R	
Documents:	Click link(s) to preview/purchase the documents Final Cover	Click HERE to purchase all documents related to this one docket entry	
Docket Entry:	*none.*		
26-OCT-2022 01:26 PM	COMPLAINT FILED NOTICE GIVEN	PODRAZA JR, JOSEPH R	
Documents:	Click link(s) to preview/purchase the documents 2022 10 26 Greenberg II Complaint FINAL.pdf	Click HERE to purchase all documents related to this one docket entry	
Docket Entry:	COMPLAINT WITH NOTICE TO DEFEND WITHIN TWENTY (20) DAYS AFTER SERVICE IN ACCORDANCE WITH RULE 1018.1 FILED.		
26-OCT-2022 01:26 PM	JURY TRIAL PERFECTED	PODRAZA JR, JOSEPH R	
Docket Entry:	8 JURORS REQUESTED.		
26-OCT-2022 01:26 PM	WAITING TO LIST CASE MGMT CONF	PODRAZA JR, JOSEPH R	

Docket Entry:	*none.*

28-OCT-2022 02:58 PM	AFFIDAVIT OF SERVICE FILED		
Documents:	🔏 Click link(s) to preview/purchase the documents Affidavit of Service	🛒 **Click HERE to purchase all documents related to this one docket entry**	
Docket Entry:	AFFIDAVIT OF SERVICE OF PLAINTIFF'S COMPLAINT UPON SAMUEL P GULINO BY PERSONAL SERVICE ON 10/28/2022 FILED.		

07-NOV-2022 01:19 PM	AFFIDAVIT OF SERVICE FILED		
Documents:	🔏 Click link(s) to preview/purchase the documents Affidavit of Service	🛒 **Click HERE to purchase all documents related to this one docket entry**	
Docket Entry:	AFFIDAVIT OF SERVICE OF PLAINTIFF'S COMPLAINT UPON ANN PONTERIO BY PERSONAL SERVICE ON 11/05/2022 FILED.		

08-NOV-2022 01:53 PM	AFFIDAVIT OF SERVICE FILED		
Documents:	🔏 Click link(s) to preview/purchase the documents Affidavit of Service	🛒 **Click HERE to purchase all documents related to this one docket entry**	
Docket Entry:	AFFIDAVIT OF SERVICE OF PLAINTIFF'S COMPLAINT UPON JOHN MCNAMEE BY PERSONAL SERVICE ON 11/08/2022 FILED.		

08-NOV-2022 02:01 PM	ATTEMPTED SERVICE - NOT FOUND		
Documents:	🔏 Click link(s) to preview/purchase the documents Affidavit of Service	🛒 **Click HERE to purchase all documents related to this one docket entry**	
Docket Entry:	TIM COONEY NOT FOUND ON 11/08/2022.		

08-NOV-2022 02:03 PM	AFFIDAVIT OF SERVICE FILED		
Documents:	🔏 Click link(s) to preview/purchase the documents Affidavit of Service	🛒 **Click HERE to purchase all documents related to this one docket entry**	
Docket Entry:	AFFIDAVIT OF SERVICE OF PLAINTIFF'S COMPLAINT UPON JOHN MCNAMEE BY PERSONAL SERVICE ON 11/08/2022 FILED.		

14-NOV-2022 09:12 AM	ENTRY OF APPEARANCE	DESIDERATO, JERRY R	
Documents:	⚖ Click link(s) to preview/purchase the documents entry of appearance JRD.pdf	🛒 **Click HERE to purchase all documents related to this one docket entry**	
Docket Entry:	ENTRY OF APPEARANCE OF JERRY R DESIDERATO FILED. (FILED ON BEHALF OF ANN PONTERIO)		

15-NOV-2022 08:24 AM	STIPULATION FILED	DESIDERATO, JERRY R	
Documents:	⚖ Click link(s) to preview/purchase the documents Stipulation Extending Time to Respond to Complaint - Ponterio.pdf	🛒 **Click HERE to purchase all documents related to this one docket entry**	
Docket Entry:	STIPULATION TO STIPULATION EXTENDING TIME TO RESPOND TO COMPLAINT FILED. (FILED ON BEHALF OF ANN PONTERIO) ENTRY OF APPEARANCE FILED ON BEHALF OF ANN PONTERIO.		

29-NOV-2022 11:03 AM	ENTRY OF APPEARANCE	KIRBY, AMY MARIE	
Documents:	⚖ Click link(s) to preview/purchase the documents EOA_Amy(Greenberg) 2308.pdf	🛒 **Click HERE to purchase all documents related to this one docket entry**	
Docket Entry:	ENTRY OF APPEARANCE OF AMY MARIE KIRBY FILED. (FILED ON BEHALF OF JOHN MCNAMEE, TIM COONEY, LYNDSEY EMERY, MARLON OSBOURNE AND SAMUEL P GULINO)		

29-NOV-2022 11:03 AM	CITY CHARGE SUBSEQUENT FILINGS	KIRBY, AMY MARIE	
Docket Entry:	*none.*		

29-NOV-2022 01:57 PM	ACCEPTANCE OF SERVICE FILED	KIRBY, AMY MARIE	
Documents:	⚖ Click link(s) to preview/purchase the documents acceptance of service - 221002308_Greenberg v. City.pdf	🛒 **Click HERE to purchase all documents related to this one docket entry**	
Docket Entry:	SERVICE OF PLAINTIFF'S COMPLAINT ACCEPTED BY TIM COONEY, SAMUEL P GULINO, MARLON OSBOURNE, LYNDSEY EMERY AND JOHN MCNAMEE ON 11/15/2022 FILED. (FILED ON BEHALF OF JOHN MCNAMEE, TIM COONEY, LYNDSEY EMERY, MARLON OSBOURNE AND SAMUEL P GULINO)		

APPENDIX F

06-DEC-2022 04:49 PM	ENTRY OF APPEARANCE-CO COUNSEL	WECK JR, DOUGLAS M	
Documents:	⚖ Click link(s) to preview/purchase the documents Weck Notice of Appearance.pdf	🛒 **Click HERE to purchase all documents related to this one docket entry**	
Docket Entry:	ENTRY OF APPEARANCE OF DOUGLAS M WECK AS CO-COUNSEL FILED. (FILED ON BEHALF OF ANN PONTERIO)		
08-DEC-2022 04:06 PM	PRELIMINARY OBJECTIONS	WECK JR, DOUGLAS M	
Documents:	⚖ Click link(s) to preview/purchase the documents Greenberg, Ponterio POs.pdf Exh A-Complaint wo Exh.pdf	🛒 **Click HERE to purchase all documents related to this one docket entry**	
Docket Entry:	58-22121858 PRELIMINARY OBJECTIONS TO PLAINTIFFS' COMPLAINT FILED. RESPONSE DATE: 12/28/2022 (FILED ON BEHALF OF ANN PONTERIO)		
08-DEC-2022 04:06 PM	JURY TRIAL PERFECTED	WECK JR, DOUGLAS M	
Docket Entry:	12 JURORS REQUESTED.		
23-DEC-2022 02:05 PM	PRAECIPE TO WITHDRAW	KIRBY, AMY MARIE	
Documents:	⚖ Click link(s) to preview/purchase the documents Praecipe to withdraw Acceptance of Service.pdf	🛒 **Click HERE to purchase all documents related to this one docket entry**	
Docket Entry:	PRAECIPE TO WITHDRAW ACCEPTANCE OF COMPLAINT-COONEY FILED. (FILED ON BEHALF OF TIM COONEY)		
23-DEC-2022 03:02 PM	LISTED FOR CASE MGMT CONF		
Docket Entry:	none.		
27-DEC-2022 12:31 AM	NOTICE GIVEN		
Docket Entry:	none.		
27-DEC-2022 09:53 AM	PRELIMINARY OBJECTIONS	KIRBY, AMY MARIE	

Documents:	☞ Click link(s) to preview/purchase the documents Greenberg v. City POs and memo.pdf	🛒 **Click HERE to purchase all documents related to this one docket entry**	
Docket Entry:	90-22124990 PRELIMINARY OBJECTIONS TO PLAINTIFFS COMPLAINT FILED. RESPONSE DATE: 01/17/2023 (FILED ON BEHALF OF JOHN MCNAMEE, LYNDSEY EMERY, MARLON OSBOURNE AND SAMUEL P GULINO)		

28-DEC-2022 02:33 PM	ANSWER TO PRELIMINARY OBJCTNS	PODRAZA JR, JOSEPH R	
Documents:	☞ Click link(s) to preview/purchase the documents 2022 12 28 Pltfs Answer to Defs Preliminary Objections (Ponterio Esq.) (002).pdf	🛒 **Click HERE to purchase all documents related to this one docket entry**	
Docket Entry:	58-22121858 ANSWER IN OPPOSITION OF PRELIMINARY OBJECTIONS FILED. (FILED ON BEHALF OF JOSHUA AND SANDRA GREENBERG ADMIN OF THE ESTATE OF ELLEN GR, SANDRA GREENBERG AND JOSHUA M GREENBERG)		

30-DEC-2022 09:28 AM	PREL OBJECT-RESP DATE UPDATED		
Docket Entry:	58-22121858 PRELIMINARY OBJECTIONS MOTION RESPONSE DATE UPDATED TO 01/17/2023.		

11-JAN-2023 01:23 PM	CASE MGMT CONFERENCE COMPLETED	SULLIVAN, JOAN	
Docket Entry:	*none.*		

11-JAN-2023 01:23 PM	CASE MANAGEMENT ORDER ISSUED		
Documents:	☞ Click link(s) to preview/purchase the documents CMOIS_26.pdf	🛒 **Click HERE to purchase all documents related to this one docket entry**	
Docket Entry:	CASE MANAGEMENT ORDER COMPLEX TRACK - AND NOW, 11-JAN-2023, it is Ordered that: 1. The case management and time standards adopted for complex track cases shall be applicable to this case and are hereby incorporated into this Order. 2. All discovery on the above matter shall be completed not later than 06-MAY-2024. 3. Plaintiff shall identify and submit curriculum vitae and expert reports of all expert witnesses intended to testify at trial to all other parties not later than 03-JUN-2024. 4. Defendant and any additional defendants shall identify and submit curriculum vitae and expert reports of all expert witnesses intended to testify at trial not later than 01-JUL-2024. 5. All pre-trial motions shall be filed not later than 01-JUL-2024. 6. A settlement conference may be scheduled at any time after 05-AUG-2024. Prior to the settlement conference all counsel shall serve all opposing counsel and file a		

settlement memorandum containing the following: (a) A concise summary of the nature of the case if plaintiff or of the defense if defendant or additional defendant; (b) A statement by the plaintiff or all damages accumulated, including an itemization of injuries and all special damages claimed by categories and amount;(c) Defendant shall identify all applicable insurance carriers, together with applicable limits of liability. 7. A pre-trial conference will be scheduled any time after 07-OCT-2024. Fifteen days prior to pre-trial conference, all counsel shall serve all opposing counsel and file a pre-trial memorandum containing the following:(a) A concise summary of the nature of the case if plaintiff or the defense if defendant or additional defendant;(b) A list of all witnesses who may be called to testify at trial by name and address. Counsel should expect witnesses not listed to be precluded from testifying at trial;(c) A list of all exhibits the party intends to offer into evidence. All exhibits shall be pre-numbered and shall be exchanged among counsel prior to the conference. Counsel should expect any exhibit not listed to be precluded at trial;(d) Plaintiff shall list an itemization of injuries or damages sustained together with all special damages claimed by category and amount. This list shall include as appropriate, computations of all past lost earnings and future lost earning capacity or medical expenses together with any other unliquidated damages claimed; and (e) Defendant shall state its position regarding damages and shall identify all applicable insurance carriers, together with applicable limits of liability;(f) Each counsel shall provide an estimate of the anticipated length of trial. 8. It is expected that the case will be ready for trial 04-NOV-2024, and counsel should anticipate trial to begin expeditiously thereafter. 9. All counsel are under a continuing obligation and are hereby ordered to serve a copy of this order upon all unrepresented parties and upon all counsel entering an appearance subsequent to the entry of this order. ...BY THE COURT: LINDA CARPENTER, J.

11-JAN-2023 01:23 PM	LISTED-PROJ. SETTLEMENT CONF.		
Docket Entry:	none.		

11-JAN-2023 01:23 PM	LISTED-PROJ. PRE-TRIAL CONF		
Docket Entry:	none.		

11-JAN-2023 01:23 PM	LISTED FOR TRIAL		
Docket Entry:	none.		

11-JAN-2023 01:23 PM	NOTICE GIVEN UNDER RULE 236		

Docket Entry:	NOTICE GIVEN ON 11-JAN-2023 OF CASE MANAGEMENT ORDER ISSUED ENTERED ON 11-JAN-2023.		

11-JAN-2023 03:10 PM	REPLY-PRELIM. OBJECT. FILED	WECK JR, DOUGLAS M	
Documents:	⚲ Click link(s) to preview/purchase the documents Greenberg, Ponterio Reply.pdf	🛒 **Click HERE to purchase all documents related to this one docket entry**	
Docket Entry:	58-22121858 REPLY IN SUPPORT OF PRELIMINARY OBJECTIONS FILED. (FILED ON BEHALF OF ANN PONTERIO)		

17-JAN-2023 03:59 PM	ANSWER TO PRELIMINARY OBJCTNS	PODRAZA JR, JOSEPH R	
Documents:	⚲ Click link(s) to preview/purchase the documents 2023-01-17 Answer to POs.pdf	🛒 **Click HERE to purchase all documents related to this one docket entry**	
Docket Entry:	90-22124990 ANSWER IN OPPOSITION OF PRELIMINARY OBJECTIONS FILED. (FILED ON BEHALF OF JOSHUA AND SANDRA GREENBERG ADMIN OF THE ESTATE OF ELLEN GR, SANDRA GREENBERG AND JOSHUA M GREENBERG)		

18-JAN-2023 09:47 AM	PRELIM OBJECTIONS ASSIGNED		
Docket Entry:	58-22121858 PRELIMINARY OBJECTIONS ASSIGNED TO JUDGE: CARPENTER, LINDA . ON DATE: JANUARY 18, 2023		

18-JAN-2023 09:47 AM	PRELIM OBJECTIONS ASSIGNED		
Docket Entry:	90-22124990 PRELIMINARY OBJECTIONS ASSIGNED TO JUDGE: CARPENTER, LINDA . ON DATE: JANUARY 18, 2023		

18-JAN-2023 12:52 PM	PREL OBJECT-ASSIGNMENT UPDATED		
Docket Entry:	58-22121858 REASSIGNED TO JUDGE CUNNINGHAM III, CHARLES J ON 18-JAN-23		

18-JAN-2023 12:55 PM	PREL OBJECT-ASSIGNMENT UPDATED		
Docket Entry:	90-22124990 REASSIGNED TO JUDGE CUNNINGHAM III, CHARLES J ON 18-JAN-23		

19-JAN-2023 04:47 PM	PRAECIPE TO REINSTATE CMPLT	PODRAZA JR, JOSEPH R	
Documents:	✎ Click link(s) to preview/purchase the documents praecipe to reissue complaint.pdf	🛒 **Click HERE to purchase all documents related to this one docket entry**	
Docket Entry:	COMPLAINT WITH NOTICE TO DEFEND WITHIN TWENTY (20) DAYS AFTER SERVICE IN ACCORDANCE WITH RULE 1018.1 REINSTATED. (FILED ON BEHALF OF JOSHUA AND SANDRA GREENBERG ADMIN OF THE ESTATE OF ELLEN GR, SANDRA GREENBERG AND JOSHUA M GREENBERG)		
03-FEB-2023 09:37 AM	ORDER ENTERED/236 NOTICE GIVEN	CUNNINGHAM III, CHARLES J	
Documents:	✎ Click link(s) to preview/purchase the documents ORDER_38.pdf	🛒 **Click HERE to purchase all documents related to this one docket entry**	
Docket Entry:	58-22121858 AND NOW, THIS 2ND DAY OF FEBRUARY, 2023, UPON CONSIDERATION OF THE PRELIMINARY OBJECTIONS OF DEFENDANT, FORMER DISTRICT ATTORNEY, ANN PONTERIO, ESQ., TO PLAINTIFF'S COMPLAINT PURSUANT TO PENNSYLVANIA RULE OF CIVIL PROCEDURE 1028 AND LOCAL CIVIL RULE NUMBER 1028(C), ANY OPPOSITION THHERETO, IT IS HEREBY ORDERED THAT: 1. THE PRELIMINARY OBJECTIONS ARE SUSTAINED; 2. PLAINTIFF'S COMPLAINT AGAINST ADA PONTERIO IS DISMISSED BECAUSE: A. ADA PONTERIO HAS ABOSLUTE HIGH-OFFICIAL IMMUNITY FROM TORT SUITS FOR ACTIONS OR OMISSIONS CLOSELY RELATED TO HER OFFICIAL DUTIES AS AN ADA; B. THE COMPLAINT'S OLY WELL-PLEADED ALLEGATIONS AGAINST ADA PONERTIO IS THAT SHE ATTENDED A MEETING IN MARCH 2011 WITH EHT PHILADELPHIA MEDICAL EXAMINER'S OFFICE AND THE PHILADELPHIA POLICE DEPARTMENT, WHICH IS INSUFFICIENT TO STATE A CLAIM FOR INTENTIONAL INFLICTION OF EMOTIONAL DISTRESS; C. ADA PONTERIO HAS IMMUNITY PURSUANT TO THE PENNSYLVANIA POLITICAL SUBDIVISION TORT CLAIMS ACT. 42 PA.C.S.A. 8541-64, AND PLAINTIFFS HAVEW NOT PLEADED ANY FACTS DEMONSTRATING A STATUTORY EXCEPTION TO THAT IMMUNITY. BY THE COURT: HON. CHARLES CUNNINGHAM, 2-2-2023.		
03-FEB-2023 09:37 AM	NOTICE GIVEN UNDER RULE 236		
Docket Entry:	NOTICE GIVEN ON 03-FEB-2023 OF ORDER ENTERED/236 NOTICE GIVEN ENTERED ON 03-FEB-2023.		
14-FEB-2023 02:31 PM	MOTION TO WITHDRAW APPEARANCE	KIRBY, AMY MARIE	

Documents:	⚘ Click link(s) to preview/purchase the documents Withdraw_Cooney_AK.pdf Motion CoverSheet Form	Click HERE to purchase all documents related to this one docket entry
Docket Entry:	25-23023025 MOTION TO WITHDRAW APPEARANCE (FILED ON BEHALF OF TIM COONEY)	

14-FEB-2023 02:31 PM	CITY CHARGE SUBSEQUENT FILINGS	KIRBY, AMY MARIE	
Docket Entry:	none.		

14-FEB-2023 04:25 PM	MOTION ASSIGNED		
Docket Entry:	25-23023025 MOTION TO WITHDRAW APPEARANCE ASSIGNED TO JUDGE: CARPENTER, LINDA . ON DATE: FEBRUARY 14, 2023		

17-FEB-2023 03:30 PM	PRAECIPE TO REINSTATE CMPLT	PODRAZA JR, JOSEPH R	
Documents:	⚘ Click link(s) to preview/purchase the documents praecipe to reissue complaint 2023-02-17.pdf	Click HERE to purchase all documents related to this one docket entry	
Docket Entry:	COMPLAINT WITH NOTICE TO DEFEND WITHIN TWENTY (20) DAYS AFTER SERVICE IN ACCORDANCE WITH RULE 1018.1 REINSTATED. (FILED ON BEHALF OF JOSHUA AND SANDRA GREENBERG ADMIN OF THE ESTATE OF ELLEN GR, SANDRA GREENBERG AND JOSHUA M GREENBERG)		

17-FEB-2023 03:45 PM	WITHDRAWAL/ENTRY OF APPEARANCE	THOMSON, AIMEE D	
Documents:	⚘ Click link(s) to preview/purchase the documents Entry_Withdraw_Greenberg.pdf	Click HERE to purchase all documents related to this one docket entry	
Docket Entry:	WITHDRAWAL OF APPEARANCE OF AMY MARIE KIRBY AND ENTRY OF APPEARANCE OF AIMEE D THOMSON FILED. (FILED ON BEHALF OF JOHN MCNAMEE, LYNDSEY EMERY, MARLON OSBOURNE AND SAMUEL P GULINO)		

02-MAR-2023 02:44 PM	ORDER ENTERED/236 NOTICE GIVEN	CARPENTER, LINDA	
Documents:	⚘ Click link(s) to preview/purchase the documents ORDER_45.pdf	Click HERE to purchase all documents related to this one docket entry	

Docket Entry	25-23023025 AND NOW, THIS 2ND DAY OF MARCH, 2023, UPON CONSIDERATION OF THE ABOVE-CAPTIONED REQUEST TO WITHDRAW AS COUNSEL, IT IS HEREBY ORDERED THAT A HEARING VIA ZOOM IS SCHEDULED FOOR MARCH 28, 2023 AT 1:00 P.M. COUNSEL/PARTIES MAY ACCESS THHE HEARING THROUGH THE COURT WEBPAGE AT WWW.COURTS.PHILA.GOV BY OPENING THE "CALENDARS" MENU ANND SELECTING "COMMON PLEAS-CIVIL REMOTE HEARING INFORMMATION". (SEE ORDER FOR TERMS) BY THE COURT: HON. LINDA CARPENTER, 3-2-2023.

02-MAR-2023 02:44 PM	NOTICE GIVEN UNDER RULE 236		
Docket Entry:	NOTICE GIVEN ON 03-MAR-2023 OF ORDER ENTERED/236 NOTICE GIVEN ENTERED ON 02-MAR-2023.		

02-MAR-2023 02:48 PM	MOTION HEARING SCHEDULED		
Docket Entry:	*none.*		

02-MAR-2023 03:59 PM	ORDER ENTERED/236 NOTICE GIVEN	CUNNINGHAM III, CHARLES J	
Documents:	Click link(s) to preview/purchase the documents ORDER_47.pdf	Click HERE to purchase all documents related to this one docket entry	
Docket Entry:	90-22124990 AND NOW, THIS 1ST DAY OF MARCH, 2023, IT IS ORDERED AND DECREED THAT SAID PRELIMINARY OBJECTIONS, ANY RESPONSE THERETO, ARE OVERRULED AND THE DEFENDANT, LINCOLN UNIVERSITY SHALL FILE AN ANSWER TO THE COMPLAINT WITHOUT FURTHER OBJECTIONS WITHIN TWENTY (20) DAYS OF THE DATE OF THIS ORDER. BY THE COURT: HON. CHARLES CUNNINGHAM, 3-1-2023.		

02-MAR-2023 03:59 PM	NOTICE GIVEN UNDER RULE 236		
Docket Entry:	NOTICE GIVEN ON 03-MAR-2023 OF ORDER ENTERED/236 NOTICE GIVEN ENTERED ON 02-MAR-2023.		

07-MAR-2023 03:44 PM	CORRECTIVE ENTRY	CARPENTER, LINDA	
Docket Entry:	PLEASE NOTE: PLEASE DISREGARD THE ORDER OF MARCH 1. 2023 UNDER CONTROL NO. 23010188 - THIS WAS ENTERED UNDER AN INCORRECT COURT TERM AND NUMBER.		

07-MAR-2023 03:52 PM	AFFIDAVIT OF SERVICE FILED	PODRAZA JR, JOSEPH R	
Documents:	✄ Click link(s) to preview/purchase the documents TIMOTHY Return of service.pdf	🛒 **Click HERE to purchase all documents related to this one docket entry**	
Docket Entry:	AFFIDAVIT OF SERVICE OF PLAINTIFF'S COMPLAINT UPON TIM COONEY BY PERSONAL SERVICE ON 03/04/2023 FILED. (FILED ON BEHALF OF JOSHUA AND SANDRA GREENBERG ADMIN OF THE ESTATE OF ELLEN GR, SANDRA GREENBERG AND JOSHUA M GREENBERG)		
17-MAR-2023 09:58 AM	WITHDRAWAL/ENTRY OF APPEARANCE	THOMSON, AIMEE D	
Documents:	✄ Click link(s) to preview/purchase the documents Entry_Withdraw_Greenberg Cooney.pdf	🛒 **Click HERE to purchase all documents related to this one docket entry**	
Docket Entry:	WITHDRAWAL OF APPEARANCE OF AMY MARIE KIRBY AND ENTRY OF APPEARANCE OF AIMEE D THOMSON FILED. (FILED ON BEHALF OF TIM COONEY)		
17-MAR-2023 10:07 AM	MOTION/PETITION/STIP WITHDRAWN	THOMSON, AIMEE D	
Documents:	✄ Click link(s) to preview/purchase the documents Greenberg Withdraw Praecipe .pdf	🛒 **Click HERE to purchase all documents related to this one docket entry**	
Docket Entry:	25-23023025 PRAECIPE TO WITHDRAW MOTION TO WITHDRAW APPEARANCE FILED. (FILED ON BEHALF OF LYNDSEY EMERY)		
22-MAR-2023 04:49 PM	JOINDER-PRELIM. OBJECT. FILED	THOMSON, AIMEE D	
Documents:	✄ Click link(s) to preview/purchase the documents Greenberg Joinder POs.pdf Joinder Proposed Order.pdf	🛒 **Click HERE to purchase all documents related to this one docket entry**	
Docket Entry:	90-22124990 JOINDER TO PRELIMINARY OBJECTIONS FILED. (FILED ON BEHALF OF TIM COONEY)		
07-SEP-2023 04:00 PM	LISTED 1-YR STAT CONF		
Docket Entry:	*none.*		
09-SEP-2023 12:31 AM	NOTICE GIVEN		

Docket Entry:	OF 1-YR STATUS CONFERENCE SCHEDULED FOR 16-OCT-2023.		
13-SEP-2023 01:22 PM	DISCOVERY MOTION FILED	PODRAZA JR, JOSEPH R	
Documents:	✍ Click link(s) to preview/purchase the documents Motion to Compel Discovery Responses.pdf	🛒 **Click HERE to purchase all documents related to this one docket entry**	
Docket Entry:	83-23092483 MOTION TO COMPEL ANSWERS AND PRODUCTION OF DOCUMENTS. CERTIFICATION DUE DATE: 09/20/2023. RESPONSE DATE: 09/27/2023. (FILED ON BEHALF OF SANDRA GREENBERG, JOSHUA AND SANDRA GREENBERG ADMIN OF THE ESTATE OF ELLEN GR AND JOSHUA M GREENBERG)		
20-SEP-2023 11:01 AM	CERT MOTION IS CONTESTED	PODRAZA JR, JOSEPH R	
Documents:	✍ Click link(s) to preview/purchase the documents Praecipe for Contested Discovery Motion.pdf	🛒 **Click HERE to purchase all documents related to this one docket entry**	
Docket Entry:	83-23092483 MOTION IS CONTESTED. (FILED ON BEHALF OF SANDRA GREENBERG, JOSHUA AND SANDRA GREENBERG ADMIN OF THE ESTATE OF ELLEN GR AND JOSHUA M GREENBERG)		
27-SEP-2023 04:43 PM	ANSWER (MOTION/PETITION) FILED	THOMSON, AIMEE D	
Documents:	✍ Click link(s) to preview/purchase the documents Greenberg MTC Opp Answer.pdf Greenberg MTC Opp MOL.pdf Greenberg MTC Opp Order.pdf	🛒 **Click HERE to purchase all documents related to this one docket entry**	
Docket Entry:	83-23092483 83-23092483 ANSWER/RESPONSE IN OPPOSITION TO MOTION/PETITION. (FILED ON BEHALF OF TIM COONEY, SAMUEL P GULINO, MARLON OSBOURNE, LYNDSEY EMERY AND JOHN MCNAMEE)		
28-SEP-2023 09:28 AM	LISTED FOR DISCOVERY HEARING		
Docket Entry:	83-23092483 DISCOVERY MOTION FILED SCHEDULED FOR A HEARING ON OCTOBER 17, 2023 AT 09:00 AM IN REMOTE HEARING VIA ADVANCED COMMUN. TECH.		
30-SEP-2023 12:30 AM	NOTICE GIVEN-DISCOVERY HEARING		
Docket Entry:	*none.*		

13-OCT-2023 09:17 AM	ENTRY OF APPEARANCE-CO COUNSEL	SHUEY ESQ, WILLIAM B	
Documents:	⚖ Click link(s) to preview/purchase the documents Greenberg - EOA Shuey.pdf	🛒 **Click HERE to purchase all documents related to this one docket entry**	
Docket Entry:	ENTRY OF APPEARANCE OF WILLIAM B SHUEY AS CO-COUNSEL FILED. (FILED ON BEHALF OF ANN PONTERIO, JOHN MCNAMEE, TIM COONEY, LYNDSEY EMERY, MARLON OSBOURNE AND SAMUEL P GULINO)		

16-OCT-2023 11:09 AM	PRAECIPE TO SUPPL/ATTACH FILED	THOMSON, AIMEE D	
Documents:	⚖ Click link(s) to preview/purchase the documents Praecipe to Supplement Greenberg II POs.pdf Supplemental Brief ISO POs Greenberg II Exhibits.pdf	🛒 **Click HERE to purchase all documents related to this one docket entry**	
Docket Entry:	90-22124990 PRAECIPE TO SUPPLEMENT/ATTACH RE: PRELIMINARY OBJECTIONS FILED. (FILED ON BEHALF OF JOHN MCNAMEE, TIM COONEY, LYNDSEY EMERY, MARLON OSBOURNE AND SAMUEL P GULINO)		

16-OCT-2023 02:33 PM	CASE RESCHEDULED BY COURT	CARPENTER, LINDA	
Docket Entry:	none.		

16-OCT-2023 02:33 PM	LISTED 1-YR STAT CONF		
Docket Entry:	none.		

17-OCT-2023 12:30 AM	NOTICE GIVEN		
Docket Entry:	OF 1-YR STATUS CONFERENCE SCHEDULED FOR 16-OCT-2023.		

17-OCT-2023 12:30 AM	NOTICE GIVEN-DISCOVERY HEARING		
Docket Entry:	none.		

17-OCT-2023 09:08 AM	CASE RESCHEDULED BY COURT		
Docket Entry:	*none.*		

17-OCT-2023 09:10 AM	LISTED FOR DISCOVERY HEARING		
Docket Entry:	83-23092483 DISCOVERY MOTION FILED SCHEDULED FOR A HEARING ON OCTOBER 24, 2023 AT 09:00 AM IN REMOTE HEARING VIA ADVANCED COMMUN. TECH.		

18-OCT-2023 12:30 AM	NOTICE GIVEN		
Docket Entry:	OF 1-YR STATUS CONFERENCE SCHEDULED FOR 19-OCT-2023.		

19-OCT-2023 12:30 AM	NOTICE GIVEN-DISCOVERY HEARING		
Docket Entry:	*none.*		

19-OCT-2023 11:19 AM	WITHDRAWAL OF APPEARANCE	SHUEY ESQ, WILLIAM B	
Documents:	Click link(s) to preview/purchase the documents WOA_Shuey - Greenberg - Ponterio.pdf	Click HERE to purchase all documents related to this one docket entry	
Docket Entry:	WITHDRAWAL OF APPEARANCE OF WILLIAM B. SHUEY FILED. (FILED ON BEHALF OF ANN PONTERIO)		

23-OCT-2023 03:50 PM	MOTION/PETITION REPLY FILED	PODRAZA JR, JOSEPH R	
Documents:	Click link(s) to preview/purchase the documents Pltfs Reply to Defs Opposition to MTC Discovery 10 23 23.pdf	Click HERE to purchase all documents related to this one docket entry	
Docket Entry:	83-23092483 REPLY IN SUPPORT/OPPOSITION TO MOTION/PEITION. (FILED ON BEHALF OF SANDRA GREENBERG, JOSHUA AND SANDRA GREENBERG ADMIN OF THE ESTATE OF ELLEN GR AND JOSHUA M GREENBERG)		

15-NOV-2023 10:55 AM	ORDER ENTERED/236 NOTICE GIVEN	CARPENTER, LINDA	

Documents:	⚡ Click link(s) to preview/purchase the documents ORDER_74.pdf	🛒 **Click HERE to purchase all documents related to this one docket entry**
Docket Entry	83-23092483 AND NOW, THIS 15TH DAY OF NOVEMBER, 2023, UPON CONSIDERATION OF PLAINTIFFS' SUBPOENAS TO PRODUCE DOCUMENTS OR THINGS FOR DISCOVERY PURSUANT TO RULE 4009.22 TO THE CITY OF PHILADELPHIA MEDICAL EXAMINER'S OFFICE (MEO) AND CITY OF PHILADELPHIA POLICE DEPARTMENT (PPD) INT HE ABOVE-CAPTIONED MATTER, IT IS HEREBY ORDER THAT MEO AND PPD WILL RESPOND TO THESE SUBPOENAS NOTWITHSTANDING THE CRIMINAL HISTORY INFORMATION ACT, 18 PA.C.S.PT. III, CH. 91...................BY THE COURT: CARPENTER,J. 11/15/23	

15-NOV-2023 10:55 AM	NOTICE GIVEN UNDER RULE 236		
Docket Entry:	NOTICE GIVEN ON 15-NOV-2023 OF ORDER ENTERED/236 NOTICE GIVEN ENTERED ON 15-NOV-2023.		

11-JAN-2024 05:02 PM	WITHDRAWAL OF APPEARANCE	THOMSON, AIMEE D	
Documents:	⚡ Click link(s) to preview/purchase the documents ADT Withdraw.pdf ADT Withdraw.pdf	🛒 **Click HERE to purchase all documents related to this one docket entry**	
Docket Entry	WITHDRAWAL OF APPEARANCE OF AIMEE D. THOMSON FILED. (FILED ON BEHALF OF JOHN MCNAMEE, TIM COONEY, LYNDSEY EMERY, MARLON OSBOURNE AND SAMUEL P GULINO)		

23-FEB-2024 12:40 PM	ENTRY OF APPEARANCE	MEDINA, MELISSA	
Documents:	⚡ Click link(s) to preview/purchase the documents 2024.02.23_EOA_Melissa.pdf	🛒 **Click HERE to purchase all documents related to this one docket entry**	
Docket Entry	ENTRY OF APPEARANCE OF MELISSA MEDINA FILED. (FILED ON BEHALF OF ANN PONTERIO, JOHN MCNAMEE, TIM COONEY, LYNDSEY EMERY, MARLON OSBOURNE AND SAMUEL P GULINO)		

15-MAR-2024 01:44 PM	DISCOVERY MOTION FILED	MEDINA, MELISSA	
Documents:	⚡ Click link(s) to preview/purchase the documents 2024.03.015 -- Motion for Protective Order -- FINAL.pdf	🛒 **Click HERE to purchase all documents related to this one docket entry**	
Docket Entry:	45-24033445 MOTION FOR PROTECTION ORDER. CERTIFICATION DUE DATE: 03/22/2024. RESPONSE DATE: 04/01/2024. (FILED ON		

	BEHALF OF TIM COONEY, SAMUEL P GULINO, MARLON OSBOURNE, LYNDSEY EMERY AND JOHN MCNAMEE)		

15-MAR-2024 01:44 PM	CITY CHARGE SUBSEQUENT FILINGS	MEDINA, MELISSA	
Docket Entry:	*none.*		

22-MAR-2024 10:51 AM	CERT MOTION IS CONTESTED	MEDINA, MELISSA	
Documents:	Click link(s) to preview/purchase the documents — Certification - contested discovery motion.pdf	Click HERE to purchase all documents related to this one docket entry	
Docket Entry:	45-24033445 MOTION IS CONTESTED. (FILED ON BEHALF OF TIM COONEY, SAMUEL P GULINO, MARLON OSBOURNE, LYNDSEY EMERY AND JOHN MCNAMEE)		

01-APR-2024 01:06 PM	ANSWER (MOTION/PETITION) FILED	PODRAZA JR, JOSEPH R	
Documents:	Click link(s) to preview/purchase the documents — Pltfs Answer In Opposition to Defs Motion 04 01 24 Control No 24033445.pdf — Exhibit A.pdf	Click HERE to purchase all documents related to this one docket entry	
Docket Entry:	45-24033445 ANSWER/RESPONSE IN OPPOSITION TO MOTION/PETITION. (FILED ON BEHALF OF SANDRA GREENBERG, JOSHUA AND SANDRA GREENBERG ADMIN OF THE ESTATE OF ELLEN GR AND JOSHUA M GREENBERG)		

04-APR-2024 11:51 AM	LISTED FOR DISCOVERY HEARING		
Docket Entry:	45-24033445 DISCOVERY MOTION FILED SCHEDULED FOR A HEARING ON APRIL 16, 2024 AT 09:00 AM IN REMOTE HEARING VIA ADVANCED COMMUN. TECH.		

05-APR-2024 07:31 AM	NOTICE GIVEN-DISCOVERY HEARING		
Docket Entry:	*none.*		

17-APR-2024 08:27 AM	ORDER ENTERED/236 NOTICE GIVEN	CARPENTER, LINDA	

Documents:	✎ Click link(s) to preview/purchase the documents ORDER_84.pdf	🛒 Click HERE to purchase all documents related to this one docket entry	
Docket Entry:	45-24033445 IT IS HEREBY ORDERED AND DECREED THAT THE DEPOSITION OF GUY D'ANDREA SHALL PROCEED AND SHALL BE LIMITED TO 4 HOURS. THE SCOPE OF SAID DEPOSITION SHALL BE LIMITED TO MR. D'ANDREA'S EXAMINATION OF THE HOMICIDE/DISTRICT ATTORNEY FILE AND CONVERSATIONS WITH DR. GIULINO OR OTHER DEFENDANTS, THE CITY AND DEFENDANTS DO NOT WAIVE OBJECTIONS. ANY ISSUES OF IMMUNITY AND OTHER DEFENSES TO BE RAISED IN SUMMARY JUDGMENT. NO EXTENSIONS TO THE CASE MANAGEMENT DEADLINES SHALL BE MADE.................BY THE COURT: CARPENTER, J. 04/16/2024		

17-APR-2024 08:27 AM	NOTICE GIVEN UNDER RULE 236		
Docket Entry:	NOTICE GIVEN ON 17-APR-2024 OF ORDER ENTERED/236 NOTICE GIVEN ENTERED ON 17-APR-2024.		

24-APR-2024 04:46 PM	MOTION FOR RECONSIDERATION	MEDINA, MELISSA	
Documents:	✎ Click link(s) to preview/purchase the documents 2024.04.24 Motion for Reconsideration - FINAL.pdf Motion CoverSheet Form	🛒 Click HERE to purchase all documents related to this one docket entry	
Docket Entry:	92-24045692 MOTION FOR RECONSIDERATION JUDGE CARPENTER'S ORDER DATED 4/16/2024 (FILED ON BEHALF OF JOHN MCNAMEE, TIM COONEY, LYNDSEY EMERY, MARLON OSBOURNE AND SAMUEL P GULINO)		

24-APR-2024 04:46 PM	CITY CHARGE SUBSEQUENT FILINGS	MEDINA, MELISSA	
Docket Entry:	none.		

25-APR-2024 03:16 PM	MOTION ASSIGNED		
Docket Entry:	92-24045692 MOTION FOR RECONSIDERATION ASSIGNED TO JUDGE: CARPENTER, LINDA . ON DATE: APRIL 25, 2024		

01-MAY-2024 03:37 PM	ORDER ENTERED/236 NOTICE GIVEN	CARPENTER, LINDA	

Documents:	☞ Click link(s) to preview/purchase the documents ORDER_89.pdf	🛒 **Click HERE to purchase all documents** related to this one docket entry	
Docket Entry:	92-24045692 AND NOW, THIS 1ST DAY OF MAY, 2024, UPON CONSIDERATION OF DEFENDANTS' MOTION FOR RECONSIDERATION, ANY RESPONSE THERETO, IT IS HEREBY ORDERED AND DECREED THAT THE MOTION IS DENIED WITHOUT PREJUDICE TO THE PARTIES TO WORK COOPERATIVELY TO COMPLETE OUTSTANDING DISCOVERY AFTER THE DISCOVERY DEADLINES. ANY ISSUES OF TRIAL READINESS MAY BE ADDRESSED AT THE PRE-TRIAL CONFERENCE. BY THE COURT: HON. LINDA CARPENTER, 5-1-2024.		

01-MAY-2024 03:37 PM	NOTICE GIVEN UNDER RULE 236		
Docket Entry:	NOTICE GIVEN ON 02-MAY-2024 OF ORDER ENTERED/236 NOTICE GIVEN ENTERED ON 01-MAY-2024.		

13-MAY-2024 01:06 PM	WITHDRAWAL OF APPEARANCE	MEDINA, MELISSA	
Documents:	☞ Click link(s) to preview/purchase the documents MM WOA.pdf	🛒 **Click HERE to purchase all documents** related to this one docket entry	
Docket Entry:	WITHDRAWAL OF APPEARANCE OF MELISSA MEDINA FILED. (FILED ON BEHALF OF JOHN MCNAMEE, TIM COONEY, LYNDSEY EMERY, MARLON OSBOURNE AND SAMUEL P GULINO)		

17-MAY-2024 12:01 PM	ENTRY OF APPEARANCE	SORATHIA, ALEENA Y	
Documents:	☞ Click link(s) to preview/purchase the documents 2024-05-17 AYS and JZ Entry of Appearance.pdf	🛒 **Click HERE to purchase all documents** related to this one docket entry	
Docket Entry:	ENTRY OF APPEARANCE OF JOSEPH ZAFFARESE AND ALEENA Y SORATHIA FILED. (FILED ON BEHALF OF LYNDSEY EMERY)		

20-MAY-2024 10:44 AM	WITHDRAWAL OF APPEARANCE	SHUEY ESQ, WILLIAM B	
Documents:	☞ Click link(s) to preview/purchase the documents 2024.05.20 Greenberg - Withdrawal_Shuey_Dr. Emery.pdf	🛒 **Click HERE to purchase all documents** related to this one docket entry	
Docket Entry:	WITHDRAWAL OF APPEARANCE OF WILLIAM B SHUEY FILED. (FILED ON BEHALF OF LYNDSEY EMERY)		

20-MAY-2024 11:00 AM	ENTRY OF APPEARANCE	MAYS, KATELYN L	
Documents:	⚲ Click link(s) to preview/purchase the documents 2024-05-20 KM Entry of Appearance.pdf	🛒 Click HERE to purchase all documents related to this one docket entry	
Docket Entry:	ENTRY OF APPEARANCE OF KATELYN L MAYS FILED. (FILED ON BEHALF OF LYNDSEY EMERY)		

22-MAY-2024 10:45 AM	ENTRY OF APPEARANCE	BAILKIN, MARC B	
Documents:	⚲ Click link(s) to preview/purchase the documents Entry of Appearance (MBB).pdf	🛒 Click HERE to purchase all documents related to this one docket entry	
Docket Entry:	ENTRY OF APPEARANCE OF MARC B BAILKIN FILED. (FILED ON BEHALF OF MARLON OSBOURNE)		

22-MAY-2024 10:54 AM	WITHDRAWAL OF APPEARANCE	SHUEY ESQ, WILLIAM B	
Documents:	⚲ Click link(s) to preview/purchase the documents 2024.05.22 Greenberg - Withdrawal_Shuey_Dr. Osbourne.pdf	🛒 Click HERE to purchase all documents related to this one docket entry	
Docket Entry:	WITHDRAWAL OF APPEARANCE OF WILLIAM B SHUEY FILED. (FILED ON BEHALF OF MARLON OSBOURNE)		

30-MAY-2024 01:39 PM	ENTRY OF APPEARANCE-CO COUNSEL	AXE, BAILEY E	
Documents:	⚲ Click link(s) to preview/purchase the documents Greenberg -- Axe EOA.pdf	🛒 Click HERE to purchase all documents related to this one docket entry	
Docket Entry:	ENTRY OF APPEARANCE OF BAILEY E AXE AS CO-COUNSEL FILED. (FILED ON BEHALF OF JOHN MCNAMEE, TIM COONEY AND SAMUEL P GULINO)		

03-JUN-2024 10:21 AM	ENTRY OF APPEARANCE-CO COUNSEL	BRAINARD, ALESSANDRA	
Documents:	⚲ Click link(s) to preview/purchase the documents EOA co-counsel AB.pdf	🛒 Click HERE to purchase all documents related to this one docket entry	
Docket Entry:	ENTRY OF APPEARANCE OF ALESSANDRA BRAINARD AS CO-COUNSEL FILED. (FILED ON BEHALF OF MARLON OSBOURNE)		

03-JUN-2024 10:46 AM	MOT-FOR EXTRAORDINARY RELIEF	BAILKIN, MARC B	

Documents:	🔗 Click link(s) to preview/purchase the documents 2024.06.03 Motion for Extraordinary Relief - FINAL.pdf Motion CoverSheet Form 🛒 **Click HERE to purchase all documents** related to this one docket entry
Docket Entry:	06-24060306 RESPONSE DATE 06/13/2024. (FILED ON BEHALF OF MARLON OSBOURNE)

08-JUN-2024 10:12 PM	ANSWER TO COMPLAINT FILED	AXE, BAILEY E	

Documents:	🔗 Click link(s) to preview/purchase the documents Greenberg -- answer (6.8.24).pdf 🛒 **Click HERE to purchase all documents** related to this one docket entry
Docket Entry:	ANSWER WITH NEW MATTER TO PLAINTIFF'S COMPLAINT FILED. (FILED ON BEHALF OF JOHN MCNAMEE, TIM COONEY AND SAMUEL P GULINO)

13-JUN-2024 09:49 AM	ANSWER (MOTION/PETITION) FILED	PODRAZA JR, JOSEPH R	

Documents:	🔗 Click link(s) to preview/purchase the documents Pltfs Response to Defs MFER 06 13 24.pdf Motion CoverSheet Form 🛒 **Click HERE to purchase all documents** related to this one docket entry
Docket Entry:	06-24060306 ANSWER IN OPPOSITION OF MOT-FOR EXTRAORDINARY RELIEF FILED. (FILED ON BEHALF OF JOSHUA AND SANDRA GREENBERG ADMIN OF THE ESTATE OF ELLEN GR, SANDRA GREENBERG AND JOSHUA M GREENBERG)

17-JUN-2024 09:36 AM	MOTION ASSIGNED		

Docket Entry:	06-24060306 MOT-FOR EXTRAORDINARY RELIEF ASSIGNED TO JUDGE: CARPENTER, LINDA . ON DATE: JUNE 17, 2024

17-JUN-2024 12:57 PM	EXTRAORDINARY RELIEF/DENIED	CARPENTER, LINDA	

Documents:	🔗 Click link(s) to preview/purchase the documents PTEXD_103.pdf 🛒 **Click HERE to purchase all documents** related to this one docket entry
Docket Entry:	06-24060306 AND NOW, THIS 17TH DAY OF JUNE, 2024, UPON CONSIDERATION OF DEFENDANTS' MOTION FOR EXTRA RELIEF, ANY RESPONSE THERETO, IT IS HEREBY ORDERED AND DECREED THAT SAID MOTION IS DENIED. BY THE COURT: HON. LINDA CARPENTER, 6-17-2024.

17-JUN-2024 12:57 PM	NOTICE GIVEN UNDER RULE 236		
Docket Entry:	NOTICE GIVEN ON 20-JUN-2024 OF EXTRAORDINARY RELIEF/DENIED ENTERED ON 17-JUN-2024.		

APPENDIX G

CAPTION

Marlon Osbourne, M.D. and the City of Philadelphia Office of the Medical Examiner, Respondents

v.

Joshua M. Greenberg and Sandra Greenberg, Administrators of the Estate of Ms. Ellen R. Greenberg, Petitioners

CASE INFORMATION

Initiating Document:	Petition for Allowance of Appeal
Case Status:	Closed
Journal Number:	
Case Category:	Civil

Case Type(s): Mandamus

CONSOLIDATED CASES | RELATED CASES

COUNSEL INFORMATION

Attorney:	Podraza, Joseph R.
	Lamb McErlane, PC
Address:	1 S Broad St Ste 1500
	Philadelphia, PA 19107
Phone No:	(610) 701-4405
Receive Mail:	Yes
Receive EMail:	Yes Email:
Representing:	Greenberg, Joshua M., Petitioner
Pro Se:	No
IFP Status:	
Representing:	Greenberg, Sandra, Petitioner
Pro Se:	No
IFP Status:	

Attorney:	Trask, William Howard
	Lamb McErlane, PC
Address:	Lamb Mcerlane Pc
	1 S Broad St Ste 1500
	Philadelphia, PA 19107
Phone No:	(215) 609-3148
Receive Mail:	Yes
Receive EMail:	Yes Email:
Representing:	Greenberg, Joshua M., Petitioner
Pro Se:	No
IFP Status:	
Representing:	Greenberg, Sandra, Petitioner
Pro Se:	No
IFP Status:	

Supreme Court of Pennsylvania		**Allocatur Docket Sheet**
		Docket Number: 332 EAL 2023
		Page 2 of 4
		December 9, 2024

COUNSEL INFORMATION

Attorney:	Diffily, Kelly Susan
	City of Philadelphia
Address:	City Of Phila Law Dept
	1515 Arch St Fl 17
	Philadelphia, PA 19143
Phone No:	(215) 683-5010
Receive Mail:	Yes
Receive EMail:	Yes Email:
Representing:	City of Philadelphia Office of the Medical Examiner, Respondent
Pro Se:	No
IFP Status:	
Representing:	Osbourne, Marlon, Respondent
Pro Se:	No
IFP Status:	

SUPREME COURT INFORMATION

Appeal From:		
Appeal Filed Below:		
Probable Jurisdiction Noted:	Docketed Date:	October 16, 2023
Allocatur/Miscellaneous Granted:	Allocatur/Miscellaneous Docket No.:	
Allocatur/Miscellaneous Grant Order:		

FEE INFORMATION

Fee Dt	Fee Name	Fee Amt	Receipt Dt	Receipt No	Receipt Amt
10/13/2023	Petition for Allowance of Appeal Filed	69.00	10/16/2023	2023-SUP-E-001283	69.00

INTERMEDIATE APPELLATE COURT INFORMATION

Court Name:	Commonwealth	Docket Number:	1461 CD 2021
Date of Order:	September 13, 2023	Rearg/Recon Disp Date:	
		Rearg/Recon Disposition:	
Judge(s):	McCullough, Patricia A.		
	Ceisler, Ellen		
	Dumas, Lori A.		
Intermediate Appellate Court Action:	Reversed/Remanded		
Referring Court:			

AGENCY/TRIAL COURT INFORMATION

Court Below:	Philadelphia County Court of Common Pleas	
County:	Philadelphia	Division: Philadelphia County Civil Division
Date of Agency/Trial Court Order:	October 21, 2021	
Docket Number:	191001241	
Judge(s):	Hill, Glynnis D.	OTN:
Order Type:	Order	

ORIGINAL RECORD CONTENT

APPENDIX G

Supreme Court of Pennsylvania		Allocatur Docket Sheet
		Docket Number: 332 EAL 2023
		Page 3 of 4
		December 9, 2024

ORIGINAL RECORD CONTENT		
Original Record Item	Filed Date	Content/Description

Record Remittal:

DISPOSITION INFORMATION		
Related Journal No:	Judgment Date:	
Category: Decided	Disposition Author:	Per Curiam
Disposition: Order Granting Petition for Allowance of Appeal	Disposition Date:	July 30, 2024
Dispositional Filing:	Author:	
Filed Date:		

DOCKET ENTRY			
Filed Date	Docket Entry / Representing	Participant Type	Filed By
October 13, 2023	**Petition for Allowance of Appeal**		
		Petitioner	Greenberg, Joshua M.
		Petitioner	Greenberg, Sandra
October 13, 2023	**Reproduced Record**		
		Petitioner	Greenberg, Joshua M.
		Petitioner	Greenberg, Sandra
October 16, 2023	**Respondent's Unopposed Application for a 30-day Extension of Time to File Their Answer**		
		Respondent	Osbourne, Marlon
		Respondent	City of Philadelphia Office of the Medical Examiner
October 18, 2023	**Order Granting Application for Extension of Time**		
			Gorman, Kaitlin A.

Comments:
AND NOW, this 18th day of October, 2023, the "Respondents' Unopposed Application for a 30-Day Extension of Time to File Their Answer to Petition for Allowance of Appeal" is GRANTED. Respondents' answer is now due in this Court on or before
November 29, 2023.

October 18, 2023	**Order Exited**		
			Office of the Prothonotary
November 29, 2023	**Answer to Petition for Allowance of Appeal**		
		Respondent	Osbourne, Marlon
		Respondent	City of Philadelphia Office of the Medical Examiner

Neither the Appellate Courts nor the Administrative Office of Pennsylvania Courts assumes any liability
for inaccurate or delayed data, errors or omissions on the docket sheets.

APPENDIX H

Page 1

1   IN THE COURT OF COMMON PLEAS
        PHILADELPHIA COUNTY, PENNSYLVANIA
2   - - -
3   JOSHUA M. GREENBERG and   :   OCTOBER TERM,
    SANDRA GREENBERG,   :   2019
4   Administrators of the   :
    ESTATE OF ELLEN R.   :
5   GREENBERG,   :
    Plaintiffs,   :
6   :
                                :
7   v.   :
                                :
8   MARLON OSBOURNE, M.D. and   :
    CITY OF PHILADELPHIA   :
9   OFFICE OF THE MEDICAL   :
    EXAMINER,   :
10   Defendants.   :   NO. 01241
11   - - -
12   Thursday, April 22, 2021
13   - - -
14   Video-recorded deposition of MARLON
15   OSBOURNE, M.D., taken remotely via Zoom, at
16   West Palm Beach, Florida, beginning at
17   10:34 a.m., reported stenographically by
18   Cheryl L. Goldfarb, a Registered Professional Reporter, Notary Public,
19   and an approved reporter of the United States District Court.
20   - - -
21   VERITEXT LEGAL SOLUTIONS
22   MID-ATLANTIC REGION
23   1801 Market Street - Suite 1800
24   Philadelphia, Pennsylvania 19103

208

APPENDIX H

Page 5

1	(It is hereby stipulated and
2	agreed by and between counsel that
3	reading, signing, sealing, certification
4	and filing are waived; and that all
5	objections, except as to the form of the
6	question, are reserved until the time of
7	trial.)
8	---
9	THE COURT REPORTER: The
10	attorneys participating in this
11	deposition acknowledge that I am not
12	physically present in the deposition room
13	and that I will be reporting this
14	deposition remotely.
15	They further acknowledge that in
16	lieu of an oath administered in person, I
17	will administer the oath remotely. The
18	parties and their counsel consent to this
19	arrangement and waive any objections to
20	this manner of reporting.
21	Please indicate your agreement
22	by stating your name and your agreement
23	on the record.
24	MS. BERKOWITZ: Ellen Berkowitz.

Page 6
1 I represent the City of Philadelphia
2 Medical Examiner and Dr. Osbourne.
3 THE COURT REPORTER: And do you
4 agree that I may swear the witness in via
5 Zoom?
6 MS. BERKOWITZ: Oh, yes. I
7 didn't say I agree. I apologize. I
8 agree.
9 MR. PODRAZA: And Joe Podraza,
10 on behalf of the plaintiffs. I agree.
11 Ellen, do we have usual
12 stipulations?
13 MS. BERKOWITZ: Yes.
14 MR. PODRAZA: Very good.
15 THE VIDEO TECHNICIAN: Good
16 morning. We are going on the record at
17 10:34 on April 22nd, 2021.
18 This is media unit one of the
19 video-recorded deposition of Dr. Marlon
20 Osbourne, taken in the matter of the
21 Estate of Ellen R. Greenberg versus
22 Marlon Osbourne, M.D., et al., filed in
23 the Philadelphia Court of Common Pleas,
24 October Term, 2019, Case Number 01241.

Page 7
1 This deposition is being held
2 virtually via Zoom videoconferencing. My
3 name is Matt MacMurchy, from the firm
4 Veritext, and I'm the videographer. The
5 court reporter is Cheryl Goldfarb, from
6 the firm Veritext.
7 I'm not authorized to administer
8 an oath. I am not related to any party
9 in this action, nor am I financially
10 interested in the outcome.
11 Counsel will now please state
12 their appearance and affiliations for the
13 record.
14 MR. PODRAZA: Joe Podraza, on
15 behalf of the plaintiffs.
16 MS. BERKOWITZ: Ellen Berkowitz,
17 on behalf of the defendants.
18 DR. OSBOURNE: Marlon Osbourne.
19 THE VIDEO TECHNICIAN: Will the
20 court reporter please swear in the
21 witness.
22 THE COURT REPORTER: Dr.
23 Osbourne, will you please raise your
24 right hand.

Page 8
1   - - -
2   MARLON OSBOURNE, M.D., after
3 having been first duly sworn/affirmed,
4 was examined and testified as follows:
5   - - -
6   THE WITNESS: I do.
7   THE COURT REPORTER: Thank you.
8   - - -
9   EXAMINATION
10   - - -
11 BY MR. PODRAZA:
12 Q.   Good morning, Dr. Osbourne. My
13 name is Joe Podraza, and I represent the Estate
14 of Ellen Greenberg.
15 First, thank you for
16 accommodating a deposition for today.
17 Second, have you ever been
18 deposed before?
19 A.   Yes.
20 Q.   So you're familiar with the
21 format generally?
22 A.   Generally, yes.
23 Q.   All right. And it's just a
24 question-and-answer format, where counsel will

Page 9
1 pose a question, to which you will then supply
2 an answer.
3 Do you understand that?
4 A.   Yes.
5 Q.   And maybe most importantly, I
6 will try not to speak over you if you, in turn,
7 will try not to speak over me, so that the
8 transcription will be clear as to
9 question/answer, without it being commingled.
10 Understandable?
11 A.   Understandable.
12 Q.   All right. Now, Doctor, is
13 there any reason today why you would not be
14 able to understand or otherwise respond to a
15 question that's posed?
16 A.   No, there is no reason.
17 Q.   All right. In preparing for
18 today, did you speak with anyone other than
19 your counsel?
20 A.   No.
21 Q.   Did you review any documentation
22 prior to your deposition today?
23 A.   I reviewed the packet that
24 included the Complaints and the exhibits and

Page 10

1 the investigative report from Mr. Olszewski.
2 Q. All right. Anything else?
3 A. Some photographs from the
4 autopsy.
5 Q. Did you have the opportunity to
6 speak with Dr. Gulino?
7 A. No, I did not.
8 Q. Are you aware, however, that
9 Dr. Gulino has been deposed in this matter?
10 A. I am aware.
11 Q. And how are you aware of that
12 fact?
13 A. When I received the e-mail with
14 the subpoenas, both subpoenas were in the same
15 e-mail.
16 Q. Okay. Why don't we start a
17 little bit with your background.
18 Where did you go to medical
19 school?
20 A. Well, it was called New Jersey
21 Medical School. It's now Rutgers New Jersey
22 Medical School.
23 Q. And post-medical school, did you
24 do a residency?

Page 12

1 completed, where did you become employed?
2 A. The Philadelphia Medical
3 Examiner's Office.
4 Q. And do you recall from when to
5 when?
6 A. From 2009 to 2014,
7 September 2009 to September of 2014.
8 Q. And after your tenure at the
9 Medical Examiner's Office in Philadelphia, did
10 you have other employment?
11 A. Yes, at the Broward
12 Q. Where?
13 A. At the Broward County Medical
14 Examiner's Office.
15 Q. Was that starting in 2014?
16 A. Yes, October 2014.
17 Q. And do you continue to be
18 employed there today?
19 A. No. I -- I left that employment
20 in September of 2019.
21 Q. And where were you employed
22 after 2019?
23 A. The West Palm Beach County
24 Medical Exam -- sorry, Palm Beach County

Page 11

1 A. Yes, at what used to be
2 Hahnemann University Hospital, Drexel College
3 of Medicine.
4 Q. And what was the residency in?
5 A. Pathology.
6 Q. And I take it you successfully
7 completed the residency?
8 A. Yes, in 2008.
9 Q. All right. And --
10 A. I'm sorry, 2004.
11 Q. Very good. And after your
12 residency, did you have any other post-medical
13 training?
14 A. Yes. I did a one-year
15 fellowship at the Miami-Dade Medical Examiner's
16 Office in Miami-Dade, Florida from 2008 to
17 2009.
18 Q. And would that complete the
19 extent then of your medical training?
20 A. Yes.
21 Q. Okay. Now, why don't we walk
22 through your employment.
23 You mentioned your fellowship
24 down at Miami-Dade. After the fellowship was

Page 13

1 Medical Examiner's Office.
2 Q. And are you presently employed
3 at that location and with that --
4 A. Yes, I am.
5 Q. -- employer?
6 Okay. Again, if you can try to
7 wait until the completion of my question before
8 you answer. Even if you can anticipate what
9 that question is, it helps with the
10 transcription for the court reporter. Okay?
11 A. I'm sorry. I understand.
12 Q. No problem. All right. Let's
13 talk a little bit about the Ellen Greenberg
14 case, which brings us here today. Before we
15 get into the specifics, I'd like to just go
16 over your recollection of the matter.
17 A. Okay.
18 Q. When do you recall you became
19 first involved in the Ellen Greenberg
20 THE WITNESS: The screen froze.
21 MS. BERKOWITZ: Your screen
22 froze?
23 THE WITNESS: I'm sorry, the
24 screen froze then it zoomed -- it

Page 14
1 fast forwarded through what you said.
2 BY MR. PODRAZA:
3 Q. Well, then let me repeat that.
4 I'd like to just go by your recollection now of
5 your involvement in the Ellen Greenberg matter
6 before we get into some specific questions.
7 And my first question to you is,
8 what's your first recollection of your
9 involvement in the Ellen Greenberg matter?
10 A. My first recollection is being
11 briefed of the circum -- the scene
12 investigation on the case on the morning of the
13 27th of January 2011.
14 Q. What does that mean, to be
15 briefed on the scene investigation?
16 A. The investigator who attended
17 the scene gave me the background information
18 and described the scene investigation that he
19 conducted --
20 Q. And who was the invest --
21 A. -- regarding the case.
22 Q. I'm sorry. Who was the
23 investigator?
24 A. Stephen Olszewski.

Page 15
1 Q. And to the best of your
2 recollection, what information did
3 Mr. Olszewski share with you?
4 A. The decedent was a female who
5 was found in her apartment in the kitchen area
6 with a -- several stab wounds to her chest.
7 And the knife was still within one of the stab
8 wounds. She was fully clothed.
9 He reports that he got
10 information from the decedent's boyfriend that
11 he returned home after going to the gym to not
12 be able to open the door because the security
13 latch was still -- was in place. And he
14 unlocked the door and seen that his significant
15 other was on the ground in the kitchen area.
16 He did not -- he could not enter
17 the room until the security latch was broken
18 in; that he -- the boyfriend said he broke down
19 after trying to call her several times to talk
20 to her and wake her up.
21 The scene investigation
22 proceeded with Mr. Olszewski's description of
23 the apartment. The other rooms and areas
24 appeared ordered. Nothing seemed out of place.

Page 16
1 His examination of the body at the scene. The
2 photographs that also accompanied I reviewed
3 later on. He also stated that the decedent was
4 fully clothed.
5 And that's pretty much the brief
6 before the autopsy continued.
7 Q. All right. At Dr. Gulino's
8 deposition a couple days ago, he made reference
9 to like a synopsis report that's available to
10 the pathologist at the time of autopsy.
11 Was such a synopsis report
12 available to you at that time?
13 A. Yes, it was.
14 Q. And did you review that report?
15 A. Yes, I did.
16 Q. And I take it, then, what's in
17 the report is fairly consistent with what
18 Mr. Olszewski shared with you that morning?
19 A. Yes.
20 Q. Were there any inconsistencies
21 between the information in the report and what
22 Mr. Olszewski shared with you that morning?
23 A. No.
24 Q. I take it then after you had

Page 17
1 your conversation with Mr. Olszewski, you
2 proceeded to do the autopsy?
3 A. Yes.
4 Q. And was there anything
5 remarkable about the autopsy that you recall?
6 A. On initial examination, several
7 stab wounds to the posterior aspect of the neck
8 were noted. As in all autopsies, we proceed
9 with first an external examination with overall
10 photographs of the body, and -- and then
11 individual photographs of each wound. Their
12 location is documented. The measurements are
13 documented from the external aspect of the body
14 before we proceed with an internal examination.
15 Other injuries, such as --
16 beyond the stab wounds, there was bruising
17 noted on the arms, the hands or the wrist area,
18 the thighs in different stages of healing.
19 The knife that was in -- well,
20 the clothing was, you know, removed. The
21 situation preserved, the knife, so that it
22 could be properly packaged and sent to -- and
23 given to the police as evidence.
24 And then we proceeded with,

APPENDIX H

1 after the photograph, taking documentation,
2 proceeded with the internal examination.
3   Q.   And was there anything
4 remarkable about the internal examination that
5 comes to mind?
6   A.   The internal examination showed
7 that there were -- the final blow, the stab
8 wound to the chest, had damaged the heart,
9 lungs, the liver. There were stab wounds to
10 the back of the neck, the majority of which
11 were shallow, only went through skin and/or
12 muscle. One did go through one of the lig –
13 the ligament that connects the -- between the
14 first cervical vertebra and the base of the
15 skull.
16   The brain when examined did have
17 some subarachnoid hemorrhage on the cerebellar
18 hemispheres.
19   Additionally, there was one
20 wound of the posterior neck that went through
21 the disc of the -- between the second and third
22 cervical vertebrae and incised the covering
23 that covers the spinal cord in that area, which
24 is called the dura. And the spinal cord in

1 investigator did not share with you knowledge
2 of the posterior wounds? Is that correct?
3   A.   I can't recall if he shared
4 knowledge of it. I would have to refer to his
5 scene investigation. And I don't -- I'm not
6 certain if I -- I don't recall specific
7 descriptions of those wounds in the scene
8 report. I can't say. I can't -- I can't
9 remember.
10   Q.   Okay. And that's fine. We'll
11 get to the investigator's report.
12   But with posterior wounds, would
13 you have expected the investigator, Olszewski,
14 to have included that in his report if he was
15 aware of them?
16   A.   Yes.
17   Q.   Okay. After you had your dis –
18 well, after you reviewed the synopsis, the
19 material in the synopsis, spoke with
20 Investigator Olszewski and then did an autopsy,
21 you reached a conclusion as to what the manner
22 of death was; is that correct?
23   A.   That is correct.
24   Q.   And at that time, it was based

1 that area appeared to be bulging from that
2 defect.
3   There was a large collection of
4 blood removed from the left chest cavity. At
5 this time, I can't remember exactly how much.
6 If I can refer, I could tell you, from the
7 autopsy report, how much blood was removed.
8   And my examination of the neck
9 did not show any significant injury or
10 hemorrhage. And there was no injury or
11 hemorrhage to the hyoid bone or thyroid
12 cartilages. And that was -- all the other
13 organs were within normal -- appeared normal.
14   Q.   You have a pretty good
15 recollection.
16   Has some of that been refreshed
17 by reviewing some of the documentation prior to
18 today?
19   A.   Yes.
20   Q.   Okay. I have a question for
21 you. You mentioned that at the time of
22 autopsy, you became familiar about the
23 posterior wounds to Ellen.
24   Am I correct that the

1 on the information that we've generally gone
2 over right now; is that correct?
3   A.   That's correct.
4   Q.   All right. And you reached the
5 conclusion of a homicide; is that correct?
6   A.   At that time, yes, that's
7 correct.
8   Q.   And we know that later, that
9 would be revised to suicide, correct?
10   A.   It was amended to suicide, yes.
11   Q.   All right. After you had
12 concluded homicide -- but let me first say,
13 were you confident at the time, based on the
14 information available to you, that the
15 determination of homicide was within a
16 reasonable degree of medical certainty?
17   A.   At the time of autopsy, I did
18 believe that I had enough information to make
19 that determination.
20   Q.   Okay. Now, based on your
21 recollection, walk us through how it came about
22 that you amended the manner of death.
23   A.   Subsequent -- well, following my
24 determination of homicide, the police were

Page 22

1   notified. I was then notified that they were
2   continuing their investigation. I had --
3   although I had, from my own examination of the
4   spinal cord, thought the injury was -- or there
5   was injury to the spinal cord, I was not
6   certain.
7   So I, with consultation with
8   other associates, decided that it should be
9   looked at by a neuropathologist. And
10 additionally in the interim, as in all cases
11 where it's non -- when it's a non-natural
12 death, toxicology is performed.
13 So with those things outlying
14 and the police request and knowing that they
15 were going to continue to do an investigation,
16 the case was made pending until all information
17 could be gathered and then revisited to
18 determine of the manner of death.
19 Q.   Now, when you -- when you
20 came -- well, you said you had a consultation
21 with personnel at the Medical Examiner's Office
22 about having the spinal cord evaluated,
23 correct?
24 A.   Correct.

Page 24

1   a meeting with the police and a representative
2   from the District Attorney's office.
3   Do you recall such a meeting
4   after you had determined the manner of death to
5   be homicide?
6   A.   Yes, it occurred after that. It
7   occurred -- that meeting occurred after the
8   case was made pending and there was more
9   information that was gathered.
10 Q.   But did that meeting occur
11 before you consulted with Dr. Rorke?
12 A.   No, not -- no, it did not happen
13 before I consulted.
14 Q.   Had you received information
15 from Dr. Rorke as to her impressions prior to
16 that meeting with the police and the DA's
17 office?
18 A.   Yes, I believe that meeting –
19 prior to that meeting, yes.
20 Q.   Were there other meetings with
21 the police and DA other than the one?
22 A.   I only recall one meeting with
23 the police and DA after I gathered information
24 and they presented the information they

Page 23

1   Q.   All right. When did that occur
2   post your determination of homicide or the
3   manner of death? Was it within days? Weeks?
4   Months?
5   A.   It was within days to -- it was
6   likely days to a week or two.
7   Q.   And what prompted you to want to
8   have the spinal cord examined?
9   A.   Again, I was not completely a
10 hundred percent certain that there was actual
11 injury to the spinal cord. And if so, the
12 question was, if there was injury, how severe
13 would it be, which the question would be, would
14 Ms. Greenberg not be able to continue to
15 inflict injury to herself because of this
16 injury.
17 Q.   And you said that it was
18 followed with a consultation that you then
19 requested involvement by a neuropathologist,
20 correct?
21 A.   Correct.
22 Q.   Who did you consult with?
23 A.   Dr. Lucy Rorke.
24 Q.   Now, Dr. Gulino had talked about

Page 25

1   gathered, to the best of my knowledge.
2   Q.   And at the meeting you had with
3   the police and the District Attorney, what was
4   the information that you gathered that was new
5   that was not present at the time that you
6   determined homicide as the manner of death?
7   A.   The information that was
8   gathered was that we had the information –
9   the -- Dr. Rorke's evaluation had been done.
10 The toxicology, I believe, had been reported by
11 that time.
12 Additionally, I had already had
13 the chance to review the psychiatry records
14 that we requested that I wasn't able to review
15 before the autopsy was performed and go through
16 the scene investigation report that was
17 completed by Mr. Olszewski and review the scene
18 photographs completely.
19 And the -- I believe that's the
20 majority. That's all the things that I brought
21 to the meeting.
22 Q.   Okay. And we'll get into more
23 detail with your interaction with Dr. Rorke in
24 a second here.

APPENDIX H

1 At the meeting, what did the
2 police or representatives from the District
3 Attorney's office present?
4 A. To my knowledge, they discussed
5 their interactions with the decedent's
6 boyfriend and the statement he gave. They also
7 stated that they were going to be evaluating
8 the knife.
9 And I'm not sure that the dating
10 evidence was available at that time, because I
11 can't place exactly when that happened and the
12 sequence of events.
13 I knew that in their
14 investigation at that point that they were
15 going to be testing the knife for DNA.
16 And we went through the entire
17 scene again to discuss what factors would
18 contribute -- what factors are associated with
19 or lead to homicide versus what lead to
20 suicide.
21 Q. And, again, we'll get into a
22 little bit more detail as we proceed here in
23 the examination.
24 After that meeting with the

1 Q. -- up to January 27 of 2011, had
2 you had a similar meeting with representatives
3 from the police department and the District
4 Attorney's Office to discuss changing the
5 manner of death from homicide to suicide?
6 A. Any case or just this case?
7 Q. Any case.
8 A. No, I'd never -- I have not had
9 a meeting to discuss changing.
10 Q. Would you agree with me that
11 suicide is not a default determination simply
12 when you feel homicide hasn't occurred?
13 A. I'm not sure I understand your
14 question.
15 Q. Sure. In other words, when you
16 were doing the autopsy and taking in all this
17 information, you were determining whether there
18 was proof of a homicide, correct?
19 A. I was determining how and under
20 what circumstances these injuries could have
21 occurred.
22 Q. And what were your -- what were
23 the -- under the manner of death, you have
24 suicide, homicide and cannot be determined or

1 police department and the DA -- yes, I'm sorry,
2 I'm reminded, can you tell me who were the
3 participants at the meeting with the police
4 department and the District Attorney's office?
5 A. Myself, Dr. Gulino. There were
6 two officers. I do not recall their names.
7 And District Attorney, who I believe is Ann –
8 I can't remember her last name at this time.
9 Q. Prior to that meeting with
10 respect to the Ellen Greenberg case, had you
11 had any similar meetings with police and/or DA
12 representatives to discuss the changing of the
13 manner of death from homicide to suicide?
14 A. I had -- well, I spoke to the
15 investigating officers when they requested it
16 be changed -- when they requested the change be
17 that the case be pending while they continue
18 their investigation. I don't remember the
19 officer's name, though.
20 Q. All right. My question was a
21 little bit more general.
22 In your time with the Medical
23 Examiner's Office in Philadelphia –
24 A. Oh, I'm sorry.

1 investigation continuing, is how that gets
2 defined, correct? Those are the three choices?
3 A. No. There are five manners of
4 death. There's natural, accident, homicide,
5 suicide or undetermined or could not be
6 determined.
7 Q. Okay. And when you were
8 considering the homicide choice versus the
9 suicide choice, did -- was it your view that if
10 you decided to --
11 MS. BERKOWITZ: Objection.
12 BY MR. PODRAZA:
13 Q. Well, when you were deciding
14 whether it was homicide or suicide, was it your
15 thought that concluding one -- or excluding one
16 by default meant the other?
17 A. I don't think I understand --
18 MS. BERKOWITZ: Joe, could
19 you -- excuse me. Could you clarify
20 whether you're talking about his initial
21 determination or his amendment? Because
22 I think the timeline is a little foggy
23 here.
24 MR. PODRAZA: Well, not really.

Page 30

1 BY MR. PODRAZA:

2 Q. But my question, Doctor, let me

3 clarify it this way. Maybe it . . .

4 I've heard folks say that before

5 you decide the manner of death is homicide, you

6 have to prove homicide from your investigation,

7 both from the autopsy as well as the other

8 information that's made available.

9 Do you agree with that

10 statement?

11 A. In general terms, yes, I agree

12 with that statement.

13 Q. And then similarly in

14 determining suicide, before that manner of

15 death is designated, that needs to be proved

16 through the autopsy as well as the other

17 information that is gathered.

18 Do you agree with that?

19 A. In general terms, yes.

20 Q. And if there is doubt as to that

21 proof of homicide or suicide or any of the

22 other manners of death, you know, compared –

23 as between competing manners of death that can

24 be selected, then the default would be to

Page 32

1 said there.

2 If, for instance, a natural

3 cause -- let's say that the manners of death,

4 the reasonable manners of death out of the five

5 that can be selected, the two competing ones

6 would be homicide and suicide.

7 I believe we just agreed that

8 before homicide can be selected, you have --

9 you have to sufficiently prove in your mind

10 it's a homicide, correct?

11 A. Yes.

12 Q. All right. And the same thing

13 with suicide. Before suicide is selected, you

14 have to sufficiently prove in your mind that

15 it's a suicide, correct?

16 A. You have to have circumstantial

17 ev -- circumstances and findings to support

18 that, yes.

19 Q. And where the situation, even

20 with all the information now made available,

21 does not enable you to feel comfortable that

22 you can prove one against the other, then the

23 determination would be investigation pending or

24 manner of death cannot be determined at this

Page 31

1 indicate cannot be determined or investigation

2 continuing, to try to unearth further

3 information.

4 Would you agree with that, sir?

5 A. Before you come to the

6 conclusion of cannot be determined, all

7 information needs to be -- all information that

8 possibly can be gathered has to be evaluated

9 and then you come to the conclusion that you

10 can't decide between two manners and/or you

11 don't have enough information to make that

12 determination.

13 And so if you're not certain at

14 the time of autopsy, then you would make the

15 case pending until you gather that information

16 and/or exhausted all ways of getting that

17 information in order to make the determination

18 of either a distinct manner or you cannot make

19 a distinction between the two and call it

20 undetermined.

21 Q. Okay. But I'm talking right now

22 a little bit more generically.

23 A. Yes.

24 Q. And I understand what you just

Page 33

1 time; is that correct?

2 A. Well, pending is just a -- it's

3 used in the interim when you're gathering

4 information. It's not a definitive cause of

5 death --

6 Q. I understand.

7 A. -- or manner of death. I'm

8 sorry.

9 Q. Right.

10 A. So that would never be a

11 definitive manner of death. And so you would

12 end up, if you cannot decide between one -- one

13 or more manners -- two or more manners, then

14 you would end up calling it undetermined.

15 Q. Okay. All right. Then let's

16 get into some of the particulars of this case.

17 The first exhibit I'd like to go

18 over with you is an exhibit we discussed with

19 Dr. Gulino, and we're going to mark as O-1, for

20 Osbourne 1. It's the death investigation

21 report or what I believe is the synopsis. And

22 we're going to put it up on the screen so

23 you'll have a chance to review it and

24 familiarize yourself with it.

APPENDIX H

Page 34
1   A.   Okay.
2   - - -
3   (Whereupon, Exhibit Osbourne 1
4   is marked for identification.)
5   - - -
6   BY MR. PODRAZA:
7   Q.   And, Doctor, if you need to
8   scroll down or see another page, just let us
9   know and we can accomplish that for you.
10   A.   Okay.
11   MS. BERKOWITZ: Could you scroll
12   down, please?
13   MR. TRASK: (Scrolling.)
14   MS. BERKOWITZ: All the way.
15   BY MR. PODRAZA:
16   Q.   Well, Doctor, have you
17   familiarized yourself so --
18   A.   No, not yet. Give me a moment.
19   MR. TRASK: Who am I listening
20   to?
21   MR. PODRAZA: The doctor. He's
22   the witness.
23   MS. BERKOWITZ: Well, the
24   attorney is allowed to see it. And I am

Page 35
1   just asking that you scroll down.
2   Could you do that, please?
3   MR. PODRAZA: Ellen, the doctor
4   hasn't completed the parts that you want
5   to scroll away from. Can we let him
6   accomplish that? And we'll do it –
7   MS. BERKOWITZ: I'd like to see
8   the whole document. If we were in
9   person, I would be able to see the entire
10   document. Could you please scroll down?
11   It's not an unreasonable request and it's
12   not burdensome.
13   MR. TRASK: (Scrolling.)
14   MS. BERKOWITZ: That's it?
15   MR. PODRAZA: It's the document
16   you produced, yes.
17   MS. BERKOWITZ: Okay.
18   BY MR. PODRAZA:
19   Q.   All right. So why don't we
20   resume back on Page 1. And, Doctor,
21   familiarize yourself with the contents of the
22   document and let us know when you need us to
23   scroll down.
24   (Pause)

Page 36
1   A.   Scroll down, please.
2   MR. TRASK: (Scrolling.)
3   (Pause)
4   THE WITNESS: Scroll down,
5   please.
6   MR. TRASK: (Scrolling.)
7   THE WITNESS: Okay.
8   BY MR. PODRAZA:
9   Q.   Now, is this the synopsis that
10   was available to you prior to your starting the
11   autopsy on January 27, 2011?
12   A.   Just the first paragraph.
13   Q.   Excuse me?
14   A.   To my knowledge, just the first
15   paragraph. I do not believe the scene
16   investigation was fully completed at the time
17   of -- before I started the autopsy.
18   Q.   Okay.
19   A.   That's why some of the
20   information was given to me verbally.
21   Q.   And of the -- besides that first
22   paragraph, the remaining parts, do you recall
23   what was supplied to you at the time of
24   autopsy?

Page 37
1   A.   As I believe I --
2   MS. BERKOWITZ: Asked and
3   answered.
4   You can answer that question.
5   THE WITNESS: Okay.
6   A.   (Continuing) I believe I
7   answered that generally the scene was like
8   explained to me as Mr. Olszewski had approached
9   it, the information he got from doing his scene
10   investigation, where wounds to the torso of the
11   decedent were identified. Her status of
12   clothing was identified -- was relayed to me.
13   The door and the story given by the boyfriend,
14   which he elicited from the boyfriend himself,
15   was given to me about having to break down the
16   door. And the general description of the scene
17   investigation, which the details are consistent
18   with what's in the scene investigation report.
19   BY MR. PODRAZA:
20   Q.   So that would be paragraphs two
21   and -- excuse me -- three and four?
22   A.   Two through -- two, three, four,
23   five and six.
24   Q.   And that would be information

Page 38

1 that was shared with you that's also
2 memorialized here in those paragraphs?
3 A. Yes.
4 Q. All right. And that would have
5 been at the time of your autopsy, or more
6 significantly, prior to your determination of
7 the manner of death being a homicide, correct?
8 A. Yes.
9 Q. And then what information on
10 this second page, starting where it says,
11 "Psychiatrist: Dr. Ellen Berman," if you could
12 review that information, what of that
13 information was shared with you prior to your
14 determination that the manner of death was
15 homicide?
16 A. I don't believe -- I'm not
17 certain any of that particular information was
18 shared with me prior to determining homicide.
19 Q. So everything from,
20 "Psychiatrist: Dr. Ellen Berman" below, you
21 don't believe was shared with you at the time
22 of the determination of homicide?
23 A. I don't recall knowing those
24 details before determining it was --

Page 39

1 determining -- making the determination of
2 homicide.
3 Q. Okay.
4 A. (Zoom audio glitch)
5 unavailable -- unavailable at autopsy.
6 Q. All right. Now, you mentioned
7 an investigator, Olszewski. If you go to the
8 first page of this. What we're calling as the
9 synopsis, Osbourne 1 --
10 A. Yes.
11 Q. -- identifies a Jaime Budd as
12 the investigator.
13 Who is Jaime Budd?
14 A. Jaime Budd is also -- was also
15 an investigator at the Philadelphia Medical
16 Examiner's Office.
17 If you read the first paragraph,
18 the investigator, Olszewski, is the individual
19 who went to the scene. She received the
20 initial information and started the case,
21 giving it a case number, getting all the
22 initial information, location. Mr. Olszewski
23 is the actual investigator who went to the
24 scene.

Page 40

1 Q. So there was only one
2 investigator who actually went to the scene?
3 A. Yes.
4 Q. Okay. And the reference then
5 to -- it's a Ms. Budd or Mr. Budd?
6 A. Ms.
7 Q. Ms. Budd. So she appears on
8 this document because she began the generation
9 of the document. Is that your --
10 A. Yes.
11 Q. -- understanding?
12 A. She's the investigator who
13 received the call, yes.
14 Q. Now, before you determined the
15 manner of death, did you have an understanding
16 as to how the scene was going to be maintained
17 by the police department?
18 A. I -- no, I do not know that I
19 knew that information.
20 Q. Does the Medical Examiner's
21 Office at all have any expectations as to how
22 the scene is maintained prior to a
23 determination of homicide or some other
24 determination for manner of death?

Page 41

1 A. I'm not certain I understand
2 your question.
3 Q. Sure. Do you -- would you
4 expect that before the determination of manner
5 of death is made, that the scene is maintained
6 to keep it from becoming polluted?
7 A. That's on a case by -- that's up
8 to the police discretion on a case-by-case
9 basis. For our purposes, that's why we have
10 our investigators go to scenes, take the
11 photographs, examine the body, to collect that
12 information for us to evaluate.
13 Additionally, we may -- or at
14 times, we do use additional information
15 provided by the police from their photographs
16 and their scene investigation. But we're
17 not -- we're not solely relying upon it.
18 Q. Are you aware if ever a forensic
19 division of the police department, either
20 homicide or other division, actually examined
21 the premises?
22 A. I -- for all scenes, there's
23 always an investigator or detective, homicide
24 detective, presence. And in this case, I

APPENDIX H

1 believe in Mr. Olszewski's report, it was
2 Detective Sierra and Peters as the homicide
3 detectives.
4 To my knowledge, we are called
5 after the scene is discovered, after police
6 identified the scene.
7 Q. All right.
8 A. Therefore, police are present at
9 the scene when our staff is there.
10 Q. And I understand that. And I
11 appreciate that clarification. But my question
12 was a little more pointed.
13 Are you aware of whether there
14 was ever a forensic examination done by the
15 Philadelphia Police Department on the -- for
16 that scene?
17 A. I don't recall specific -- I
18 don't recall that specific information. I
19 would likely -- knowing that investigation
20 continued, at some point I believe, I would
21 likely believe they would have had some
22 investigation of that manner.
23 Q. Do you have a recollection, at
24 that meeting with the Philadelphia Police

1 Q. And am I correct, then, that
2 it's only a pathologist who could -- who could
3 determine the manner of Ellen's death?
4 A. Yes.
5 Q. And that's not the role of the
6 police department; is that correct?
7 A. It is not the role of the police
8 department. That's correct.
9 Q. Now, what I'd like to do is to
10 focus on the Report of Examination that you
11 made. And we're going to mark that as
12 Osbourne 2.
13 I'll ask you to take a moment to
14 review the document to familiarize yourself
15 with it. And then I'm going to have some
16 specific questions about it. Okay?
17 A. Okay.
18 ---
19 (Whereupon, Exhibit Osbourne 2
20 is marked for identification.)
21 ---
22 BY MR. PODRAZA:
23 Q. And when you would like, we can
24 scroll down and move to the next pages,

1 Department and the representative from the DA's
2 office, of information that was obtained by the
3 police department based on its forensic
4 examination of the premises?
5 A. I do not have a recollection of
6 specific information from a forensic
7 investigation at that point.
8 Q. Do you recall if anyone from the
9 Philadelphia Police Department or associated
10 with the city at any time told you that a
11 homicide forensic examination had been done of
12 the premises?
13 A. I don't specifically recall
14 being told a forensic examination had been
15 done. I know homicide detectives had attended
16 the scene. What -- I'm not -- I do not have at
17 this time or have not reviewed at this time any
18 investigations by the police generated from the
19 report. So at this time, I can't recall. I
20 can't recall.
21 Q. Now, prior to Ellen's body being
22 removed from the premises and brought to the
23 morgue, has a pathologist examined her body?
24 A. Prior to? No.

1 whenever you prefer.
2 A. Okay.
3 (Pause)
4 Scroll down, please.
5 MR. TRASK: (Scrolling.)
6 (Pause)
7 THE WITNESS: Scroll down,
8 please.
9 MR. TRASK: (Scrolling.)
10 THE WITNESS: Scroll down,
11 please.
12 MR. TRASK: (Scrolling.)
13 (Pause)
14 THE WITNESS: Scroll down,
15 please.
16 MR. TRASK: (Scrolling.)
17 (Pause)
18 THE WITNESS: Scroll down,
19 please.
20 MR. TRASK: (Scrolling.)
21 (Pause)
22 THE WITNESS: Scroll down,
23 please.
24 MR. TRASK: (Scrolling.)

Page 46

1 (Pause)
2 THE WITNESS: Scroll down,
3 please.
4 MR. TRASK: (Scrolling.)
5 (Pause)
6 THE WITNESS: Scroll down,
7 please.
8 MR. TRASK: (Scrolling.)
9 (Pause)
10 THE WITNESS: Okay.
11 BY MR. PODRAZA:
12 Q. Okay. And before I actually ask
13 you some questions about the report, in your
14 experience when you were with the Medical
15 Examiner's Office in Philadelphia, did the
16 medical examiners, investigators, regularly
17 pronounce the manner of death on the scene
18 prior to autopsy?
19 A. I don't understand your
20 question.
21 Q. Sure. When the investigator,
22 like Mr. Olszewski, goes to the scene, was it
23 your experience, while you were at the office,
24 that the investigator would determine the

Page 48

1 Q. And you've already had the
2 benefit of reading it yourself.
3 The question I have is, there's
4 a reference to "incises the dura covering the
5 subjacent spinal cord."
6 Do you see that language?
7 A. Yes.
8 Q. All right. And am I correct,
9 then, that that language is conveying that the
10 dura, or the sheath around the spinal cord, was
11 cut?
12 A. Yes.
13 Q. And in your experience -- well,
14 when I spoke to Dr. Gulino about this, I asked
15 him whether that would be painful. And he
16 said, yes, it would be.
17 Do you agree with that?
18 A. Yes.
19 Q. I also asked him whether it
20 could be unrelenting intense pain, and he
21 agreed with that.
22 Do you agree with it?
23 A. It may be.
24 Q. And I asked him whether it could

Page 47

1 manner of death on scene prior to autopsy?
2 A. I wouldn't classify it as
3 determining the manner of death. I would say
4 they would infer the type of case it possibly
5 could be.
6 Q. But we can agree that they would
7 not determine the manner of death, correct?
8 A. No, they don't make the
9 determination.
10 Q. All right. And was it your
11 experience that police officers on the scene
12 would make a determination as to the manner of
13 death prior to autopsy?
14 A. Again, only the medical -- only
15 the medical examiner can make a determination
16 of manner of death. Individuals attending a
17 scene may infer what type of case they're
18 dealing with and call it a homicide, suicide,
19 accident, based on the scene that they
20 approached and interpreted it as.
21 Q. Okay. What I'd like to now do
22 is your report, if we could focus on wound "T",
23 which -- as in Thomas.
24 A. Yes.

Page 49

1 be incapacitating pain in the sense that while
2 the person could still move, the pain is so
3 intense that it essentially makes them
4 immobile.
5 Would you agree with that?
6 A. I don't know that I can make
7 that determination.
8 Q. But you would agree with me that
9 under the proper circumstances, the cut of the
10 dura could incapacitate a person?
11 A. It may, yes.
12 Q. And would you also agree with me
13 that it not only could incapacitate a person,
14 but could make a person become unconscious?
15 A. Simply cutting the dura?
16 Q. Yes, cutting the dura and the
17 nerves around the dura, as Dr. Gulino said –
18 MS. BERKOWITZ: Objection.
19 BY MR. PODRAZA:
20 Q. -- under the right
21 circumstances, couldn't that cause somebody to
22 become unconscious just from the sheer
23 intensity of the pain?
24 MS. BERKOWITZ: Objection.

APPENDIX H

Page 50
1 BY MR. PODRAZA:
2 Q. You can answer.
3 A. I don't know that -- I don't –
4 I don't know that I can answer that
5 definitively yes or no.
6 Q. Could you -- would you agree
7 that the cutting of the dura may lead to the
8 loss of blood pressure?
9 A. It can affect blood pressure,
10 yes.
11 Q. And would you also agree that
12 the cutting of the dura could lead to the loss
13 of spinal fluid?
14 A. It can lead to the loss of
15 spinal fluid. That is correct.
16 Q. Now, Doctor, did you ever
17 attempt to reenact the wounds?
18 A. No, I did not.
19 Q. Did you ever determine that each
20 wound could physically be done by Ellen even if
21 she was capable of movement?
22 A. I -- can you rephrase the
23 question, please?
24 Q. Sure. First I asked you, did

Page 52
1 length of Ellen's arm or fingers, et cetera,
2 would facilitate such a wound, correct?
3 A. I did not do that.
4 Q. All right. Now, would you agree
5 with me, however, if there was a wound or more
6 than one wound that Ellen could not physically
7 do, that this could not then be a suicide as
8 manner of death, correct?
9 A. If that could be absolutely
10 proven. I don't exactly know how you would do
11 that, though, to prove that fact.
12 Q. I'm not asking that. My
13 question to you, sir, is, if it could be proven
14 that one or more of the wounds that Ellen
15 sustained could not have been inflicted by
16 her --
17 MS. BERKOWITZ: Objection.
18 BY MR. PODRAZA:
19 Q. -- would you agree with me that
20 the manner of death as suicide would be
21 improper or incorrect?
22 A. It would just mean she . . .
23 (Pause)
24 I -- I would have to agree.

Page 51
1 you ever reenact the wounds, and your answer
2 was no.
3 Is that correct?
4 A. That's correct, I never
5 reenacted the wounds.
6 Q. All right. And you also then
7 didn't do anything to physically determine that
8 Ellen could physically administer each of the
9 wounds, correct?
10 A. To my knowledge, in my opinion,
11 I didn't believe that there was any reason, but
12 for the fact that she would be incapacitated,
13 that she would not be able to do so.
14 Q. But you did nothing beyond just
15 simply believing that. In other words, you
16 took no steps to support it through an analysis
17 or beyond that, correct?
18 A. No --
19 MS. BERKOWITZ: Objection.
20 A. (Continuing) -- I did not.
21 BY MR. PODRAZA:
22 Q. All right. So you never took,
23 for instance, the knife and attempted to see
24 what angles it would be at and whether the

Page 53
1 Q. Now, what I'd like to now do
2 is -- oh, by the way, the autopsy report that
3 you just reviewed, can we agree that this was
4 the final report that you completed, correct?
5 A. That's correct.
6 Q. The report went through
7 different iterations prior to it becoming
8 final; is that correct?
9 A. Please rephrase what you mean by
10 "iterations".
11 Q. In other words, when you
12 generated the autopsy report, as time went on,
13 you would add some information on that you may
14 not have known previously, correct?
15 A. The report is final when it is
16 finalized. It's just a working document until
17 that point.
18 Q. That's a good way to put it.
19 So within the computer system in
20 the Medical Examiner's Office, you had a
21 working document that was generated on or about
22 January 27, 2011, and that proceeded until it
23 became this final work product; is that right?
24 A. That's correct.

Page 54

1 MR. PODRAZA: Okay. Now, I'd
2 like to show you what we are going to
3 mark as Osbourne 3.
4 Will, can we have Osbourne 3,
5 please?
6 MR. TRASK: (Screen sharing
7 document.)
8 - - -
9 (Whereupon, Exhibit Osbourne 3
10 is marked for identification.)
11 - - -
12 BY MR. PODRAZA:
13 Q. And this is the Findings and
14 Opinions that was completed by you; is that
15 correct, sir?
16 A. Correct.
17 Q. All right.
18 A. On January 27.
19 Q. Right. This is pre-amendment,
20 correct?
21 A. This is pre-amendment,
22 pre-report being written.
23 Q. So there is no autopsy report at
24 this time; is that correct?

Page 55

1 A. No. The procedure in
2 Philadelphia was to create a findings document
3 at the completion of the autopsy, documenting
4 findings and what your cause and manner of
5 death were, if you could determine that at the
6 time.
7 Q. I see.
8 A. So this is -- this was done for
9 every single case after the autopsy is
10 performed.
11 Q. I see. So this -- what I mean
12 by "this," we're looking at Osbourne 3 -- was
13 actually completed and generated on January 27,
14 2011, post-autopsy, correct?
15 A. Correct. On the bottom of the
16 page is a printed date that verifies that.
17 Q. All right. But the autopsy
18 report would still be in a -- what do you call
19 it? -- a non-final condition; is that correct?
20 A. Yes, the actual report would be
21 non-finalized at that point. Yes.
22 Q. Okay. And you make reference
23 to, "There is an incised wound to the right
24 occipital scalp."

Page 56

1 Is that the gash on the -- on
2 Ellen's head?
3 A. Yes.
4 Q. Why were you making reference to
5 that in your Findings and Opinions?
6 A. Because the distinction between
7 a stab wound and an incised wound, an incised
8 wound has dimensions that are longer on the
9 skin surface than it is deep. That is a
10 different type of wound. That's why it was
11 singled out separate from the other described
12 stab wounds to the chest, abdomen and back of
13 the neck. Because stab wounds have a depth
14 than is greater than their -- than their
15 dimensions on the skin surface.
16 Q. Well, I guess my -- my question
17 is a little bit more general, not the
18 terminology that you used.
19 Maybe the best way to present it
20 is this: When you were indicating your
21 findings, were you highlighting those which
22 you believed supported the conclusion of
23 homicide?
24 A. Yeah -- as it is listed, yes,

Page 57

1 those are the findings that I believed
2 supported homicide at the time.
3 Q. Okay. And you concluded
4 homicide with all the information that we
5 reviewed earlier in this deposition that you
6 got from the investigator, from the synopsis
7 and the completion of the autopsy, correct?
8 A. Correct.
9 Q. Now, I'd like to get into a
10 little bit more detail then with Dr. Rorke.
11 We're now post-autopsy, we're post-Findings and
12 Manners (sic), which is Osbourne 3, and you
13 determined homicide.
14 Why did you want to speak -- or
15 take me from there. How does Dr. Rorke become
16 involved?
17 A. Dr. Rorke becomes involved
18 because I described injury that I was
19 obviously -- that was grossly seen was a defect
20 to the dura. The question, in fact, was
21 whether the spinal cord was injured.
22 I, in my training at that time,
23 did not feel confident to make that
24 determination by myself. So in discuss -- in

APPENDIX H

1 consultation with my chief and the other
2 doctors, it was decided to have Dr. Rorke
3 evaluate it.
4 Given the time frame in that
5 period of time and the weather conditions, I
6 decided to take the spinal cord to Dr. Rorke's
7 office, which was located in her pathology
8 department at Children's Hospital of
9 Pennsylvania, which was right across the -- it
10 was not very far. It was a walkable distance.
11 However, she would have had to
12 walk across the parking lot, and there had been
13 some heavy snow. So the concern was, it would
14 be easier for me, a younger person, to walk
15 across that distance.
16 So I took the spinal cord to her
17 to have her look at the spinal cord to see if
18 there's distinct injuries to it grossly.
19 Q.   Was that the sole purpose for
20 the examination by Dr. Rorke?
21 A.   Yes.
22 Q.   Did you tell Dr. Rorke at that
23 time that the individual subject to the autopsy
24 had 20 separate stab wounds?

1 correct?
2 A.   I am aware of that, yes.
3 Q.   All right. Dr. Gulino described
4 sometimes there are full detailed examinations
5 by a neuropathologist and sometimes there's
6 what he called a curbside examination.
7 Were you requesting a curbside
8 examination by Dr. Rorke?
9 A.   Yes, that's what -- that's
10 what's . . .
11 Q.   And that's essentially a
12 look-see, but not fully thorough in the
13 completion of the exam, correct?
14 A.   Well, it's -- sometimes we
15 answer a specific question. And in this case,
16 it was, was this injured?
17 Q.   Well, did Dr. Rorke do either
18 histologic or microscopic examination?
19 A.   No, she did not.
20 Q.   Doesn't the cut of a spinal cord
21 versus cut of the sheath require histologic
22 microscopic examination?
23 A.   Again, the reason I did bring it
24 to Dr. Rorke was to have her evaluate it for

1 A.   Well, I mean, I did discuss the
2 case with her and told her she had a cluster of
3 wounds to the back of her neck, yes, and one of
4 the -- one of them caused this injury.
5 Q.   Had you had prior interactions
6 with Dr. Rorke?
7 A.   Yes.
8 Q.   And in those prior interactions,
9 had Dr. Rorke generated a written report
10 following her completion of her examination?
11 A.   Those prior interactions
12 occurred in our office during our scheduled
13 neuropathology brain-cutting sessions. And the
14 entire setup was there for her to do so.
15 So those -- up until that point,
16 that was the extent -- the exposure I had had
17 to Dr. Rorke and the process.
18 Q.   And did she generate a report
19 after each time you had interaction with her
20 regarding an autopsy?
21 A.   Regarding the case that she
22 evaluated, yes.
23 Q.   You're aware that there's no
24 report generated in this case by Dr. Rorke,

1 that purpose. I believe if she could not have
2 made that determination, she would have gone
3 ahead with the histology.
4 Q.   I asked you -- my question was,
5 based on your experience, would you agree that
6 the determination of whether the spinal cord
7 was cut or just the sheath would require
8 histologic microscopic examination?
9 A.   I wouldn't say it requires it in
10 every single instance, no.
11 Q.   You're saying that Dr. Rorke was
12 comfortable giving you an opinion on the
13 condition of the spinal cord without histologic
14 microscopic examination?
15 A.   That is what occurred.
16 Q.   How long was this meeting with
17 Dr. Rorke?
18 A.   I would be guessing if I offered
19 a time frame. It was more than five minutes,
20 likely less than an hour and a half. I don't
21 know exactly how long it lasted.
22 Q.   Well, from the time that you
23 handed the specimen to Dr. Rorke to examine to
24 the time Dr. Rorke gave you her opinion, what

Page 62

1 would be the approximate amount of lapsed time?
2 MS. BERKOWITZ: Objection.
3 A. Again, I can't give you an exact
4 amount of time. I don't recall exactly how
5 long we were there in discussion while she
6 dissected the spinal cord personally.
7 BY MR. PODRAZA:
8 Q. Was the -- was a determination
9 being made by Dr. Rorke an important one in
10 your assessment of this case?
11 A. It was an important question
12 that I'd like -- I would want -- I wanted
13 answered, yes.
14 Q. And because of its importance,
15 didn't you want her to do a thorough
16 comprehensive examination so that you would
17 know that what she was relaying to you was
18 correct?
19 A. I believed I was doing the
20 appropriate thing by having her examine it,
21 and to her discretion determine what
22 examination needed to occur, as I am not a
23 neuropathologist.
24 Q. So is it your testimony that you

Page 63

1 left it to Dr. Rorke to elect the methodology
2 she would employ in examining the specimen in
3 order to give you an opinion as to whether the
4 spinal cord was involved or not?
5 A. That would be correct, as I do
6 with all consultants.
7 Q. How often had you consulted with
8 Dr. Rorke when she did a curbside versus a
9 fully comprehensive examination?
10 A. For my cases, I can only recall
11 that one. I don't know if she's done it for
12 others.
13 Q. Now, even assuming that
14 Dr. Rorke had told you that the spinal cord was
15 not involved due to the cut, she certainly
16 confirmed your finding that the dura was cut,
17 correct?
18 A. Correct.
19 Q. All right. Did you ask
20 Dr. Rorke what would be her belief of the
21 consequences of the dura being cut to Ellen?
22 A. I believe I did. And besides
23 the discussion of pain to varying degrees,
24 there was no -- there was -- she did not -- I

Page 64

1 was not -- there was no indication that she
2 would not have or have lost any motor function.
3 She did indicate it might possibly have led to
4 a decreased sensation, but no loss -- not
5 necessarily a loss of motor function, as I
6 recall.
7 Q. But you say decrease in
8 sensation. I asked Dr. Gulino that question as
9 to whether a cut of the dura would generally
10 make a person less -- could lead them to not
11 feel pain, and he said no.
12 Are you suggesting that the cut
13 of the dura could render --
14 A. The screen is frozen.
15 Q. -- someone incapable of feeling
16 pain so that they could continue to
17 self-inflict without feeling pain?
18 MR. PODRAZA: Doctor, I think
19 you've frozen.
20 MS. BERKOWITZ: He's frozen.
21 THE WITNESS: The screen was
22 frozen for there -- for a moment. I'm
23 sorry.
24 THE COURT REPORTER: Repeat

Page 65

1 that, Joe, because --
2 MS. BERKOWITZ: Can you repeat
3 that question, Joe?
4 MR. PODRAZA: Can you read that
5 back?
6 THE COURT REPORTER: No. Joe,
7 he was talking over you at one point and
8 I think you should repeat it.
9 BY MR. PODRAZA:
10 A. I asked Dr. Gulino the question
11 as to whether a cut of the dura could render
12 someone incapable of feeling pain, and he said
13 no.
14 Do you agree or disagree --
15 MS. BERKOWITZ: Objection.
16 BY MR. PODRAZA:
17 Q. -- with his statement?
18 A. I agree with it. When you're
19 dealing with pain, when I say sensation, it's
20 tactile or like touch, not pain.
21 Q. So what you're saying is,
22 Dr. Rorke confirmed that Ellen Greenberg could
23 have still had the use of the movement of her
24 arms?

Page 66

1   A.   Correct.
2   Q.   But Dr. Rorke didn't say to you,
3   oh, and in addition to that, the cut to the
4   dura would have -- could have --
5   A.   The screen is frozen again.
6   MR. PODRAZA: Let's see when he
7   comes back.
8   MS. BERKOWITZ: Do you want him
9   to leave and come back in?
10   MR. PODRAZA: I'll leave it
11   to -- you know, we've been at this now
12   for like a little over an hour. Maybe if
13   we take a ten-minute break --
14   MS. BERKOWITZ: Okay.
15   MR. PODRAZA: -- and he'll be
16   able to log back in.
17   MS. BERKOWITZ: Okay. All
18   right. I'm going to call him and let him
19   know. Okay.
20   THE VIDEO TECHNICIAN: The time
21   is 1:15 -- or, I'm sorry, the time is
22   11:49. We are going off the video
23   record. This concludes media unit one.
24   - - -

Page 68

1   examination, correct?
2   MS. BERKOWITZ: Objection.
3   A.   Correct.
4   BY MR. PODRAZA:
5   Q.   All right. And the conclusion,
6   according to you, by Dr. Rorke was that Ellen
7   would have been able to move her extremities
8   despite the cut to the dura, correct?
9   A.   Correct.
10   Q.   And Dr. Rorke never said to you
11   that in addition, the cut to the dura would
12   have rendered Ellen without feeling so that the
13   subsequent wounds would not have been felt by
14   her, correct?
15   A.   That's correct.
16   Q.   Now, I'm -- just for my own
17   edification, if the status of the spinal cord
18   was of such importance to you, why didn't you
19   ask Dr. Rorke to do a full, thorough
20   examination versus the curbside examination?
21   MS. BERKOWITZ: Asked and
22   answered, I believe.
23   A.   I at that time left the
24   discretion of the examination to the

Page 67

1   (Whereupon, a recess was taken
2   from 11:49 a.m. to 12:05 p.m.)
3   - - -
4   THE VIDEO TECHNICIAN: The time
5   is 12:05. We are on the video record.
6   This begins media unit two.
7   BY MR. PODRAZA:
8   Q.   Okay. Doctor, unfortunately,
9   your screen froze just before our break. So I
10   just want to clean up my understanding of your
11   testimony.
12   First, according to you, you
13   went to Dr. Rorke to examine the spinal column
14   specimen of Ellen to determine if the cut to
15   the dura involved the spinal cord, correct?
16   A.   Correct.
17   Q.   And the reason you did that is
18   because if the spinal cord was involved, that
19   could factor into whether it's a homicide or
20   not, correct?
21   A.   Correct.
22   Q.   All right. And the examination
23   by Dr. Rorke was what we would call the
24   curbside examination versus a thorough full

Page 69

1   consultant.
2   BY MR. PODRAZA:
3   Q.   Did you make it clear to
4   Dr. Rorke that there was time for her to
5   evaluate the specimen in the manner that she
6   felt best in order to thoroughly determine the
7   condition of the spinal column?
8   A.   I don't believe that I had to
9   explicitly say that to her. I had had dealings
10   with her before. However, they were in a
11   different context or location.
12   At the time in my practice, I
13   believed that if I'm showing the specimen to
14   the consultant, they needed to do, to their
15   discretion, what needed to be done to provide
16   an answer for the question being asked.
17   Q.   Well, Doctor, can we at least
18   agree that notwithstanding the opinion you
19   claim Dr. Rorke gave you --
20   MS. BERKOWITZ: Objection.
21   BY MR. PODRAZA:
22   Q.   -- the cut of the dura still
23   could have been done by an attacker, not Ellen,
24   correct?

Page 70
1   A.   I don't understand your
2   question.
3   Q.   Sure. By the opinion that
4   Dr. Rorke gave you, that doesn't definitively
5   establish that Ellen cut the dura, correct?
6   A.   It does not definitively
7   establish -- it only informs me as to the
8   amount of damage that was done to the spinal
9   cord, as was the question, and whether or not
10 Ellen could con -- could potentially have the
11 use of her upper extremities to -- past that
12 point of receiving that injury.
13 Q.   And it doesn't tell you who cut
14 the dura, correct?
15 A.   It does not.
16 Q.   And, therefore, even after your
17 discussions with Dr. Rorke, the dura could have
18 been cut by an attacker, correct?
19 A.   That wasn't the scope of
20 understanding what -- that wasn't the scope of
21 the question that was being pre -- posed to
22 Dr. Rorke.
23 Q.   But the information that she
24 relayed to you did not discount the possibility

Page 72
1   occur?
2   A.   I don't recall, but it had to
3   have been sometime after toxicology was
4   received, to have a complete discussion of all
5   the information that was gathered, prior to
6   amending the case to suicide. The meeting
7   happened prior to amending the case to suicide.
8   Q.   How --
9   A.   And all of the information would
10 have been presented by both sides at that
11 meeting.
12 Q.   And how soon before the
13 amendment was made to your findings as to the
14 manner of death did this meeting with the
15 police department and District Attorney's
16 epresentative occur?
17 A.   I don't -- I don't even recall
18 exactly the time frame between having Dr. Rorke
19 look at the spinal and having this meeting. I
20 really don't.
21 Q.   Is it possible, then, that the
22 meeting with the police department and the
23 District Attorney representative occurred
24 before you sought a consult by Dr. Rorke?

Page 71
1   of an attacker causing that wound to the dura,
2   correct?
3   A.   That specific information did
4   not, in a general way, discount that, no.
5   Q.   Now, I'd like to -- well, let
6   me -- in a chrono -- from a chronological
7   standpoint, when you claim you spoke with
8   Dr. Rorke or met with Dr. Rorke, was that
9   before or after the meeting with the
10 Philadelphia Police Department and the
11 representative from the DA's office?
12 A.   To the best of my knowledge, I
13 believe that was before.
14 Q.   And how -- how long before the
15 meeting with the police and the DA's office did
16 this meeting you claim occur with Dr. Rorke?
17 A.   Again, I believe I showed
18 Dr. Rorke -- or I brought the spinal cord to
19 Dr. Rorke days after or within a week after the
20 autopsy being performed. I don't recall ten
21 years later specifically what day it was.
22 Q.   Okay. And then how far
23 afterward did the meeting with the Philadelphia
24 Police Department and the DA representative

Page 73
1   A.   No, because I had the
2   information from Dr. Rorke to give -- to
3   discuss with them.
4   Q.   Then my question was, when you
5   amended the findings to suicide as the manner
6   of death, how far earlier did you meet with the
7   police department and the representative from
8   the District Attorney's office? Was it days?
9   Weeks? Months?
10 A.   It --
11 MR. PODRAZA: I believe he's
12 frozen again.
13 A.   (Continuing) It was likely a
14 week.
15 Am I frozen?
16 BY MR. PODRAZA:
17 Q.   You were, but you did come back.
18 A.   Oh, good.
19 Q.   Now, prior to the meeting, had
20 you decided to amend the determination, the
21 manner of death, and change it from homicide to
22 suicide?
23 A.   Prior to the meeting?
24 Q.   Yes. And this is the meeting

Page 74

1 with the police department and the
2 representative from the District Attorney's
3 office.
4 A. Actually, the meeting of the
5 case was pending for the additional
6 information. So the potential to amend it was
7 always there once the case was pending.
8 Q. Well, my question to you is,
9 based on the information you had at the time
10 you were going to that meeting, had you decided
11 to change the manner of death from homicide to
12 suicide?
13 A. To the best of my knowledge, I
14 don't know that I made a definitive decision
15 prior to that meeting to change it.
16 Q. Then at the meeting, what is the
17 best of your recollection of what was said by
18 each of the participants?
19 A. As I stated earlier, I discussed
20 the findings I had -- interaction I had with
21 Dr. Rorke regarding the spinal cord. The
22 investigative officers reviewed and answered
23 questions regarding the scene yet again, about
24 the door and the -- offering information about

Page 76

1 could -- and I don't know exactly how to say
2 that. I don't want to say itemize or --
3 basically collect all the evidence that
4 supports homicide and weigh it against whateve
5 evidence supports suicide, to see how I
6 would -- to see which determination I would
7 make.
8 Q. Now, what about the scene did
9 the police department or the representative
10 from the DA's office share with you that you
11 did not already know?
12 A. Again, I don't know that there's
13 anything specifically that we discussed that
14 they provided that I did not already know
15 versus re -- going over again and verifying
16 what was already collected by our investigator
17 through their investigation. I can't speak to
18 specifics that they gave.
19 Q. Did you -- this was an important
20 meeting, correct?
21 A. Yes.
22 Q. Did you create a record in
23 writing of the meeting and what was being
24 shared, what was new, what was already known,

Page 75

1 the boyfriend having had the, I believe, front
2 desk person witness him breaking down the door,
3 to verify that.
4 Additionally, and I'm not
5 certain if the actual final DNA information was
6 given to me at that time or they -- having been
7 told it was forthcoming at that time. I'm not
8 certain.
9 And additionally, discussing
10 with Dr. Gulino what to weigh -- or to decide
11 and weigh out exactly what information,
12 findings would support or are leaning towards
13 or support or confirm a homicide versus a
14 suicide, and to take it upon myself to weigh
15 out both scenarios based upon the information
16 and all of the information gathered and the
17 autopsy findings at that point.
18 Q. So --
19 A. And then to come to a conclusion
20 based upon that information.
21 Q. But you hadn't come to a
22 conclusion at the meeting; is that correct?
23 A. No. We were exchanging
24 information, thus to get to the point where I

Page 77

1 and, you know, the discussions that occurred
2 among the group?
3 A. I don't have -- I don't have
4 notes from that meeting, no.
5 Q. Why not?
6 A. I do not have meeting – notes
7 from that meeting.
8 Q. Why not?
9 A. I do not have notes from that
10 meeting.
11 Q. And my question to you is, if
12 it's such an important meeting, why is there no
13 written record that can then be included so
14 that we would know what information was being
15 shared at that time, to assess how it is that
16 you will ultimately reach a conclusion?
17 A. To answer your question, I
18 personally did not take notes at that meeting.
19 However, all of the information gathered was
20 documented in other forms elsewhere. I did not
21 take notes at that meeting. I do not have any
22 notes to refer to regarding that meeting.
23 Q. What then about the door were
24 you told at that meeting that you didn't

Page 78
1   already know?
2   A.   Again, I believe it was just
3   confirming that the door, even though the
4   photographs were there and Mr. Olszewski's
5   interpretation was that it was broken in, it
6   was also the police's opinion that it was also
7   broken in.
8   Q.   And that was information you
9   already knew at the time you had determined
10 that this was a homicide, correct?
11 A.   I knew what Mr. Olszewski had
12 provided through photographs and his
13 interpretation.
14 Q.   Okay. And that was just -- and
15 the police were just corroborating what
16 Mr. Olszewski had told you predetermination of
17 the manner of death being a homicide, correct?
18 A.   Correct.
19 Q.   And then you mentioned that the
20 boyfriend had been accompanied by a member of
21 the personnel at the front desk.
22 Was that new information
23 supplied to you at that meeting?
24 A.   I'm -- not new. I believe

Page 80
1   having accompanied the boyfriend.
2   MS. BERKOWITZ: Again, objection
3   as to form.
4   MR. PODRAZA: Why don't you let
5   me finish the question, please, Counsel.
6   BY MR. PODRAZA:
7   Q.   So is it fair that perhaps the
8   information about somebody accompanying the
9   boyfriend was supplied by the police department
10 or the representative from the DA's office at
11 the meeting we're talking about?
12 A.   I believe it was corroborated by
13 someone at that meeting. I believe
14 Mr. Olszewski -- and I don't know if it's a
15 conversation I had prior to autopsy or just
16 after autopsy with Mr. Olszewski regarding the
17 door, that that information I did receive
18 verbally. But I do not believe that I
19 definitively knew that until I saw his report.
20 And then subsequently, that's what was also
21 given to me by the police who were
22 investigating.
23 Q.   Definitively knew what?
24 A.   That someone was present when

Page 79
1   Mr. Olszewski had mentioned that. I'm not
2   certain if it was in his report. But it was
3   also corroborated at that meeting.
4   Q.   And the reason I ask is, when
5   you look at the synopsis, there's no mention of
6   somebody accompanying the boyfriend to the
7   apartment. And if you'd like, we can put up
8   the synopsis. But then later in the completed
9   Olszewski report, there is that reference. And
10 I was wondering if that means then that the
11 information of the -- somebody accompanying the
12 boyfriend was --
13 MS. BERKOWITZ: Object to the
14 form. That was about three questions.
15 THE WITNESS: I'm sorry. And
16 like half of that was frozen for me.
17 BY MR. PODRAZA:
18 Q.   My question is, I'm trying to
19 understand when the information about somebody
20 accompanying the boyfriend was given to you.
21 Because when you look at the synopsis, there's
22 no reference to anybody accompanying the
23 boyfriend. But the final report by
24 Investigator Olszewski does reference somebody

Page 81   1   the boyfriend broke the door down.
2   Q.   And was that an important fact
3   being shared with you?
4   A.   It --
5   Q.   I'm sorry?
6   A.   It adds to the circumstances.
7   Q.   How so?
8   A.   Because when we're dealing with
9   the determination -- determining if someone did
10 something to themselves versus someone else
11 doing something to them, there has to be a way
12 of that other person to be present in that
13 space.
14 Thus far, looking at the scene
15 investigation, the house was orderly. Nothing
16 was disheveled. Nothing was stolen. They
17 lived on a very high -- on a high floor. The
18 only other access to the apartment would have
19 been, I believe, through the balcony, which was
20 closed. And I don't believe anyone could have
21 gotten there through that.
22 So the only way to enter the
23 room would be through the front door. And with
24 that particular security lock, as I asked more

Page 82
1 than once, could it have been possible to lock
2 it from the inside and not be in the room, I
3 was told no. It's not possible to have that
4 security latch on and somehow leave it -- leave
5 the apartment with that latch still in place.
6 So that's why it was important
7 to find out if it was broken, if anyone was
8 there to see it be broken, or is it just the
9 story we're getting from the decedent's
10 boyfriend that it was broken by him.
11 Q. So would it be fair to say that
12 the corroboration of somebody accompanying the
13 boyfriend made you maybe trust more the
14 information that was being conveyed?
15 A. From the boyfriend?
16 Q. Yes.
17 A. Yes.
18 Q. You also said that there may
19 have been DNA information shared at the
20 meeting.
21 Do you recall the nature of that
22 information that would have been shared?
23 A. I can't recall specifically
24 whether they had the report at the time or

Page 84
1 be able to defend either determination, and it
2 had to be based upon the information that was
3 collected or had been provided. And going from
4 the position of homicide, what salient features
5 or information was still pointing towards
6 homicide versus all the information that was
7 collected that doesn't support or does not
8 validate that decision.
9 If I'm equivocal on both, I
10 should be determining it as undetermined. But
11 if there is no information that you have a
12 question about that's still lingering that
13 supports your homicide determination, at that
14 point weigh that against the information that
15 you have that supports suicide or does not
16 exclude suicide.
17 Q. And did Dr. Gulino indicate,
18 directly or indirectly, his views on how he
19 would have weighed the evidence with respect to
20 determining manner of death?
21 A. I don't believe he specifically
22 gave me what he thought he would call it. He
23 left it up to me to decide what to call it, but
24 be careful in making sure that whatever you

Page 83
1 whether they told me the report was
2 forthcoming. I can't remember.
3 Q. Now, when did you have your
4 conversation with Dr. Gulino about marshaling
5 the considerations with respect to a
6 determination or amendment of the manner of
7 death?
8 A. It was, I believe, at least two,
9 possibly -- at least two conversations. Part
10 of it happened during that meeting. And then
11 sometime after that meeting, when I had
12 received all the information, again the
13 discussion was to evaluate all of the
14 circumstances and evidence that points to
15 homicide and weigh it against all of the
16 evidence and circumstances that point to
17 suicide, if there are -- if there were any at
18 that point based on --
19 Q. And I appreciate the summary of
20 the discussions with Dr. Gulino. But can you
21 be more specific? What did Dr. Gulino express
22 to you about the evidence and manner of death?
23 A. Dr. Gulino expressed that in
24 making this determination, that I would need to

Page 85
1 call it, you can defend your decision, because
2 unduly -- if you call it -- if it remains
3 homicide, someone could be unduly incarcerated
4 and/or wrongful charges adjudicated against
5 them if you do not have enough to clearly
6 support homicide.
7 Q. Did Dr. Gulino share with you
8 knowledge or an awareness of the boyfriend of
9 Ellen's?
10 A. I don't understand your
11 question.
12 Q. That he was aware of or he knew
13 Sam Goldberg or the Goldberg family?
14 A. I -- that's news to me. I never
15 had knowledge of him knowing that family
16 whatsoever.
17 Q. Did he express any -- did he
18 express to you having had discussions with
19 others, besides just the police department
20 representatives or the representative from the
21 DA's office, about the case, outside of the
22 Medical Examiner's Office?
23 A. To my knowledge, no, I'm not
24 aware of any conversations with anyone else.

Page 86

1   Q.   Did you discuss the case with
2   others in the office?
3   A.   Yes, I discussed the case with
4   my colleagues, the other associate medical
5   examiners.
6   Q.   And who would that be?
7   A.   I'm sorry? I presume –
8   Q.   Who would that be?
9   A.   That would be Dr. Gary Collins,
10   Dr. Aaron Rosen and Dr. Edward Lieberman.
11   Q.   Was there anybody else in the
12   Medical Examiner's Office that you discussed
13   the case with, like investigator or other
14   personnel?
15   A.   Mr. Olszewski, the investigator.
16   Beyond that, no, not in particular. No, I
17   don't recall discussing it with anyone else in
18   the office.
19   Q.   When did you discuss it with
20   Drs. Collins, Lieberman and the other
21   gentleman?
22   A.   Well, every day after the
23   autopsy was performed. I believe at that time,
24   our afternoon meeting was at 2:00 p.m. The

Page 87

1   cases were presented and we discuss
2   determination of cause and manner of death.
3   So the case was then during that
4   meeting with them present. And throughout the
5   course of the two months it took to finalize --
6   two or three months it took to finalize the
7   case, I would have had at least one or two
8   conversations with each of them as to the case
9   and the information I had at the time.
10   I can't recall specific
11   conversations with individuals about a singular
12   case ten years later after doing thousands of
13   cases.
14   Q.   Well, give me your best
15   recollection of what the other doctors were
16   saying to you about the determination of the
17   manner of death in Ellen's case.
18   MS. BERKOWITZ: Objection.
19   A.   I really honestly can't recall
20   their individual positions on the case. I
21   think the consensus initially was that it was
22   very, very weird. Although we do have a scene
23   that doesn't lend itself to someone else being
24   there present, that's why the presence of the

Page 88

1   wounds on the neck and the injury was unique.
2   And so that is why the position
3   of homicide was kind of held because sans any
4   other information letting us know that someone
5   else -- well, let me rephrase.
6   The opinion of homicide based
7   upon the autopsy findings initially outweighed
8   what we were discovering in the actual scene
9   investigation based -- just based upon the
10   unique nature of the wound pattern, if that is
11   understandable.
12   Q.   Yes. Let me just see if I can
13   break that down, perhaps, into layperson terms.
14   If I understand what you just
15   said, that if you look just at the autopsy
16   anatomical features of Ellen, that would weigh
17   towards homicide, correct?
18   A.   Correct.
19   Q.   But then when you take into
20   account the other information that you're being
21   supplied with the scene, that made you adjust
22   what you would otherwise have just been viewing
23   as the manner of death just based on the
24   anatomical characteristics, correct?

Page 89

1   A.   Well, I mean, it's not simply
2   just -- it's the -- any and all cases are
3   usually taken -- you take into consideration
4   the autopsy findings, which they themselves
5   don't necessarily always define exactly what
6   the cause or manner of death is, but also the
7   scene investigation.
8   And, again, a majority of the
9   time, some determinations that are made based
10   on autopsy findings have consistent
11   circumstances that go along with it.
12   Here, the circumstances of the
13   scene investigation and all of the other
14   information collected did not hold up against
15   just the unique pattern that we're seeing in
16   this particular case.
17   And so that was the dilemma, to
18   decide or discern what still, outside of just
19   the autopsy, supported homicide versus is there
20   anything that would dis -- anything from the
21   autopsy that rules out suicide completely
22   and/or in addition to all of the other
23   information that does not support homicide.
24   Q.   You yourself didn't do any

Page 90
1   independent investigation as to the accuracy of
2   the information you were given about the scene,
3   correct?
4   THE WITNESS: Frozen again.
5   MR. PODRAZA: I think they need
6   better Wi-Fi in Florida.
7   THE VIDEO TECHNICIAN: Counsel,
8   do you want to go off the video record
9   while he figures that out?
10 THE WITNESS: I'm sorry.
11 MR. PODRAZA: Are we back?
12 THE WITNESS: We're back. I'm
13 sorry, I don't know what's going on with
14 my signal. It doesn't look like it's
15 going in and out. I don't know why it
16 keeps freezing.
17 MR. PODRAZA: Doctor, I think
18 you have to tell your employer you need
19 better Wi-Fi.
20 THE WITNESS: Well, I'm not
21 in -- I was working at home, which it
22 should be fine.
23 THE VIDEO TECHNICIAN: Counsel,
24 we are still on the video.

Page 92
1   would have to factor. It's information that's
2   pertinent to the case.
3   Q.   And how would it have factored
4   into your determination?
5   A.   The possibility that someone
6   else could be in the room would still be there.
7   Q.   And would you then have changed
8   your initial determination of homicide to
9   suicide if those were the facts?
10 A.   If those were the facts, then I
11 don't know if I would go and -- and re -- I
12 don't know if I would go to undetermined or I
13 would leave it homicide. I'm not certain. But
14 those were not the facts presented to me.
15 Q.   I understand that.
16 And my next question to you is,
17 if information had been supplied to you which
18 drew into question whether the fiancé was
19 accompanied by someone else, where the fiancé
20 had broken through the door, whether the lock
21 was engaged at the time Ellen was being
22 stabbed, would that also have factored in and
23 kept you from changing the manner of death from
24 homicide to suicide?

Page 91
1   MR. PODRAZA: All right.
2   BY MR. PODRAZA:
3   Q.   Do you remember my last
4   question, Doctor?
5   A.   I do not, no.
6   Q.   All right. My last question
7   was, you yourself didn't independently
8   investigate the accuracy of any of the
9   information you were being supplied, what
10 you're calling scene investigation, correct?
11 A.   No. I rely upon my
12 investigators and the police and what's
13 collected as evidence and information from them
14 to make determinations in all cases.
15 Q.   Okay. So if, for instance,
16 the -- the fiancé was not accompanied by
17 another person, the fiancé did not break
18 through the door, the lock was not engaged at
19 the time Ellen was being stabbed, would those
20 considerations have factored into your ultimate
21 determination on the manner of death in this
22 case?
23 A.   If those were the -- if that was
24 information collected, and it would factor. It

Page 93
1   A.   I don't think I understand your
2   question.
3   Q.   In other words, you -- well,
4   I'll try to -- I'll try to articulate this
5   better.
6   If -- if you were told there was
7   a question as to whether the fiancé was
8   accompanied by someone, whether the fiancé
9   broke through the door, whether the lock was
10 engaged when the wounds were administered to
11 Ellen, if those were in question and not
12 decided, would you have changed your initial
13 determination of homicide to suicide while
14 those questions remained open?
15 A.   No, I would not. I would then
16 have somewhere closer to undetermined if those
17 things are still in question. But that was not
18 the case.
19 Q.   No, I understand.
20 And who was relaying to you that
21 it was without question that the fiancé was
22 accompanied by a security guard, it was without
23 question that the fiancé broke through the
24 door, and it was without question that the lock

Page 94

1 was engaged at the time Ellen was being
2 wounded? Who told you that?
3 A.   That information was told to me
4 by Mr. Olszewski and also from the
5 investigating officers.
6 MR. PODRAZA: I hate to do this,
7 but I think I may have to take a bathroom
8 break. I don't know. I have a little
9 bit more to go. I didn't know if we
10 wanted to do a lunch break or . . .
11 You know, Doctor, I don't want
12 to impose too much on your time. Are
13 there any thoughts? Do we want to take
14 maybe a 20-minute break for lunch and
15 resume after that?
16 MS. BERKOWITZ: That's fine.
17 THE WITNESS: That's fine.
18 MR. PODRAZA: Or do you want to
19 do it --
20 MS. BERKOWITZ: Is that okay,
21 Dr. Osbourne?
22 THE WITNESS: Yes, that's okay.
23 MR. PODRAZA: Do you want to
24 resume at 1:15? That gives a half an

Page 96

1 to revisit the -- your Report of Examination or
2 what I call the autopsy report, which we've
3 marked as O-2, Osbourne 2.
4 Where in the document do you
5 indicate --
6 A.   Yes.
7 Q.   -- the time of death?
8 A.   The time -- this document
9 doesn't have the first page. So that would be
10 on the very first page.
11 The document, I forget, it was
12 Osbourne 3, that was done on the day of
13 autopsy. And the demographic paragraph at the
14 top has the time of death.
15 MR. PODRAZA: Could we have
16 Osbourne 3?
17 A.   (Continuing) There should be a
18 separate (Zoom audio glitch) one for this
19 report.
20 THE VIDEO TECHNICIAN: Doctor, I
21 didn't catch your answer. I heard "a
22 separate," and then it cut out.
23 A.   (Continuing) There should be a
24 separate accompanying first page, similar to

Page 95

1 hour, basically?
2 THE WITNESS: Yes.
3 MS. BERKOWITZ: That's fine.
4 Thank you.
5 MR. PODRAZA: All right. That
6 sounds great. Thank you.
7 THE VIDEO TECHNICIAN: The time
8 is 12:38. Going off the video record.
9   - - -
10 (Whereupon, a luncheon recess
11 was taken from 12:38 p.m. to 1:15 p.m.)
12   - - -
13 THE VIDEO TECHNICIAN: The time
14 is 1:15. We are on the video record.
15 BY MR. PODRAZA:
16 Q.   Good afternoon, Doctor. I'd
17 like to revisit what I'm calling the autopsy
18 report, which was Osbourne 2.
19 MR. PODRAZA: I think he's
20 frozen.
21 BY MR. PODRAZA:
22 Q.   Are you with us, Doctor?
23 A.   I am now.
24 Q.   All right. As I said, I wanted

Page 97

1 the previous exhibit, that goes along with this
2 report and the date it was signed.
3 BY MR. PODRAZA:
4 Q.   Am I correct, Doctor, you said
5 that Osbourne 3 would contain the answer to the
6 question?
7 A.   I believe that that was the
8 Findings and Opinions that you showed me
9 earlier? Yes.
10 Q.   We should have that up for you
11 in a moment.
12 A.   Okay.
13 Q.   All right. Doctor, where then
14 on Osbourne 3 will we find the indication of
15 the time of Ellen's death?
16 A.   The date and time is at the top,
17 towards the right. (Zoom audio glitch.)
18 January 26th 6:40 p.m. by
19 Medic-5 at the address.
20 Q.   Well, that's when she was
21 declared dead, correct?
22 A.   Yes.
23 Q.   I'm asking you, when was the
24 time of her death?

Page 98

1   A.   That is the time of death.
2   Q.   She would have been dead before
3   6:40 p.m., correct?
4   A.   The time of death that we use is
5   the time of death when someone pronounces
6   someone dead. Did she die -- could she have
7   died before that time? Yes. But the official
8   time of death is the time of pronouncement.
9   Q.   So your understand --
10   A.   (Simultaneous talking.)
11   Q.   I'm sorry, sir. Your
12   understanding, then, of that date and time is
13   when, in fact, Ellen expired?
14   A.   That is the recorded date and
15   time of death, yes.
16   Q.   And did you have any indication
17   as to when one or more of the wounds was
18   inflicted on Ellen based on your evaluation at
19   autopsy?
20   A.   Before that time on that date.
21   Q.   And how --
22   A.   If you're asking how far in
23   advance of that time?
24   Q.   Yes.

Page 100

1   Office makes at the scene?
2   A.   They describe the rigor
3   mortis -- their interpretation of rigor mortis
4   and livor mortis. And all of that is taken
5   into context with the body positioning, the
6   body habitus, to possibly give an estimated
7   time of how long someone had been dead (Zoom
8   audio glitch).
9   But we don't -- we can't always
10   say --
11   THE COURT REPORTER: I'm sorry.
12   A.   (Continuing) -- if it's been an
13   amount of --
14   THE COURT REPORTER: I'm sorry.
15   A.   (Continuing) -- time that
16   passed --
17   THE COURT REPORTER: I'm sorry.
18   I'm sorry. I'm sorry. You're cutting in
19   and out. You're cutting in and out.
20   Maybe call in?
21   THE WITNESS: Do you want me to
22   call in instead of digital?
23   MR. PODRAZA: We can hear you
24   now.

Page 99

1   A.   I'd have to refer to
2   Mr. Olszewski's scene investigation. I did my
3   examination of her body on the following day.
4   And so any of the signs that we look for to try
5   to figure out or narrow down exactly the -- the
6   changes in the body since the time of death
7   would not necessarily be accurate on my
8   examination of the body in the morning, hours
9   after this had occurred.
10   Q.   Okay.
11   A.   So that's why -- another reason
12   why investigators go to scenes, and they're
13   there as soon as possible, when the body is
14   pronounced, to assess those things such as
15   rigor mortis, livor mortis, which all have to
16   be taken into context with the body and the
17   activity that could have preceded their death,
18   their body habitus. There's a lot of different
19   factors that go into it.
20   So they're just estimation or
21   best guesses, if we do have those things to go
22   by to determine how long someone had been dead.
23   Q.   And that's a determination that
24   the investigator from the Medical Examiner's

Page 101

1   THE WITNESS: Okay.
2   BY MR. PODRAZA:
3   Q.   Let me just follow up, and
4   perhaps it's more of a nomenclature.
5   There's a difference, as I
6   understand your testimony, between how long
7   someone's been dead and the time of death; is
8   that correct?
9   A.   There may be. I'm just trying
10   to answer the question you posed to me, if the
11   time that's recorded as her date and time of
12   death was when she actually died.
13   Q.   Okay. And what would we look at
14   in order to determine if and when the wounds
15   were administered to Ellen?
16   A.   I don't understand your
17   question. The wounds were obviously
18   administered before that date and time.
19   Q.   Right. And as the pathologist,
20   isn't it your job to make an estimate as to
21   when the stabbing or the wounds occurred, to
22   the best of your medical judgment?
23   A.   In what context?
24   Q.   Well, you called it a homicide.

Page 102

1 Didn't you want to -- isn't it important in a
2 homicide to have an indication of when the
3 incident occurred?
4 A. That's created from timelines of
5 information gathered through investigation as
6 to when the person was last known alive, last
7 person to see them, when they were discovered,
8 when they were pronounced, and also factoring
9 in what the investigators record as their
10 interpretation of the rigor mortis, livor
11 mortis at the time of death.
12 Q. Well, the -- we can turn to --
13 well, let me just ask you this way: As you sit
14 here today, did you ever make a determination,
15 within a reasonable degree of medical
16 certainty, as to when the wounds to Ellen
17 approximately occurred on January 26, 2011?
18 A. In what context do you want me
19 to give you? Within hours or minutes or . . .?
20 Q. Whatever context you provided
21 it. Did you ever make that determination?
22 Prior to -- prior to when she was declared
23 dead, did you give your best medical judgment
24 as to when Ellen sustained the stab wounds that

Page 104

1 discovered, and the other factors such as rigor
2 mortis, livor mortis, if someone was there to
3 assess those things at the time of their
4 discovery.
5 Q. And if rigor mortis was found in
6 the hands, would that help assess from the time
7 of the finding or that determination as to when
8 the stabbing occurred?
9 A. In general terms, rigor mortis
10 can set in anywhere between two to four hours.
11 It's fixed by six hours and goes away by
12 hours. That's the general terms. But,
13 again, things like body habitus, activity prior
14 to death, health prior to death, whether
15 they're affected or not, ambient temperature,
16 all the things factor into how fast rigor
17 mortis can set in and/or become fixed and then
18 go away. So everything is taken into context.
19 Q. If we could go back to the
20 autopsy report, which is Osbourne 2.
21 A. Yes.
22 Q. Page 5 of the report.
23 MR. PODRAZA: Will, if we can
24 have that.

Page 103

1 presented on autopsy?
2 A. The injuries that Ellen
3 occurred -- sustained occurred on that day, to
4 the best of my ability. I cannot narrow down
5 the specific hour or the time other than
6 looking at the timeline from the last time she
7 was heard or spoken to, to when she was
8 discovered --
9 Q. But my question was --
10 A. -- which would be a few hours –
11 which would be within a few hours.
12 Q. -- did you -- did you anywhere
13 record that information? In other words, that
14 determination, based on a reasonable degree of
15 medical certainty, as to when you best, under
16 the circumstances, believed the stabbing
17 occurred?
18 A. That information is not
19 generally recorded specifically in any one
20 particular place. When asked and questioned,
21 the interpretation of how long someone -- when
22 something could have occurred is done by taking
23 into context the last time they were known
24 alive, when they were discovered, how they were

Page 105

1 MR. TRASK: (Screen sharing
2 document.)
3 MR. PODRAZA: And if we can go
4 down to "Other Injuries."
5 MR. TRASK: (Scrolling.)
6 BY MR. PODRAZA:
7 Q. Doctor, do you see the section
8 that you dictated of "Other Injuries"?
9 A. Yes.
10 Q. Okay. They make references to
11 bruises throughout Ellen's body, correct?
12 A. Correct.
13 Q. And can we agree that there were
14 extensive bruises across Ellen's body in
15 varying degrees of healing?
16 A. There were bruises across her
17 body in various degrees of healing, yes.
18 Q. And they were found on her legs,
19 correct?
20 A. On her, according to the report,
21 they were found on her right thigh, above the
22 right knee, on the right forearm and the right
23 upper arm --
24 Q. And --

APPENDIX H

Page 106
1 A. -- and the lower quadrant of the
2 abdomen.
3 Q. Could the bruising pattern
4 reflect abuse that she had sustained?
5 A. I -- without -- the bruising is
6 blunt trauma to the body. I do not know how it
7 was inflicted, when it was inflicted, because
8 the majority of the bruising appears to be
9 resolving and/or going through changes which
10 happened sometime before that day.
11 Q. Did you make any inquiry
12 whatsoever to be able to assess the possible
13 significance of the bruising on Ellen's body?
14 A. I don't understand your
15 question.
16 Q. Well, did you make any inquiries
17 as to whether she was involved in physical
18 activities that could lead to bruising, things
19 of that nature, to kind of assess what the
20 cause of the bruising was?
21 A. I believe I had asked the
22 investigator to find out, through talking to
23 the family, about anything -- if they knew
24 anything about the bruising.

Page 108
1 minute.
2 (Pause)
3 THE VIDEO TECHNICIAN: I'm going
4 to go off the video record.
5 MS. BERKOWITZ: No, he's back.
6 THE VIDEO TECHNICIAN: Oh.
7 MS. BERKOWITZ: He's back and
8 moving.
9 THE WITNESS: The screen keeps
10 freezing.
11 MR. PODRAZA: And I think you
12 just froze again.
13 THE WITNESS: I did for a
14 second, yes.
15 MR. PODRAZA: Okay. Can you
16 hear me now, Doctor?
17 THE WITNESS: I can hear you,
18 yes.
19 BY MR. PODRAZA:
20 Q. Okay. Doctor, when you issued
21 your Findings and Opinions and indicated manner
22 of death as homicide, you included as one of
23 the significant findings, "Multiple contusions
24 on upper and lower extremities in various

Page 107
1 Again, I don't think our efforts
2 to speak to the boyfriend were met
3 successfully. And that would have been a
4 question I would have had the investigator ask
5 him. But I don't know that any answer was ever
6 garnered from the boyfriend at that time
7 regarding the bruising.
8 Q. Did the bruising have any
9 significance to you medically?
10 A. Medically? It indicates that
11 there was a blunt trauma that she received to
12 those parts of her body. And because they're
13 in varying stages, it did not all happen at the
14 same time.
15 Q. But yet you indicated, when you
16 ruled the manner of death to be homicide, you
17 made specific reference to the bruising as one
18 of the factors in support of the homicide.
19 Why did you do that?
20 THE WITNESS: Am I frozen again?
21 MS. BERKOWITZ: Is he frozen?
22 THE VIDEO TECHNICIAN: Yes, his
23 video is frozen again.
24 MS. BERKOWITZ: Give him a

Page 109
1 stages of resolution."
2 Why did you include that
3 finding?
4 A. Because it was an autopsy
5 finding. Any and all trauma that's documented
6 is listed in the findings section.
7 Q. And did you believe that that
8 finding was supportive of your determination of
9 homicide?
10 A. That -- those individual
11 findings themselves?
12 Q. Well, maybe not individually.
13 A. In and of themselves, I don't
14 think they -- in and of themselves, they
15 indicated that she sustained trauma prior to –
16 at some point in time before her death. And, I
17 mean, the majority of them were resolving, so
18 (Zoom audio glitch) days before her death.
19 I don't know that I specifically
20 had the thought that those contributed to the
21 determination of homicide at that time.
22 THE COURT REPORTER: You cut out
23 and I'm missing parts of the testimony.
24 I don't know if anyone else was hearing

Page 110
1   it. I'm sorry.
2   MR. PODRAZA: Matt, were you
3   able to catch it on video?
4   THE VIDEO TECHNICIAN: No.
5   There was definitely a part in the middle
6   of his testimony that cut out.
7   BY MR. PODRAZA:
8   Q.   Doctor, I apologize, we're going
9   to have to ask you to re-answer the question.
10 A.   Repeat that?
11 Q.   Yes.
12 A.   Okay. So can you repeat the
13 question? I'm sorry.
14 MR. PODRAZA: Sure.
15 MS. BERKOWITZ: Could you read
16 back the question?
17 MR. PODRAZA: Yes, if you would,
18 Cheryl.
19 MS. BERKOWITZ: Thank you.
20 (Pause)
21 THE WITNESS: Hello?
22 MS. BERKOWITZ: She's going to
23 read it back.
24 THE COURT REPORTER: I'm finding

Page 112
1   Q.   Did you biopsy any of the
2   bruises?
3   A.   No, I did not.
4   Q.   Why not?
5   A.   Because as stated, the majority
6   of them were in states of -- various stages of
7   healing. They were resolving. So I did not
8   believe that they were pertinent to or related
9   to the actual acute injuries that she sustained
10 at the time of death.
11 Q.   Doctor, could the bruises have
12 indicated defensive injuries?
13 MS. BERKOWITZ: Objection.
14 A.   I do not believe --
15 BY MR. PODRAZA:
16 Q.   You may answer.
17 MS. BERKOWITZ: You can answer.
18 A.   No. Because the majority of
19 them were not sustained at the time of the
20 injuries because they had resolution, meaning
21 that they were sustained at some point in time
22 prior to when the stab wounds were inflicted.
23 BY MR. PODRAZA:
24 Q.   Well --

Page 111
1   it.
2   THE WITNESS: Okay. I'm sorry.
3   I thought I froze again.
4   - - -
5   (Whereupon, the court reporter
6   read back the following:
7   "QUESTION: And did you believe
8   that that finding was supportive of your
9   determination of homicide?
10 "ANSWER: That -- those
11 individual findings themselves?
12 "QUESTION: Well, maybe not
13 individually.")
14   - - -
15 A.   (Continuing) Okay. So the
16 bruising that is described I don't necessarily
17 believe strengthened or weakened the opinion to
18 determine that it was homicide. They were
19 findings that were documented because they were
20 present in the autopsy, the significance of
21 which I could not ascertain because of the fact
22 that they were -- the majority of them were
23 resolving.
24 BY MR. PODRAZA:

Page 113
1   A.   Because I believe the stab
2   wounds were inflicted that day. And you
3   wouldn't get that level of resolution in the
4   majority of those bruises in just a day.
5   Q.   How about those which were of
6   more recent vintage, did they support or could
7   they possibly support a finding of defensive
8   injuries?
9   A.   Bruises I don't typically
10 consider to be specifically defensive injuries,
11 especially when there's a sharp or penetrating
12 object that could be -- that is used as the
13 weapon.
14 In those cases, the majority of
15 the time in my cases that I have seen, when
16 they are sharp or penetrating injury, the
17 defensive wounds or the wounds on the parts of
18 the body that someone would use to defend
19 themselves would have sustained sharp force
20 injuries, if a sharp object was used.
21 And conversely, if a gun was
22 used, a penetrating or graze-type gunshot wound
23 would be associated in those areas that they
24 would use to defend themselves.

Page 114
1 MR. PODRAZA: Doctor, I'd like
2 to show you what we're going to mark as
3 Osbourne 8. And these are photographs
4 from the time of autopsy.
5   - - -
6 (Whereupon, Exhibit Osbourne 8
7 is marked for identification.)
8   - - -
9 BY MR. PODRAZA:
10 Q.   Do you recognize the tag,
11 Doctor?
12 A.   Yes, I do.
13 Q.   All right. And do you see that
14 there's a bruise above the tag, correct?
15 A.   Correct.
16 Q.   All right. And was it per your
17 direction that the photograph was taken?
18 A.   Yes.
19 Q.   All right. And if -- if what
20 you were photographing was insignificant, you
21 wouldn't have wasted the time of the technician
22 to take the picture, correct?
23 A.   Injuries that are documented on
24 the body are photographed.

Page 115
1 Q.   Regardless of whether you think
2 they're significant or not?
3 A.   Yes.
4 Q.   What does the photograph depict
5 to you?
6 A.   In this photograph? I think the
7 actual focus of the photograph is not
8 necessarily the contusion, because we don't see
9 the full scope of the contusion. I think it's
10 more of the palm of the hand --
11 Q.   Okay. Well --
12 A.   -- and the fingertips.
13 Q.   -- we'll continue here because
14 the photograph is like a series.
15 Do you see that focus is on the
16 bruise?
17 A.   That is more -- that's more on
18 the bruise.
19 Q.   Correct. And in your opinion,
20 when you were doing the autopsy, what was your
21 understanding as to the cause of that bruise?
22 A.   A blunt trauma.
23 Q.   Caused by what?
24 A.   I do not know.

Page 116
1 Q.   Did you do any type of
2 investigation to try to find out?
3 MS. BERKOWITZ: Objection.
4 A.   Specifically for that particular
5 bruise? No.
6 BY MR. PODRAZA:
7 Q.   Would you agree with me that
8 that bruise is of recent vintage?
9 A.   It is -- appears to be more
10 recent than the other bruises, yes.
11 Q.   Did it occur to you, Doctor,
12 that perhaps it also indicates that Ellen's
13 wrists were restrained and that the bruise
14 reflects, perhaps, pressure of a thumb
15 restraining her arms?
16 A.   It appears to be round. I do
17 not believe that it singularly represents any
18 type of restraint, per se --
19 MR. PODRAZA: Could we see the
20 next one?
21 A.   (Continuing) -- just by a single
22 digit.
23 BY MR. PODRAZA:
24 Q.   And how --

Page 117
1 A.   The other bruises --
2 Q.   Would that demonstrate to you,
3 Doctor, the possibility that Ellen was
4 restrained, her arms were restrained, and
5 that's a bruise that resulted from the
6 restraint of her arms?
7 A.   I did not appreciate that or
8 think of that, think that that was the case
9 related to that particular bruise.
10 Q.   Upon reflection now, do you
11 believe it's possible that that bruise reflects
12 perhaps restraint of Ellen's arms?
13 A.   Upon reflection, there's
14 actually three bruises that are distinctly seen
15 there. Two have resolved or almost completely
16 resolved and there is one recent one.
17 So, again, that might be an area
18 that might have been involved in some sort of
19 restraint outside of that day. And so I cannot
20 place exactly what caused that specific bruise,
21 the darker red one that you are referring to.
22 Q.   Would you agree with me, Doctor,
23 that the -- the purpose of an autopsy, however,
24 is to try to determine as many answers to what

Page 118

1   happened to the victim as possible?
2   A.   To the best of my ability, yes,
3   it is.
4   Q.   And do you agree with me that it
5   would be important to explore the possibility
6   that the victim was restrained at the time of
7   the incident?
8   A.   A single bruise on the forearm
9   does not indicate to me a pattern of restraint.
10   MR. PODRAZA: Can we see the
11   next photograph?
12   MR. TRASK: (Screen sharing
13   photograph.)
14   MR. PODRAZA: And then the next
15   photograph?
16   MR. TRASK: (Screen sharing
17   photograph.)
18   MR. PODRAZA: Is that it? If
19   you go up.
20   MR. TRASK: (Scrolling.)
21   BY MR. PODRAZA:
22   Q.   In addition to the single
23   bruise, there seems to be bruises towards the
24   palm.

Page 120

1   (Whereupon, Exhibit Osbourne 5
2   is marked for identification.)
3   - - -
4   BY MR. PODRAZA:
5   Q.   Doctor, I want to show you
6   another photograph from the autopsy.
7   A.   Okay.
8   Q.   Do you recognize the anatomy?
9   A.   Yes. That's the front of the
10   neck dissection.
11   Q.   So it's the front of the neck of
12   Ellen; is that correct?
13   A.   Yes, it is.
14   Q.   All right. And the skin's been
15   peeled back, correct?
16   A.   The skin has been peeled back,
17   yes.
18   Q.   All right. And what is the
19   impression in the center of the photograph?
20   A.   It's an area of hemorrhage on
21   top of the -- it looks like anterior neck
22   muscles -- well, anterior neck, deep to the
23   anterior neck muscles, because those have been
24   reflected and are upward in the photograph.

Page 119

1   Do you see that there, Doctor?
2   A.   Vaguely, faintly, yes. I -- if
3   you're talking about the bottom of the
4   photograph that's not a clean photograph, then
5   yes --
6   Q.   And --
7   A.   -- as opposed to the one that's
8   being photographed higher up on the wrist.
9   Q.   In your opinion, is it possible
10   that those bruises are demonstrating restraint
11   of Ellen?
12   A.   I can't say definitively that
13   they are or not -- or are not.
14   Q.   But in your differential
15   diagnosis, wouldn't you include the possibility
16   of restraint based upon those bruises being
17   present?
18   A.   As I said, I cannot say I know
19   that they are or not.
20   MR. PODRAZA: Can I have
21   Photograph 5?
22   MR. TRASK: (Screen sharing
23   photograph.)
24   - - -

Page 121

1   Q.   Just so that we understand,
2   there's no stab wound that's being depicted
3   here, correct?
4   A.   No, it's not a stab wound.
5   Q.   All right. Is the hemorrhage,
6   as far as you understand, caused by pressure on
7   Ellen's neck?
8   A.   It's caused by blunt trauma that
9   results from breaking of vessels --
10   Q.   And could that --
11   A.   -- in that area.
12   Q.   And could that possibly have
13   been cause -- can that occurrence happen when
14   somebody places their hands around someone's
15   neck and exerts great force on the neck?
16   A.   You can get hemorrhages of the
17   neck when there is strangulation or not.
18   Q.   Did you consider whether this
19   hemorrhage demonstrated or a part of the
20   differential diagnosis included strangulation?
21   A.   If you mean "consider," did I
22   recognize that this possibly could be? And I
23   would say yes. But, again, when you have
24   strangulation, there are other things that come

APPENDIX H

1 into play. If the person -- if -- given the
2 person that is not particularly incapacitated,
3 there would be other things that are associated
4 with strangulation. They would show more than
5 one single spot of hemorrhage on top of the
6 muscle, which is what this depicts.
7 Q.   Well, let me ask you this,
8 Doctor: If there's no wound here, meaning no
9 stab wound, why autopsy this part of her
10 anatomy?
11 A.   As a part of a complete autopsy,
12 looking at a neck dissection, especially in the
13 case of potentially maybe a homicide, is
14 routinely -- well, it's part of my routine to
15 do.
16 Q.   Were you able to rule out
17 strangulation of Ellen; and if so, how?
18 A.   Strangulation by itself
19 typically would not have just one single -- one
20 single area of hemorrhage. Potentially it can.
21 But the majority of the cases of strangulation
22 have, to varying degrees, petechiae of the
23 conjunctiva of the eyes, petechiae on the face.
24 You have marks on the neck, anterior/posterior.

1 about it?
2 A.   Yes, it would be.
3 Q.   Now, Doctor, would you agree
4 with me that if Ellen had been strangled or at
5 least incapacitated by somebody placing great
6 force on her neck in order to create that
7 hemorrhage, that that would not constitute a
8 suicide?
9 A.   If that were the case.
10 Q.   Okay. And would you agree with
11 me that if, at the time the wounds that Ellen
12 sustained, someone was restraining her arms,
13 would that also be a factor militating or going
14 against a finding of suicide?
15 MR. PODRAZA: I'm sorry, sir, I
16 think you froze again.
17 THE WITNESS: Am I frozen again?
18 MR. PODRAZA: You are. I'm
19 sorry, you're going to have to repeat
20 your answer.
21 I think you froze again, sir.
22 THE WITNESS: Yeah, I was
23 waiting for it to see if I was frozen
24 again.

1 You can have fractures of the hyoid bone. You
2 can have fractures of the thyroid cartilage.
3 You can have more extensive hemorrhages within
4 and -- within and on top of the muscles of the
5 anterior neck.
6 And so in context to this case,
7 with all these other sharp force injuries, a
8 single spot of hemorrhage on the muscle did not
9 equate to me to strangulation --
10 Q.   Am I correct --
11 A.   -- or a component of it.
12 Q.   I'm sorry, Doctor, I didn't mean
13 to interrupt.
14 Am I correct that nowhere in
15 your autopsy report is there any discussion
16 about the possibility of strangulation?
17 A.   Not in the report, there is no
18 discussion of a possibility of strangulation.
19 Q.   And if you had considered that
20 as being a possibility, would that be something
21 that you would normally include in your
22 report --
23 A.   Yes.
24 Q.   -- and have a discussion with

1 A.   You were asking about the
2 bruising on the arms and if that would -- I'm
3 sorry?
4 BY MR. PODRAZA:
5 Q.   If, at the time the wounds were
6 being inflicted on Ellen, her arms were
7 restrained, would you agree that that would go
8 against the finding of suicide?
9 A.   If I -- if her arms are being
10 restrained, that would go against suicide, yes.
11 Q.   Now, having raised these issues
12 with you, would you think that further
13 investigation as to whether strangulation
14 occurred, at the time of what happened to Ellen
15 occurred, should be done?
16 And maybe that's an inartful
17 question.
18 A.   As I was saying earlier, a
19 single spot of hemorrhage on a neck muscle does
20 not equate to strangulation. There are other
21 things that people take into consideration that
22 usually are [present when someone has been
23 strangled, especially if there is nothing to
24 incapacitate them. Therefore --]

Page 126
1 THE COURT REPORTER: Excuse me.
2 You touched the speaker, I think, on the
3 pad, and you went out.
4 THE WITNESS: Oh, I'm sorry.
5 THE COURT REPORTER: I'll read
6 what I have.
7   ---
8 (Whereupon, the court reporter
9 read back the following:
10 "ANSWER: As I was saying
11 earlier, a single spot of hemorrhage on a
12 neck muscle does not equate to
13 strangulation. There are other things
14 that people take into consideration that
15 usually are --")
16   ---
17 A. (Continuing) -- external signs
18 of injuries on the neck. There's the petechiae
19 that I explained earlier of the conjunctiva, on
20 the face itself. And in some instances, there
21 are more extensive hemorrhages within the
22 actual layers of the anterior strap muscles.
23 And additionally, there's also at times
24 fractures of the hyoid bone and/or thyroid

Page 128
1 A. I said we don't know what caused
2 them.
3 Q. All right. Well, Doctor, I'd
4 like to go back to your autopsy report. And in
5 particular, I'd like to draw your attention to
6 the section titled, "External Examination,"
7 which is Page 1 of your report.
8 A. Yes.
9 MS. BERKOWITZ: Can you pull it
10 up, please?
11 MR. TRASK: (Screen sharing
12 document.)
13 BY MR. PODRAZA:
14 Q. Do you see that section there,
15 Doctor?
16 A. Yes.
17 Q. The second full sentence is,
18 "The atraumatic scalp is covered by brown
19 hair."
20 Have I read that accurately?
21 A. Yes, you read that accurately.
22 Q. All right. And "atraumatic"
23 means no trauma, correct?
24 A. That's correct.

Page 127
1 cartilage.
2 Those additional things, the
3 only finding that was salient in this case to
4 the neck anteriorly was that spot of hemorrhage
5 on that particular muscle, which in and of
6 itself does not equate to strangulation --
7 BY MR. PODRAZA:
8 Q. So you would not even --
9 A. -- in my opinion. In my
10 opinion, it does not.
11 Q. So you would not even include
12 the possibility of strangulation based on the
13 hemorrhage within your differential diagnosis?
14 A. Not that one singular spot of
15 hemorrhage, no.
16 Q. Now, you saw the wrists and the
17 bruises on the wrist. I thought we established
18 that within your differential diagnosis, you
19 would include the possibility of restraint.
20 Am I correct or incorrect?
21 A. I believe you're incorrect. I
22 do not believe that those constitute restraint
23 patterns.
24 Q. Okay. If we go back --

Page 129
1 Q. Now, I'd like to draw your
2 attention to your description of wound "J", as
3 in Joseph.
4 A. Yes.
5 Q. Do you see that there, sir?
6 A. Yes, I do.
7 Q. It's described as an "Incised
8 Wound 'J' of Scalp," meaning a cut of the
9 scalp, correct?
10 A. That's correct.
11 Q. And can we agree that --
12 A. So "atraumatic" was a
13 typographical error.
14 Q. I'm sorry, I didn't catch that.
15 I'm sorry, Doctor.
16 A. The description of the scalp in
17 the external examination was a typographical
18 error.
19 Q. All right. So we can agree that
20 the scalp, in fact, had --
21 A. The description of the scalp
22 being atraumatic would be a typographical
23 error.
24 Q. Is that because of, you know,

Page 130

1 boilerplate language that exists that just gets
2 lifted? Is that the result of why there's a
3 typographical error? Or was that part of
4 dictation just not being accurately –
5 A. It was something that should
6 have been corrected, and it was a typographical
7 error.
8 THE WITNESS: I think I'm frozen
9 again.
10 MS. BERKOWITZ: No, you're not.
11 THE WITNESS: I'm sorry, was
12 there a question? Because I think I
13 froze there.
14 MR. PODRAZA: No, no. That's
15 quite all right.
16 THE WITNESS: Okay.
17 BY MR. PODRAZA:
18 Q. Do -- did any of the wounds –
19 well, let me step back.
20 When we deposed Dr. Gulino, we
21 discussed that at least one of the wounds
22 involved the vertebral-basal artery system.
23 Do you agree with that?
24 A. Yes.

Page 132

1 A. There is no real way to remove
2 that area of the brain without, to some degree,
3 affecting that system in removing the brain.
4 And so I removed the brain in the fashion that
5 I always have, with care, the results of which
6 is the photographs that subsequently followed
7 of the brain that were taken after it was
8 removed.
9 You can't -- sometimes you can't
10 preserve everything the way you're taking it
11 out. Some things are observed inside too, and
12 then you take out -- you have to take it out to
13 examine it further.
14 And so I -- to answer your
15 question, I removed it in the fashion that I am
16 normally used to removing the brain. Now,
17 every brain is different and there may be some
18 difficulties removing brains at times. So you
19 can't factor in or account for that. But the
20 job is to examine all parts of the body,
21 including the brain, so it has to be done.
22 Q. Can you show where in your
23 autopsy report you indicate that you examined
24 the basal artery, vertebral artery and found no

Page 131

1 Q. Okay. And on autopsy, the brain
2 was removed from the skull, correct?
3 You may be --
4 A. You're breaking up. I'm sorry.
5 Q. Okay. Upon autopsy, the brain
6 was removed from the skull, correct?
7 A. Correct.
8 Q. All right. Who removed the
9 brain from the skull?
10 A. Excuse me. I did.
11 Q. And in doing so, did you invoke
12 or follow care not to disturb the
13 vertebral-basal artery system?
14 A. I'm sorry, you're breaking up.
15 Q. Can you hear me now?
16 A. I didn't get the full
17 question --
18 Q. That's all right.
19 A. -- if you asked one.
20 Q. Oh, okay. Well, my question
21 was, in removing the brain, were you careful to
22 not disturb the vertebral-basal artery system,
23 given the fact that it might be involved with
24 one of the wounds?

Page 133

1 cut or damage to either?
2 A. It would be in the
3 neuropathology section at the end of the
4 report.
5 MR. TRASK: (Scrolling.)
6 BY MR. PODRAZA:
7 Q. Okay. And just tell us when you
8 want us to stop, Doctor.
9 A. You can keep going. I think
10 it's the last paragraph.
11 MR. TRASK: (Scrolling.)
12 A. (Continuing) Okay. So that's
13 the examination of those systems, and they have
14 no atherosclerosis or aneurysm.
15 Now, if you go to specific (Zoom
16 audio glitch) that's related to --
17 BY MR. PODRAZA:
18 Q. I'm sorry, Doctor. You froze
19 again. You're going to have to start your
20 answer again, please.
21 A. The basal artery, its
22 tributaries and branches have no
23 atherosclerosis or aneurysm. If there was
24 injury, I would have described it in the

Page 134

1 evidence of injury section related to the stab
2 wound that was associated with that area.
3 So if there is any injuries
4 described, it would be in the area -- evidence
5 of injury section where the stab wounds are
6 described.
7 Q. What would --
8 A. Otherwise, there was no injury
9 identified.
10 Q. Well, Doctor, what would be the
11 consequences of the -- one or both --
12 A. Specifically to the basal
13 artery, there was no injury.
14 Q. My question to you is, if the
15 basal artery --
16 A. I'm sorry, go ahead.
17 Q. Can you hear me?
18 A. Yes.
19 Q. Okay. If the basal artery had
20 been cut, what would have been the
21 consequences?
22 A. There would have been massive
23 hemorrhage in the posterior fossa, like
24 resulting in subarachnoid and subdural

Page 135

1 hemorrhage.
2 Q. And, therefore, whether the
3 artery was cut or not was a significant
4 determination upon autopsy with respect to the
5 consequences of that wound, correct?
6 A. Correct.
7 Q. And if the arteries were intact,
8 you would have specifically noted that, as well
9 as you would have specifically noted if it was
10 cut, correct?
11 A. I would specifically note it if
12 it was cut in the evidence of injury section.
13 Otherwise, the descriptions are as if there was
14 no other trauma, and we're looking for other
15 types of natural disease. Therefore, we're
16 specifically talking about the basal artery,
17 which is a distinct artery that is different
18 than the smaller arteries along the parts of
19 the brainstem and the cerebellum that were
20 described in the evidence of injury as being
21 injured.
22 Those were the only vessels that
23 I appreciated were injured, resulting in the
24 small amount of some focal subarachnoid

Page 136

1 hemorrhage in those areas. It did not extend
2 to the basal artery.
3 Q. Doctor, have you ever received
4 any written warnings or reprimand for the
5 quality of your work when you were at the
6 Philadelphia Medical Examiner's Office?
7 A. No.
8 Q. Were you ever criticized for
9 sloppy recordkeeping?
10 A. No.
11 Q. Ever criticized for incomplete
12 autopsy records?
13 A. No.
14 Q. Were you ever criticized for any
15 discrepancies in your report, like indicating
16 no trauma when trauma was present?
17 A. No.
18 Q. Have you ever had any criticism
19 at all of your work when you were working at
20 the Philadelphia Medical Examiner's Office?
21 A. No, not to my knowledge. No.
22 Q. I would imagine that if you did
23 receive written reprimands or written warnings,
24 that's something you wouldn't forget, right?

Page 137

1 A. Absolutely. So no, I did not
2 have that.
3 Q. All right. And when you were at
4 the Philadelphia Medical Examiner's Office, who
5 was your supervisor?
6 A. When I started there, Dr. Gulino
7 did not have a deputy chief, so he was directly
8 supervising all the associates. And then I
9 forget if it was in 2012 or maybe 2013, he made
10 one of the associates a deputy. So that would
11 have been Gary -- Dr. Gary Collins.
12 Q. Okay. And --
13 A. And I think it was for a year or
14 two years before I left.
15 Q. All right. I'm sorry. From
16 when to when would Dr. Collins, to the best of
17 your knowledge, have been your supervisor?
18 A. At least a year, if not two. I
19 believe Gulino made him deputy sometime in
20 2012. So I think it would be two years or over
21 two years.
22 Q. And before that, your
23 supervisor, I'm sorry, would have been
24 Dr. Gulino?

APPENDIX H

Page 138
1   A.   Dr. Gulino directly, yes.
2   Q.   Do you know where Dr. Collins is
3   presently, since I understand there's been a
4   big turnover in the Medical Examiner's Office
5   since 2011?
6   A.   Oh, there's turnover in every
7   office everywhere. But Dr. Gary Collins is the
8   chief in Baltimore -- no, I'm sorry, not
9   Baltimore -- Delaware currently. He's Chief
10 Medical Examiner in Delaware.
11 Q.   Do you recall, sometime after
12 amending the manner of death from homicide to
13 suicide, having had a telephone call with
14 Dr. Ross?
15 A.   With Dr. Ross, no.
16 Q.   If I suggested that such a call
17 occurred in 2013, would that help refresh your
18 recollection?
19 A.   I do not recall a phone call
20 with Dr. Ross in 2013.
21 MR. PODRAZA: All right. Let me
22 show you what we have marked as
23 Osbourne 7, and maybe this might help.
24 - - -

Page 139
1   (Whereupon, Exhibit Osbourne 7
2   is marked for identification.)
3   - - -
4   BY MR. PODRAZA:
5   Q.   This is an e-mail dated May 14,
6   2013 from Dr. Gulino to "robtom". I'll
7   represent to you that's an individual named Tom
8   Brennan.
9   A.   Yes.
10 Q.   And as you can see there,
11 Dr. Gulino says, "Dr. Ross may contact
12 Dr. Osbourne, who did the autopsy, directly to
13 ask any questions regarding the autopsy or
14 other issues about which he has questions."
15 Do you recall –
16 A.   Yes.
17 Q.   -- ever speaking with Dr. Gulino
18 and being apprised that you might get a call
19 from another pathologist to discuss the -- or
20 discuss Ellen's case?
21 A.   I don't particularly remember
22 that. I do remember -- I don't remember
23 being -- I don't remember any communication
24 directly with a Dr. Ross, per se. And I don't

Page 140
1   have a recollection of the conversation.
2   Q.   What do you have a recollection
3   of?
4   A.   To the best of my knowledge, the
5   only person that I've spoken to was Mr. Brennan
6   on two occasions.
7   Q.   And when were they, you know, to
8   the best of your recollection?
9   A.   One occurred when I was working
10 at Broward County Medical Examiner's Office --
11 well, actually, both occurred then. I believe
12 there was one in -- sometime in 2018. And then
13 I received a second call in 2019, in September,
14 informing me that I would be receiving some
15 paperwork from the family. And that was the
16 extent of that call.
17 Q.   Okay.
18 A.   The one in 2018 was a discussion
19 asking me about the case, to the best of my
20 knowledge, at that time. And he had questions
21 specifically to how the autopsy was performed
22 and information that I had received.
23 Q.   And what questions did
24 Mr. Brennan pose to you?

Page 141
1   A.   He asked about me determining it
2   homicide and then how did it get changed from
3   homicide to suicide. And I explained the
4   police asking for the case to be pending while
5   they continued their investigation.
6   I explained how I had the spinal
7   cord evaluated by Dr. Rorke, how toxicology
8   played a role, the additional information given
9   to me by the police through follow-up
10 investigation. And then how the decision
11 was -- I made the decision based upon the
12 information that I had collected and weighing
13 all the factors involved to make the
14 determination of suicide thereafter.
15 Q.   Is there anything else that
16 occurred in the conversation with Mr. Brennan
17 then?
18 A.   I -- I don't recall any other
19 information.
20 Q.   Do you recall making the
21 representation that you changed the manner of
22 death from homicide to suicide because the
23 police wanted that to be done, or words to that
24 effect?

243

Page 142

1   A.   No. I did state that I made
2   my -- I explained how I made my change, and
3   that it was based upon the information that I
4   collected from the spinal cord injury
5   evaluation by Dr. Rorke and how toxicology came
6   back with no particular drug that would lead to
7   being incapacitated. The fact that I did not
8   believe that someone who was not incapacitated
9   would not have defensive wounds, to some
10   degree, anywhere on her body. And also the
11   fact that there was nothing that would preclude
12   her from continuing to stab herself based upon
13   Dr. Rorke's evaluation and her motor function
14   still being intact.
15   Additionally, the scene does not
16   speak of another person being present in the
17   room, because it was not disheveled, not –
18   nothing was stolen, and the actual statements
19   from the boyfriend and the door and the scene
20   findings, where it doesn't seem like anyone
21   else could have been in the room to inflict
22   those injuries other than Ms. Greenberg
23   herself. And that is how I came to the
24   conclusion of suicide.

Page 143

1   Q.   Doctor, do you know any of the
2   members of the Goldberg family?
3   A.   No, I do not.
4   Q.   Have you ever had any
5   interaction, even indirectly, with any members
6   of the Goldberg family, the Hankin family?
7   A.   No.
8   Q.   How about any interactions,
9   directly, indirectly, with a gentleman by the
10   name of James Schwartzman?
11   A.   Schwartzman. The name vaguely
12   sounds familiar. But I do not recollect what
13   interaction I had at all. It just sounds
14   familiar. I am not certain that I even –
15   yeah, I'm not really certain that I had an
16   interaction with that person. Just that the
17   name sounds familiar.
18   Q.   Did you have any inter -- did
19   you have any interaction with any individuals
20   who were either representatives or agents or
21   otherwise associated with the Goldbergs,
22   Hankins or Schwartzman family?
23   A.   Again, the only person I had
24   spoken to regarding that -- in that regard was

Page 144

1   Mr. Brennan, as he presented himself as a
2   representative for the family.
3   MR. PODRAZA: All right. At
4   this time, if I could just have five
5   minutes. That may be all the questioning
6   I have at this time. But if we could
7   take maybe a ten-minute break.
8   THE WITNESS: Okay.
9   MR. PODRAZA: All right.
10   THE VIDEO TECHNICIAN: The time
11   is 2:09. Going off the video record.
12   This concludes media unit two.
13   - - -
14   (Whereupon, a recess was taken
15   from 2:09 p.m. to 2:29 p.m.)
16   - - -
17   THE VIDEO TECHNICIAN: The time
18   is 2:29. We are on the video record.
19   This begins media unit three.
20   MR. PODRAZA: Thank you, Doctor.
21   At this time, I have no further questions
22   for you.
23   THE WITNESS: Okay.
24   MS. BERKOWITZ: Okay. Great.

Page 145

1   - - -
2   EXAMINATION
3   - - -
4   BY MS. BERKOWITZ:
5   Q.   Doctor, have you had any other
6   cases this old that you've been called to
7   testify about?
8   A.   No. This is the oldest.
9   Q.   Is it fair to say it's hard to
10   remember everything?
11   A.   Oh, yes, that's fair.
12   Q.   All right. Earlier you or
13   Mr. Podraza, I can't remember which, used this
14   term, talked about you and Dr. Gulino
15   marshaling evidence, you know, to support
16   either conclusion. And you -- you also said
17   you talked to your colleagues.
18   Could you discuss this process?
19   A.   The --
20   Q.   Not in this case. In general,
21   right?
22   A.   Okay. So in general, what
23   happens is, most offices are staffed by more
24   than one pathologist. You have a chief, who's

APPENDIX H

1　at the top. You have associates.
2　In my experience, I guess I've
3　been very fortunate, I've had very good
4　colleagues to work with. And everyone is very
5　collegial.
6　Usually there's a meeting
7　where -- at some point in time, either in the
8　morning or in the evening, after cases have
9　been done. The cases are discussed so that
10　everyone is aware, can put in their input.
11　It's been valuable over the
12　years to have different individuals with
13　different backgrounds and different
14　experiences, which only helps to improve your
15　practice by having other perspectives.
16　When I worked in Philadelphia,
17　the doctors that were there were Dr. Gulino,
18　who was chief, who had had several years of
19　experience; Dr. Lieberman, who had had decades
20　of experience; additionally myself and
21　Dr. Rosen, who were pretty new; and Dr. Collins
22　had had a few years of experience. So there
23　was a good mix of different individuals with
24　different experiences.

1　Q.　Okay. So in those meetings, if
2　somebody were off base, what would happen?
3　A.　The -- if someone was coming to
4　the wrong -- well, what might be considered the
5　wrong conclusion or not necessarily evaluating
6　all of the information, there were challenges
7　by not only Dr. Gulino, but other more senior
8　staff to fully assess and look at things from a
9　different perspective, point out things that
10　may need to have been looked at further, what
11　needs to go back -- go back and be done.
12　You know, a lot of times if you
13　came to a conclusion of a case and you didn't
14　do a specific histologic study, they would say
15　go back and do that.
16　You would -- Dr. Gulino
17　practiced in the way of you're never wrong as
18　long as you can justify with some medical
19　knowledge and information how you came to the
20　conclusion you came to and be able to defend
21　it.
22　Q.　Okay.
23　A.　That was the big takeaway from
24　my training, my experience there.

1　Some of the approaches in
2　training styles were similar, because myself,
3　Dr. Gulino and Dr. Lieberman all trained in
4　Miami, which had their own perspective in the
5　way of training and how to attack and look at
6　and assess cases. However, they all came with
7　their other individual, you know, nuances that
8　they learned throughout the years practicing in
9　different offices.
10　I valued -- what happens -- what
11　happened in Philadelphia, for the most part is,
12　in the afternoon, after -- I believe it was
13　2 o'clock, we had a 2 o'clock meeting to review
14　all the cases that had been done and present
15　them to the group and Dr. Gulino. And at that
16　time, anyone who thought that something was
17　missing or omitted or -- would suggest a way of
18　approaching a case, would bring it up at that
19　time. We'd also go over toxicology cases, some
20　of which were easy, some of which were
21　difficult, in that meeting, and then to bring
22　up any other issues going on in the office.
23　And that meeting occurred, usually without
24　fail, every single day, Monday through Friday.

1　Q.　And to be able to defend it,
2　that would be to a reasonable degree of medical
3　certainty?
4　A.　Yes, that's correct.
5　Q.　Okay. You initially concluded
6　that this case was a homicide –
7　A.　Yes.
8　Q.　-- correct?
9　A.　Correct.
10　Q.　And what was the medical
11　evidence? What was your medical evidence to
12　support it being a homicide?
13　A.　The medical evidence supporting
14　it being a homicide, notwithstanding the known
15　circumstances at the time, was the number
16　not necessarily the number, but the dispersion
17　of the wounds in areas -- in an untypical area
18　of the body, the posterior neck.
19　My salient and ongoing question
20　of the injury to the spinal cord that I thought
21　was severe, but to the extent that it actually
22　impacted the spinal cord, I did not know. But
23　that withstanding, also the question of whether
24　the other wounds subsequent to the final wound

Page 150

1   could have been inflicted after sustaining that
2   injury to the spinal cord. And so my initial
3   impression and thought was that it could not.
4   But, again, on reflection and --
5   Q.   Okay. I'll get to that in a
6   minute.
7   A.   Okay.
8   Q.   So is an autopsy -- well, let's
9   go to the spinal cord.
10   What -- did you make an -- did
11   you make an assumption about the cord before
12   you saw Dr. Rorke?
13   A.   Yes.
14   Q.   And what was that assumption?
15   A.   My assumption is that it was
16   injured based on the gross findings at autopsy
17   that I observed.
18   Q.   What did you think that the
19   injury was going -- what was the significance
20   of the injury, in your mind?
21   A.   Well, that's the question I did
22   not know, how significant an injury would be.
23   And it was pointed out that maybe it -- it
24   would behoove me to find out exactly if there

Page 152

1   what is the significance of damage to the
2   spinal cord or there not being damage to the
3   spinal cord?
4   A.   Well, if there was distinct
5   damage to the spinal cord and I was -- and
6   there was no way she could continue to inflict
7   those wounds to herself, it would support it
8   being -- those wounds being inflicted by
9   someone else.
10   Q.   Okay.
11   A.   Especially the actual lethal
12   one, which was the one where the knife was
13   still in her body.
14   If there was -- if there was no
15   injury or the injury was not significant enough
16   to impair her from being able to continue to
17   stab herself, the possibility of suicide still
18   remained.
19   Q.   Okay. Thank you.
20   THE WITNESS: Can I get a pause
21   for a few moments? My tablet is dying.
22   I need to charge it just a bit --
23   MS. BERKOWITZ: Oh, yes.
24   THE WITNESS: -- before we lose

Page 151

1   was an injury, how significant that could have
2   affected Ms. Greenberg's ability to inflict the
3   other wounds to herself and/or, you know, that
4   would then point to someone else inflicting the
5   wounds at that point.
6   And this was all outside of the
7   already known scene investigation, which does
8   not lend to the fact that someone else was
9   there.
10   Q.   Okay. So what question were you
11   trying to answer exactly?
12   A.   If the spinal cord was injured
13   and how severe the injury was. At that time, I
14   had been practicing for about a year and a half
15   outside of fellowship. So the suggestion to
16   bring to someone who has seen several brains
17   and spinal cords was made to -- either to shore
18   up my initial impression and/or necessarily if
19   it was not appropriate, refute that or, you
20   know . . .
21   Q.   And, I'm sorry, I think you're
22   speaking medically.
23   In terms of -- in terms of
24   whether it would be a homicide or a suicide,

Page 153

1   the thing.
2   MS. BERKOWITZ: Okay.
3   THE VIDEO TECHNICIAN: The time
4   is 2:39. Going off the video record.
5   - - -
6   (Whereupon, a discussion was
7   held off the record.)
8   - - -
9   THE VIDEO TECHNICIAN: The time
10   is 2:41. We are on the video record.
11   BY MS. BERKOWITZ:
12   Q.   Dr. Osbourne, we were just
13   talking about Dr. Rorke.
14   Did her response to you inform
15   your determination of suicide --
16   A.   Yes.
17   Q.   -- ultimately?
18   A.   Yes, it did.
19   Q.   Why?
20   A.   In that she did not find direct
21   injury to the spinal cord. And also that
22   also -- that supported the idea that
23   Ms. Greenberg could continue to inflict
24   injuries beyond the one that was that

Page 154

1   particular injury that was sustained to the
2   spinal cord.
3   Given the totality of all the
4   injuries, the majority of the injuries were
5   shallow and did not affect specific individual
6   organs pertaining to the posterior neck, except
7   for the one to the spinal cord and the one that
8   went into the cranium.
9   The -- but the more concerning
10 one for me was the spinal cord injury. And
11 then additionally, the two -- two to the
12 anterior torso went into the actual body
13 cavities.
14 Q.   Okay. You were asked about
15 reenactment.
16   Is this something that you do as
17 standard practice?
18 A.   No, not particularly. And it's
19 a case-by-case basis, when there's a real
20 belief that something could or could not have
21 happened.
22 Q.   Did you have a reason -- is
23 it -- is it mandatory for medical examiners to
24 do a reenactment?

Page 156

1   not tell you how that happened. You need other
2   information to tell you whether the person that
3   pulled the trigger of the gun was the actual
4   individual who is dead or someone else.
5   Q.   And how do you --
6   A.   And so that's -- and we get that
7   information from our medical-legal
8   investigators going to scenes, the police in
9   their investigations, any and all medical
10 information that's pertinent to the decedent.
11 A lot of times, especially when
12 dealing with someone who may have taken their
13 own life, there are other ancillary things.
14 Like we find out if they've ever had mental
15 issues, like depression and/or other mental
16 issues. But those are not the end-all be-all.
17 They're just additive things to help discern
18 whether . . .
19   And also additionally, the
20 characteristics of the described injury also
21 help. So if the contact gunshot wound and the
22 person has -- and the gun is there and it's
23 their residence, those factors add to helping
24 determine it's suicide versus the gun not being

Page 155

1   A.   No, I don't believe it's
2   mandatory.
3   Q.   Did you have a reason to believe
4   that a reenactment was necessary in this case?
5   A.   No. I believe, as I said
6   earlier, I did not think it was not possible
7   for her to reach or stab herself in the area of
8   her neck that was affected. It's -- the
9   question mainly was, after a certain wound to
10 the posterior neck was sustained, could she
11 have continued to injure herself further.
12 Q.   Okay. Could you explain the
13 difference between the cause of death and the
14 manner of death?
15 A.   Okay. So the cause of death is
16 that disease and/or injury that immediately
17 leads to the person's death. The manner of
18 death is something that was created as a matter
19 of statistical tracking, and it basically
20 explains how the injury or disease came about.
21 And so, for example, you can
22 have a gunshot wound to the head. That in
23 and of -- in having -- doing an autopsy with a
24 gunshot wound to the head in and of itself does

Page 157

1   there, it's an open area, nowhere near where
2   they live, and the gunshot wound is not within
3   a certain range to make it clear that the
4   person could have done it themselves. And that
5   would be more of a homicide.
6   Q.   All right. So is it fair to say
7   that it's ordinary for medical examiners or
8   pathologists to consider information beyond the
9   autopsy itself?
10 A.   It's not only ordinary, it's
11 routine and customary. Even in natural deaths,
12 we don't take everything by face value. And
13 the examination doesn't necessarily give us all
14 the information. We do request medical
15 records, talk to family about social history.
16 All of those things factor into making the
17 determination.
18 The --
19 Q.   And --
20 A.   -- prevailing idea is that the
21 autopsy may be about 20 percent of the case and
22 80 percent of the case is circumstances.
23 Q.   Okay. You -- Mr. Podraza asked
24 you about a meeting with the DA and Dr. Gulino

Page 158
1   and the police.
2   What was your understanding –
3   who convened that meeting?
4   A.   I mean, I think Dr. Gulino
5   organized it. But it was something that was
6   understood to occur after we gathered -- after
7   both sides gathered information. And it was
8   coordinated between the SA and Dr. Gulino and
9   the police and myself --
10 Q.   At that --
11 A.   -- for the timing of it.
12 Q.   At that meeting, did the police
13 instruct you to change the manner of death?
14 A.   No.
15 Q.   Did they ask you to change the
16 manner of death?
17 A.   No.
18 Q.   What would your response have
19 been if they had given you such an instruction?
20 A.   I would not have dealt to just
21 them a simple request. Again, every case is an
22 individual case and all of the information
23 needs to be interpreted and weighed to
24 determine what the manner of death or how the

Page 160
1   investigation.
2   Going back, and additionally the
3   homi -- anything that I thought were the
4   salient features to support homicide after
5   reviewing everything was subsequently, in my
6   mind, discounted.
7   The things that I thought would
8   make this a homicide is the fact that somebody
9   else had to be inside the build -- inside the
10 apartment to do this to her. With the
11 affirmation that the door had to be broken in,
12 the lock couldn't have been locked from the
13 inside and someone else be -- get outside of
14 that, and she's the only one found in the
15 apartment, with nothing disturbed, nothing out
16 of place, no other way of getting in there, it
17 doesn't lend to the fact that someone else was
18 there to do it. So that was discounted.
19 The other thing about her not
20 being able to inflict all of the injuries
21 herself was also discounted by review of the
22 spinal cord, where there was no injury and
23 nothing -- and according to Dr. Rorke, she
24 would still be able to use her extremities.

Page 159
1   injury that occurred, to a reasonable degree of
2   medical certainty, could have happened.
3   And so it may have been their
4   instance (sic) or in their minds that they
5   believed it was a suicide at that point. But
6   that was not what I determined at that moment.
7   I took all of the information that was gathered
8   and then sat with the information to see what
9   still supported homicide versus what supported
10 suicide, and if there was anything that would
11 make it equivocal so I could make a
12 determination.
13 Q.   Mr. Podraza asked you about the
14 category could not be determined. You started
15 on one side with homicide and you wound up -- I
16 mean, I guess in my mind, it's a continuum, you
17 wind up on the other side with suicide.
18 Why did you not pick could not
19 be determined?
20 A.   Because at that point, the
21 factors that made me determine that it was
22 homicide mostly are based upon the autopsy
23 findings in lieu of -- not certainly in lieu
24 of, but outside of considering the scene

Page 161
1   So, therefore, there was, in my
2   mind -- unless she was incapacitated, which
3   toxicology also did not support, because the
4   levels of drugs in her system were either in a
5   trace state or very subtherapeutic or low
6   level. So therefore, I do not believe she was
7   incapacitated by drugs to be in a state where
8   she could not, A, fight off an attacker,
9   therefore it explains away the fact -- or
10 supports the -- I mean, not necessarily
11 supports, but she was not in a state where I
12 believe she was incapacitated by either some
13 outside substance, drugs and/or other factors
14 whereby she would not be able to fight off an
15 attacker who was trying to stab her as many
16 times as she had been stabbed. Because no one
17 would stand there and allow themselves to be
18 stabbed that many times but for being
19 incapacitated by drugs or some other means.
20 Q.   Like your concern about the
21 spinal injury?
22 A.   Yes. And not -- yes.
23 Q.   Did you see evidence of
24 restraint in your autopsy?

Page 162

1   A.   I did not believe those bruises
2   were significant enough to come -- or equate to
3   a restraint pattern, in my opinion.
4   Q.   What would a restraint pattern
5   look like generally?
6   A.   Restraint patterns, usually if
7   it's something other than the hands, like a
8   ligature, would leave ligature abrasions,
9   circumferential typically. Hand restraint
10   patterns would lead to bruising more than a
11   single or a -- a single bruise on one side of
12   the hand. It would have to be, in my opinion,
13   several round bruises that some consider
14   consistent with fingers. And, again, things
15   like ligature, like a zip tie or a rope or
16   anything else, would give you some kind of
17   abrasion.
18   Q.   Okay.
19   A.   That would be noted. Again, I
20   didn't appreciate or did not think that
21   restraint was part of this case –
22   Q.   Okay.
23   A.   -- per se.
24   Q.   Thank you.

Page 163

1   A.   Is --
2   THE WITNESS: I think you froze
3   there for a moment.
4   MS. BERKOWITZ: No. I just
5   wasn't talking. Maybe.
6   THE WITNESS: Oh, okay.
7   MS. BERKOWITZ: Okay.
8   BY MS. BERKOWITZ:
9   Q.   Is the death certificate, is the
10   finding of manner of death on the death
11   certificate binding on anyone?
12   MR. PODRAZA: Well, objection.
13   That's going to call for a legal
14   conclusion. But he can answer.
15   BY MS. BERKOWITZ:
16   Q.   In your experience.
17   MR. PODRAZA: Same objection.
18   A.   In my experience, the manner of
19   death, as I said, on the death certificate is
20   an opinion based upon your -- the -- it is an
21   opinion based upon the -- I'm sorry, I just
22   lost my train of thought.
23   BY MS. BERKOWITZ:
24   Q.   The manner of death.

Page 164

1   A.   Is an opinion made by a medical
2   professional based upon their evaluation of all
3   the information, and to a reasonable degree of
4   medical certainty, that's what they feel how
5   the injury occurred.
6   Its main purpose is for
7   statistical purposes, and, therefore, is not
8   definitively or legally binding. It can be
9   changed if and/or there's any new information,
10   upon additional review at any point in time.
11   And so it is again just an opinion.
12   Q.   In your experience, have there
13   been instances where the manner of death said
14   one thing and the District Attorney or the
15   prosecutor in whatever jurisdiction we're
16   talking about took a different view?
17   A.   In, for example, a large amount
18   of cases where we find death, someone is in a
19   car accident, blunt force injuries is the
20   manner -- is the cause of death, the manner of
21   death for us is almost always an accident,
22   unless we know and have evidence and
23   information for a fact that the car was being
24   used as a weapon. Those cases are almost

Page 165

1   always classified as an accident.
2   However, the local jurisdiction
3   can determine that there are other factors
4   involved and charge vehicle homicide to
5   whatever degree they would like.
6   So additionally, there are cases
7   where for us, any time someone else is shot by
8   another person, it's a homicide. But
9   situationally, if an officer is trying to
10   apprehend someone and they fire and kill
11   someone, that may or may not be considered
12   legally a homicide or even adjudicated. And
13   those cases, sometimes they're justifiable.
14   Additionally if you have a home
15   invasion where a person is shot during the home
16   invasion, the invader is shot during the home
17   invasion, then the actual person who shot them,
18   the homeowner, may or may not be charged with
19   that homicide. But for us, it's always a
20   homicide.
21   Q.   Okay. Are you familiar the
22   NAME's guide?
23   A.   The NAME's guidelines? Yes.
24   Q.   What are they?

Page 166
1   A. The NAME stands for the National
2   Association of Medical Examiners. It's the
3   medical body, association body for forensic
4   pathologists. And they put forth guidelines as
5   to the best way to practice and how to approach
6   determining cause or manner of death.
7   Q. Are they binding?
8   MR. PODRAZA: Objection. Calls
9   for a legal conclusion.
10 MS. BERKOWITZ: No, it doesn't
11 call for a legal conclusion. He's a
12 medical examiner. Are they binding on
13 him.
14 MR. PODRAZA: Objection. Still
15 calls for a legal conclusion.
16 MS. BERKOWITZ: You can answer.
17 MR. PODRAZA: Same objection.
18 MS. BERKOWITZ: Except if he's
19 there.
20 THE VIDEO TECHNICIAN: It looks
21 like we lost Dr. Osbourne's video.
22 MS. BERKOWITZ: Well, and audio,
23 apparently.
24 THE VIDEO TECHNICIAN: Do you

Page 168
1   establishing homicide or suicide?
2   A. Yes.
3   Q. Okay. Could you say what they
4   are?
5   A. I'm sorry?
6   Q. What is the standard for
7   determination --
8   A. Typically, it needs to have a
9   preponderance of evidence where the majority of
10 the information you've collected leads you to
11 one determination.
12 And so in numbers terms, if
13 we're saying you're equivocal, you can't
14 decide, it's 50/50, that's for being
15 undetermined. Preponderance could be varying
16 degrees above 51 percent up to about
17 75 percent. Overwhelming preponderance would
18 be about 75 percent.
19 And then so, you know, you have
20 to at least get in the range of having a
21 preponderance of the evidence pulling in one
22 direction.
23 Q. Okay. In this case, after
24 discussing your investigation with police,

Page 167
1   want to go off the video record while we
2   wait?
3   MS. BERKOWITZ: Sure.
4   THE VIDEO TECHNICIAN: The time
5   is 2:58. Going off the video record.
6   - - -
7   (Whereupon, a discussion was
8   held off the record.)
9   - - -
10 THE VIDEO TECHNICIAN: The time
11 is 3:02. We are on the video record.
12 BY MS. BERKOWITZ:
13 Q. Are medical -- is the NAME's
14 guide binding on medical examiners?
15 MR. PODRAZA: Objection. Calls
16 for a legal conclusion.
17 BY MS. BERKOWITZ:
18 Q. You can --
19 A. No. They're guidelines for
20 medical examiners to exercise the best
21 practices, but they're no -- they're not
22 binding.
23 Q. Okay. When -- and are you
24 familiar with the NAME's guide standard for

Page 169
1   reviewing toxicology, meeting with Dr. Rorke
2   and everything else, you amended the death
3   certificate, correct?
4   A. I'm sorry?
5   Q. You amended --
6   A. I didn't hear the last part of
7   your statement.
8   Q. You amended the death
9   certificate at the end of all of that
10 information gathering, correct?
11 A. Yes.
12 Q. Can you not hear me?
13 A. I can barely hear you. I don't
14 know why my phone is doing this. Give me one
15 moment.
16 Q. Okay.
17 (Pause)
18 A. I'm sorry, continue.
19 Q. You ultimately, after gathering
20 information, you amended the death certificate
21 in this case?
22 A. Yes, that's correct.
23 Q. And you testified that you had
24 discussions with colleagues and with Dr. Gulino

Page 170
1 about this case?
2 A. That's correct.
3 Q. And you reached a conclusion.
4 When you amended the death
5 certificate to change the manner of death to
6 suicide, did you reach that determination by a
7 preponderance of evidence?
8 A. Yes.
9 Q. And was that to a reasonable
10 degree of medical certainty?
11 A. Yes.
12 MS. BERKOWITZ: Okay. I do not
13 have any other questions.
14 MR. PODRAZA: No follow-up.
15 Thank you, Doctor, for taking
16 the time to be deposed today.
17 THE WITNESS: Okay. Thank you.
18 MS. BERKOWITZ: Thank you,
19 Dr. Osbourne.
20 THE WITNESS: Okay. Goodbye.
21 THE VIDEO TECHNICIAN: The time
22 is 3:06. We are going off the video
23 record. This concludes the video
24 deposition of Dr. Marlon Osbourne.

Page 172
1 CERTIFICATE
2
3 I do hereby certify that I am a
4 Notary Public in good standing, that the
5 aforesaid testimony was taken before me,
6 pursuant to notice, at the time and place
7 indicated; that said deponent was by me duly
8 sworn to tell the truth, the whole truth, and
9 nothing but the truth; that the testimony of
10 said deponent was correctly recorded in machine
11 shorthand by me, to the best of my ability, and
12 thereafter transcribed under my supervision
13 with computer-aided transcription; that the
14 deposition is a true and correct record of the
15 testimony given by the witness; and that I am
16 neither of counsel nor kin to any party in said
17 action, nor interested in the outcome thereof.
18 WITNESS my hand and official
19 seal this 26th day of April, 2021.
20
21
22 *Cheryl L. Goldfarb*
23 Notary Public
24

Page 171
1 THE COURT REPORTER: Is there
2 any rush for the transcript?
3 MR. PODRAZA: You know, Cheryl,
4 at this point, no. I think regular time
5 will be fine for us.
6 MS. BERKOWITZ: I think three to
7 five days would be great.
8 THE COURT REPORTER: Thank you.
9 - - -
10 (Witness excused.)
11 - - -
12 (Whereupon, the deposition was
13 concluded at 3:06 p.m.)
14 - - -
15
16
17
18
19
20
21
22
23
24

ACKNOWLEDGMENTS

Nancy Grace

First, my deepest and enduring thanks to my longtime friend and editor, Gretchen Young, who has had great faith in me and the telling of Ellen's story in order to bring her voice to life in our plea for justice. Gretchen, for so many years and through so many books, starting with *Objection!* you have changed my world. Thank you and love to Cabbie.

To Benee Knauer, you have immersed yourself in Ellen's story and dedicated your time, your energy, and your heart, sometimes at great sacrifice to yourself and your dear family, into the uphill road to justice. I pray your devotion and the countless hours you poured into *What Happened to Ellen* will somehow, finally, turn the tide for Ellen and her family. God bless you and thank you.

To Sandee and Josh Greenberg, thank you for the countless hours and deep emotional toll you paid in telling Ellen's story. Keep the Faith and Godspeed forward in the fight for Ellen.

To Dee Emmerson a/k/a "Blondie," a/k/a "Moon Pie," ever since you stepped into our place in NYC seventeen years ago and counting, you have been my partner in crime. How can I ever thank you enough? I can't! But I will continue to try!

To wonderful and faithful friends at *Crime Stories with Nancy Grace*, to my trusted partner and dear friend, Chris Balfe, to my friend, sounding board and longtime podcast and Executive Audio Producer, Jackie Howard, to my Managing Editor and friend, Wilson Garrett, and to longtime Executive Video Producer Liz Yuskaitis: many people dream, fewer have the opportunity to realize their dreams. You turn dreams and ideas into investigations that may, possibly, alter the course of justice. I am so deeply grateful. Thank you.

To my longtime colleague, trusted counselor, and most important, my dear friend, Josh Sabarra, my love and gratitude. Words are not enough.

And of course, to David. It's nothing without you and the twins, the joys of my life.

And to my Father God and Christ, thank you for these and all your many other blessings.

Benée Knauer

Enormous thanks to the indefatigable, tireless champion of rights and justice for victims, Nancy Grace, to whom I will be forever grateful for having me along on this important, heartbreaking, and empowering ride. Fighting for justice for Ellen Greenberg has become a calling. Josh Sabarra, you rock and roll; you are my partner in crime.

Huge thanks to the brilliant Gretchen Young, editor/publisher extraordinaire, the lovely Madeline Sturgeon and their amazing team at Regalo Press. Endless gratitude to the family and friends of Ellen Greenberg—the courageous, unstoppable, and amazing Sandee and Josh, Debbie, Alyson, and Pam, who shared their memories and heartache and love, who were so generous with their time and their hearts and their grief. They are warriors, who won't ever give up fighting the good fight. It is an honor to know you. I am with you all the way. Endless thanks to Joseph Podraza, the Greenberg family attorney, for all of your help and time and willingness to keep answering and explaining. Your mission is astounding; you help to make this all possible.

To the masterminds of science and compassion whose keen and exhaustive works change all of our lives. For their time, impactful explanations, and dedication to, and passion for, such profoundly imperative work, massive thanks to Joseph Scott Morgan, D. Michelle DuPre, Tom Brennan, and Graham Hetrick. I have learned so much from you.

To the magnificently talented writers I have the privilege to work with every day, I have even more respect and admiration for you, if that is somehow possible. You do it with grace and style and richness of spirit. What a great pleasure it is to collaborate and learn from you all. You inspire me; you are cherished friends, wonderful people and cohorts, and I thank you and love you.

To my truly amazing family and dearest friends, the all-time greatest of the all-time greatest group of beautiful people, a loving, kickass support system I am so unbelievably fortunate to call my own, I can never repay you. Big, giant love and kisses and hugs and gratitude to Renny (sonnyboy) and Silvio, our rock and matriarch, the original voracious reader, Mom, Dad watching over us, how we miss you, Debbie, Caron, Tammy, Ben, Howard, Jeff, Phyllis & Ed, Pearl, Silvia & Leah, Lonn, Ariel, Evynn, Laura, Meredith, Christina, Sophia, Peter, Jesse, Elizabeth, Andrew, Jake, Lou, Sarah, Candice, Doug, Sammie, Liam, Liev, Zuri, Yara, Madison, Parker, Alyssa, the eminent, steadfast, and loyal, Victoria Sanders and Diane Dickensheid, brother, David Mack, confidante and champion, May Cobb, saintly and huge-hearted, Veronika Oaks-Juranyi, Rebecca Hanover, beautiful, inside and out, wonderful spirit and sidekick, Raj Tawney, and Tara & Bill Delaney, mensches of the highest order.

Rest in peace, Ellen Greenberg, bright, shining soul. Justice is coming...